The Public Administration Workbook

Seventh Edition

Dennis L. Dresang

University of Wisconsin–Madison

Longman

Boston   Columbus   Indianapolis   New York   San Francisco   Upper Saddle River
Amsterdam   Cape Town   Dubai   London   Madrid   Milan   Munich   Paris   Montreal   Toronto
Delhi   Mexico City   Sao Paulo   Sydney   Hong Kong   Seoul   Singapore   Taipei   Tokyo

To
Maxine, Lee, Steve, Amber, Anna,
and Erin

Acquisitions Editor: Reid Hester
Project Editor: Toni Magyar
Senior Marketing Manager: Lindsey Prudhomme
Production Manager: Meghan DeMaio
Creative Director: Jayne Conte
Cover Designer: Bruce Kenselaar
Cover Illustration/Photo: © Stormur/Veer
Project Coordination, Text Design, and Electronic Page Makeup: Shiny Rajesh/Integra Software
  Services Pvt. Ltd.
Printer and Binder: Edwards Brothers
Cover Printer: Lehigh-Phoenix Color

Library of Congress Cataloging-in-Publication Data

Dresang, Dennis L.
  The public administration workbook / Dennis L. Dresang— 7th ed.
    p. cm.
  Includes bibliographical references and index.
  ISBN-13: 978-0-205-01996-0 (alk. paper)
  ISBN-10: 0-205-01996-X (alk. paper)
  1. Public administration—Problems, exercises, etc.   I. Title.
JF1338.A2H78 2012
351—dc22

                                        2010043394

1 2 3 4 5 6 7 8 9 10—EB—14 13 12 11

Longman
is an imprint of

www.pearsonhighered.com   ISBN-13: 978-0-205-01996-0
                                 ISBN-10:   0-205-01996-X

Brief Contents

Contents

Preface

Public administration is applied social science. That provides an opportunity for learning by doing—which is both an effective and an engaging way of gaining new knowledge and understanding.

The design of this book is such that it allows students to learn what public administration is by actually using the basic tools of the trade. They could get an understanding of organization, work flow, budgeting, and administrative law simply by reading a good textbook. But they are much more likely to enjoy the learning experience and to retain the lessons by completing the analyses and the tasks that professionals do in their jobs.

Learning by doing is best when it has a context. Students should know the social science and the theories that are being applied. To provide this context, a concise discussion of relevant concepts and studies introduces each exercise. Some instructors use standard public administration textbooks along with *The Public Administration Workbook*. Others work inductively with students to draw general lessons from the exercises. There are discussion questions at the end of each exercise that can be used for this purpose.

To provide maximum flexibility for instructors, most of the exercises in this book have been designed so that they can be done by students in small groups in class or individually, as out-of-class assignments. *The Public Administration Workbook* is ideal for the growing number of online courses. Exercises that do require in-class efforts and role plays are the ones on contract management (Exercise 8), administrative law (Exercise 9), emergency management (Exercise 10), and collective bargaining (Exercise 15). Many instructors assign several exercises as out-of-class

assignments and use the others in class with students working on them in small groups. You will find that the small groups provide an added dash of realism, as students learn the delicate arts of compromise and cooperation—so essential to good public administrative practice. Much of what administrators and analysts do is, after all, in teams and committees. In addition, there is the opportunity to discuss the tendencies for groupthink and ways of avoiding this. Whatever one's preferences and constraints, the accompanying *Instructor's Manual,* which has been revised for this edition of the workbook, provides detailed suggestions for using (and modifying) the exercises to fit a variety of course needs.

Those instructors who have used previous editions of *The Public Administration Workbook* will note the following changes:

- The forms and databases for the exercises are available online in an electronic format. Want to assign and have students turn in assignments from the workbook online? Register at the Pearson Instructor Resources Center at http://www.pearsonhighered.com/irc and download the "Forms and Data Sets to Accompany to *The Public Administration Workbook, 7/e.*" Use of the electronic forms and databases mimics what in reality public administrators and analysts do and cuts out much of the busy-work that is necessary when these exercises are done in a more traditional manner. There are advantages also when it comes time for grading student work.
- The budget exercises on performance and zero-base budgeting have been consolidated. This is

the common pattern in practice and will help instructors build all of the exercises into their course schedule.

- The emergency management exercise is now on a criminal and public safety issue, rather than bioterrorism. Students in criminal justice programs will find this more relevant and it will generally apply to the work that public administrators commonly do.

- The exercise on administrative law includes an option for having students promulgate as well as adjudicate an administrative rule.

- The personnel management exercises use a police dispatcher job as an example to illustrate job descriptions, classifications, and the like. This replaces the use of a budget analyst job, which is more of a challenge for students to understand.

- Web links have been added to each exercise that provide more information and examples.

- Throughout the text, I have updated material and cited the most recent scholarly literature.

The emphasis in the suggested readings continues to include the classics.

Those who have used previous editions of this book will join me in thanking Mark W. Huddleston. It was Mark who initially came up with the idea for the *Workbook* and who authored the first four editions. Mark went from a faculty position to university administration and is now the president of the University of New Hampshire. Understandably, he phased out of his role as an author. We are indebted to him for his contribution to the teaching of public administration and congratulate him on his success as an administrator.

I am immensely grateful to the following colleagues who provided invaluable feedback on the sixth edition and suggestions for shaping the seventh: Craig Curtis, Bradley University; Beth Walter Honadle, University of Cincinnati; Doug Shumavon, University of Ohio; and Jonathon West, University of Miami.

Dennis L. Dresang

Introduction

OVERVIEW OF *THE PUBLIC ADMINISTRATION WORKBOOK*

One thing that makes public administration fun to learn is that you can roll up your sleeves and actually *do* some of it in the classroom. What would otherwise be simply a collection of arcane concepts and impenetrable jargon can become accessible and—lo and behold!—even interesting when you slide behind an administrator's desk and become familiar with some of the principal techniques of public management.

The exercises in this book introduce you to 18 of the most important skills in the professional administrator's kit bag. Part One includes four exercises in decision making, the core activity of all public administrators. Exercise 1 introduces you to some techniques designed to test the cost-effectiveness of different options and to make rational decision making more probable. Exercise 2 builds on this and raises the issues of policy evaluation: Did the policy you chose in Exercise 1 work? Exercise 3 deals with choices that can be made in designing organizations so that they can implement policies effectively and efficiently, and Exercise 4 wrestles with how to act ethically when making decisions and providing services.

To understand management fully, it is important to appreciate the differences as well as the similarities in the spectrum of administrative tasks. A key requirement for all administrators is the ability to communicate clearly. Exercise 5 in Part Two introduces you to the style and format of written communication in organizations. The rest of Part Two provides you with an explanation of the nature of different managerial challenges and an opportunity to develop some of

the skills and techniques in the tool kits of public administrators. Exercise 6 focuses on operational management, the provision of ongoing services or production—the kind of organizational activity that typically comes to mind when we think of public- or private-sector administration. Projects, the topic of Exercise 7, have a distinct beginning and end and present different managerial needs than do ongoing work. Increasingly, governments in the United States contract with private and not-for-profit organizations for services, projects, and consultation. Contract management is the subject of Exercise 8. Administrative law, the focus of Exercise 9, is primarily about making and enforcing rules. Whether because of terrorism, natural disasters, or accidents, emergencies occur and call for immediate, ad hoc organizations to respond. Exercise 10 simulates an emergency.

Part Three includes five exercises in public personnel administration. You begin by learning how to conduct a job analysis and by writing a job description, the foundations of virtually everything else in personnel management. You then design a performance appraisal system, plan for filling the many vacancies that will be left by baby boomer retirements, and then go through the process of selecting someone to fill a particular vacancy. Finally, you are thrown into the thick of a labor–management dispute and have to negotiate a new contract with a union of firefighters.

Part Four introduces you to the field of public budgeting. Three successive exercises based on the same organization—a newly consolidated county library system—provide you with a tour of the five major budget formats used in the United States: line-item budgeting, performance budgeting, program budgeting, zero-base budgeting, and outcome-based budgeting. You begin by compiling a basic line-item budget for the library system and proceed by transforming the budget, step-by-step, into the remaining formats.

THEORY AND TECHNIQUE IN PUBLIC ADMINISTRATION

Techniques alone do not make a discipline, of course. It is essential that you understand the theory behind each technique so that you know when, why, and how to use it. In fact, the primary reason for doing these exercises and learning these techniques is to learn the theory. After all, techniques come and go with fair frequency—even faster, believe it or not, than theories. And you will seldom find exactly the same technique, used in exactly the same way, in any two governmental jurisdictions. But if you know the theory that generates the technique, you are way ahead of the game. You can walk into almost any administrative office, shuffle a few of your categories, and figure out in no time what your administrative colleagues are doing.

So why learn these techniques at all, you ask? Simple. They provide a useful and even enjoyable entrée to the theories themselves. It's much more fun to learn about zero-base budgeting by writing a zero-base budget than it is just to read about one. Moreover, you'll remember much more about zero-base budgeting that way. And that's the important thing.

To help you make the connection between *theories* of public administration and *techniques* of public administration, each exercise is preceded by a brief theoretical introduction. You should read these carefully. They contain valuable hints about how to complete the exercise and also explain why the technique is important and how it is anchored in the field of public administration.

Assuming that your interest in one or more of these subjects will be sufficiently aroused that you'll want to know more about it, each exercise is followed by a short bibliographic essay directing you to further reading that you will find useful.

One last point before you begin: it is possible to do almost all of the exercises on your own, outside of class. In fact, only four of them actually require a group effort. Nevertheless, you should, whenever your instructor allows, work on these exercises in small groups. Not only will you learn more and have more fun, but it is more realistic as well—administrators typically work in teams and committees!

PART I
Decision Making and Policy Analysis

ADMINISTRATORS AND THE POLICY PROCESS

The classical view of American constitutional democracy that is presented in high school civics textbooks does not have much to say about bureaucracy and public administration. Congress and other legislative bodies, we are told, follow the wishes of the citizenry and make the laws, while the president, governor, mayor, and other executives, under the watchful eye of the courts, implement laws. To the extent they are recognized at all, public administrators are understood to be somewhere in the background, working under the direct control of the executive to carry out the technical details of legislation. Elected officials make policy; administrators simply administer it.

This is not a very accurate description of the actual relationship between politics and administration in the United States—or anywhere, for that matter. It seriously understates the role of public administrators in the governmental process. Administrators do not just carry out policy; they make policy. Indeed, few areas of American life and few Americans are untouched by administrative decisions. From highway safety and the regulation of oil drilling to the processing of Social Security checks and student loans, public administrators make choices that have significant effects on all of us.

The term that we use to describe the latitude or freedom that administrators have to act on their own is *administrative discretion*. How is it that administrators have come to exercise such discretion? The Constitution, after all, creates no such role for

them. The main reason is the complexity of modern government. It is no longer possible (and perhaps no longer desirable) for legislators and other elected officials to issue precise and detailed instructions to administrators about many questions of public policy. Even if they were so inclined, they have neither the time nor the expertise to do so. Consequently, they rely on administrators. Although Congress and the president still try to set the broad goals of public policy (e.g., "air transportation should be as safe as possible"), they often leave it to professional administrators to make the rules that give the policy meaning (e.g., "airlines must install seats and carpeting made only of noncombustible materials").

Policy decisions are seldom self-implementing. Administrators are the ones who actually have to get their hands dirty and put decisions into effect. They have to identify and clean up toxic waste dumps, plan soil conservation projects, manage job training schemes, and fly reconnaissance aircraft. Even given clear goals and even absent formal delegations of authority, administrators cannot do these jobs without exercising considerable discretion. No statute—no matter how detailed—no rule book—no matter how thick—can anticipate all contingencies and program all administrative actions.

Administrators not only exercise discretion in implementing existing laws, but they also play a key role in the development of new laws and policies. Bureaucracies are the eyes and ears of government. It is often the bureaucracy that first becomes aware of problems in need of governmental attention. The administrator who defines a problem and structures the information on which a decision is made has a subtle, though powerful, impact on the decision

3

itself. For example, an employee in a department of transportation that notices that police are issuing a high number of speeding tickets in a particular location could—or could not—identify this to his or her superiors as a problem. If it is considered a problem, it could be defined as an issue of law enforcement (speed trap?), safety (need stop lights, speed bumps, or road redesign to slow traffic), or traffic flow (speed limit is too low). Although politicians in an open society have multiple sources of information—the press, interest groups, and individual citizens—public administrators occupy a strategic position.

The point of this analysis is very simple: Administrators are key actors in American government. Directly and indirectly, formally and informally, they make decisions and take actions that fundamentally shape the character and direction of public policy. The essence of public administration is problem solving. This implies that we, as students of public administration, need to pay close attention to the processes of administrative policy formulation and implementation. Administrators use specific techniques that, ideally, ensure that decision making proceeds in orderly and rational ways. The exercises in Part One introduce some of these techniques.

FURTHER READING

An excellent text and reference for policy analysis is David L. Weimer and Aidan R. Vining, *Policy Analysis: Concepts and Practice*, 5th ed. (Upper Saddle River, NJ: Prentice-Hall, 2010). Useful overviews of the role of public administrators in the political process are Emmette S. Redford, *Democracy in the Administrative State* (New York: Oxford University Press, 1969); Kenneth J. Meier and Lawrence O'Toole, *Bureaucracy in a Democratic State: A Governance Perspective* (Baltimore: Johns Hopkins University Press, 2006); and John Kingdon, *Agendas, Alternatives, and Public Policies*, 2nd ed. (New York: Longman, 2002). For a classic analysis of the roots and implications of administrative power, see Norton E. Long, "Power and Administration," *Public Administration Review* 9 (Autumn 1949), pp. 8–27. Mark H. Moore, *Creating Public Value* (Cambridge, MA: Harvard University Press, 1995), draws on case studies to discuss administrative discretion and the role administrators can and do play in policy making. Paul A. Sabatier offers a broadly theoretical overview of policy making in *Theories of the Policy Process*, 2nd ed. (Boulder, CO: Westview Press, 2007).

Exercise 1

Rational Decision Making

WHAT IS RATIONALITY?

We all like to believe that we think and act rationally and resent it if someone suggests we are doing otherwise. But what exactly does *rational* mean? In everyday discourse, we use the term fairly loosely and say that someone is rational if he or she acts reasonably, logically, and normally. We label as *irrational* any behavior that we find strange or abnormal, which, depending on one's perspective, may encompass everything from paying $125 for a concert ticket to exhibiting active fantasies about being chased by creatures from Venus.

For the student of public administration, rationality has a more precise meaning. We say that a decision is rational if there is a systematic relationship between an end being pursued and the means used to get there. More specifically, a rational decision is one that entails selecting the best alternative to reach a particular goal.

Most discussions of this subject treat rational decision making in administration as a seven-step process:[1]

1. Define the objective or problem.
2. Identify possible solutions.
3. Evaluate the alternative solutions.
4. Select the best option.
5. Announce the selection.
6. Implement the decision.
7. Evaluate the results.

You may object that this definition of administrative rationality isn't really much more precise or objective than the definition of rationality in general. After all, who is to say what alternative is best in any particular circumstance? Doesn't it depend a lot on the values we hold?

This objection has some merit. It is certainly true that estimates of the worth of an alternative will vary from person to person or from agency to agency. It is even true that we often don't know what our objectives are or how we should define the problem, much less which alternative might best get us the results we want. Moreover, any effort to apply this definition in an administrative context has to come to grips with the fact that decisions are often made collectively, with many different people applying many different values to many different goals.

Sometimes the challenge of group decision making is to find common ground when individuals in the group hold diverse views. More commonly, the impediment to rational group decision making is the tendency to emphasize reaching a consensus over making a good decision. This tendency, which is called *groupthink*, is based on our desire to get along with others and/or to defer to those who have more authority or expertise than we have.[2] Groupthink has been identified as having contributed to cases—like the surprise attacks on Pearl Harbor in 1941 and on the World Trade Center and the Pentagon in 2001—in which, at

---

[1]Irving L. Janis and Leon Mann, *Decision Making. A Psychological Analysis of Conflict, Choice and Commitment* (New York: Free Press, 1977); and Herbert A. Simon, *Administrative Behavior: A Study of Decision-Making Processes in Administrative Organization*, 3rd ed. (New York: Free Press, 1976).

[2]Irving Janis, *Groupthink*, 2nd ed. (Boston: Houghton Mifflin, 1983).

least in retrospect, wrong decisions were made despite credible warnings.[3]

While it may be impossible to make (or even identify) purely rational decisions, it is possible and necessary to try to make relatively or intended rational decisions. In fact, it may be useful to talk not about rational *decisions* but about a rational *process for making decisions.* If we make an effort to clarify and rank our goals and then search for and evaluate alternatives, we may not always be pleased with the outcome. But chances are that we will be better off than we would have been had we proceeded blindly or instinctively, with no attention to goals, alternative strategies, or consequences.

We do not pursue a rational process of decision making instinctively. Fear, pressure to conform, and time constraints prompt us to take shortcuts or to reach a conclusion without thinking through all the possible ramifications. Psychologists have developed techniques that as individuals, small groups, and organizations we can use to avoid these pitfalls. The list of various techniques of rational decision making is virtually endless. It includes, among other things, simulations and game theory, operations research, systems analysis, linear programming, and decision trees, as well as myriad techniques bequeathed by microeconomists. Although each item has a distinctive flavor and is suited for only certain limited applications, all have in common the purpose of expanding the decision maker's awareness of choices and their consequences.

COST–BENEFIT AND COST-EFFECTIVENESS ANALYSIS

Cost–benefit analysis is one of the most common techniques of rational decision making.[4] It is aimed at determining whether a particular investment of public funds is worthwhile. As its name suggests, cost–benefit analysis requires the decision maker to compare the total costs and benefits of a proposed program.

Wherever possible, hard, quantifiable measures of both benefits and costs are to be used. If the ratio of benefits to costs is favorable—that is, if the investment has a net positive return—the program is justified.

Cost–benefit analysis first came into widespread use by the federal government in water resource management programs in the 1930s. The U.S. Army Corps of Engineers and Bureau of Reclamation used variations of this technique when deciding where and how to construct municipal water, irrigation, and flood control projects. Cities often use cost–benefit analysis today when considering major capital investments, such as constructing a new municipal parking garage or a convention center.

Cost-effectiveness analysis is an outgrowth of systems analysis.[5] Although related to cost–benefit analysis, cost-effectiveness analysis is more concerned with the systematic comparison and evaluation of alternatives. The question for the cost-effectiveness analyst is, given the goal of reaching *x,* which of alternatives *a, b,* and *c* (or which combination thereof) will accomplish the job at the least cost? Note that the benefits of *x* are assumed. Cost-effectiveness analysis is often used in policy areas, such as social welfare or defense, where benefits are taken for granted but are not subject to hard measurement. This shifts attention to the relatively solvable problem of achieving these benefits at the lowest possible cost.

The relative benefits conferred by each alternative, even if not precisely quantifiable, cannot be totally ignored, however. For instance, a state agriculture or public health department may set for itself the goal of eliminating avian influenza within certain affected counties. It "costs out" three main alternatives (see Figure 1.1), each of which is probably capable of accomplishing the goal: (1) a total import–export quarantine on the affected areas, (2) a limited inspection and flock destruction program, and (3) destruction of all poultry within the target areas.

Should they now just pick the cheapest alternative (apparently alternative 2, all things considered)? Not necessarily. Alternative 3, although more expensive, confers additional benefits to

[3]Janis (1983) and *Report of the National Commission on Terrorist Attacks Upon the United States* (Washington, DC: Government Printing Office, 2005) and www.9–11commission.gov/report/index.htm.
[4]Edward M. Gramlich, *A Guide to Benefit-Cost Analysis,* 2nd ed. (Englewood Cliffs, NJ: Prentice Hall, 1990); and Robert H. Haveman and Julius Margolis, eds., *Public Expenditure and Policy Analysis,* 2nd ed. (Chicago: Rand McNally, 1977).

[5]Richard D. Bingham and Marcus E. Ethridge, eds., *Reaching Decisions in Public Policy and Administration, Methods and Applications* (New York: Longman, 1982); and Frank Fischer, *Evaluating Public Policy* (Chicago: Nelson-Hall, 1995).

1.	**Quarantine**	
	Income loss	$2,300,000
	Tax loss	460,000
	Administration	500,000
	Total	$3,260,000
2.	**Limited Inspection**	
	Income loss	$ 600,000
	Tax loss	90,000
	Administration	1,500,000
	Total	$2,190,000
3.	**Flock Destruction**	
	Income loss	$2,300,000
	Tax loss	460,000
	Administration	3,000,000
	Total	$5,760,000

Figure 1.1
Cost-Effectiveness of Avian Influenza Remedies:
Three Alternatives

the extent that it offers a greater probability of success. Alternative 1 is cheaper than 3 but may be slightly less beneficial. But who knows? One of the reasons the state agriculture department is using cost-effectiveness analysis is that it cannot quantify benefits precisely. The point of the example is that ends and means or objectives and program strategies can never be wholly separated, even in the most careful analyses. Because we can never be sure of consequences and because we find it difficult to calculate benefits, we almost always find ourselves trading off a little of our objective here for a little of an alternative there. This is the essence of systems analysis.

Ends and means are in a constant state of flux as one searches for an optimal balance. This was dramatically visible when Hurricane Katrina devastated New Orleans in 2005. A major factor in the devastation was that, based in large part on cost-effectiveness analysis, levees built to keep water flooding into certain neighborhoods were designed to withstand the effects of a category 3 storm and Katrina was a category 5 (the highest) storm. The

thinking had been to avoid the very high costs of levees that might hold in a category 5 storm because such storms were unlikely, albeit not impossible. The discussions of how to rebuild in the aftermath of Hurricane Katrina have, not surprisingly, been to revisit the objectives as well as the alternatives.

Where does this leave administrative agencies that strive to make decisions rationally? Not with any easy answers, to be sure. But the act of undertaking cost-effectiveness and similar analyses will help officials think through their objectives and clarify their alternatives.

FURTHER READING

Classical theoretical discussions of administrative decision making may be found in David Braybrooke and Charles E. Lindblom, *A Strategy of Decision* (London: Collier-Macmillan, 1963); Charles E. Lindblom, "The Science of 'Muddling Through,'" *Public Administration Review* 19 (Spring 1959), pp. 48–62; and Herbert A. Simon, *Administrative Behavior*, 3rd ed. (New York: Free Press, 1976).

A good introduction to and survey of techniques of decision making is Richard D. Bingham and Marcus E. Ethridge, eds., *Reaching Decisions in Public Policy and Administration: Methods and Applications* (New York: Longman, 1982). Warren Walker, *The Policy Analysis Approach to Public Decision-Making* (Santa Monica, CA: Rand, 1994), also provides a useful introduction to much of this material. Deborah Stone, *Policy Paradox: The Art of Political Decision Making* (New York: W.W. Norton, 2001), provides some cautionary notes.

Many technical treatises on cost–benefit analysis are available. Two of the most accessible are Anthony Boardman, David Greenberg, Aidan Vining, and David Weimer, *Cost-Benefit Analysis: Concepts and Practice*, 3rd ed. (Upper Saddle River, NJ: Prentice-Hall, 2005), and Harry Campbell and Richard P.C. Brown, *Benefit-Cost Analysis: Financial and Economic Appraisal Using Spreadsheets* (New York: Cambridge University Press, 2005). Also interesting is R. Shep Melnick, *The Politics of Benefit-Cost Analysis* (Washington, DC: Brookings Institution, 1991).

Overview of Exercise

You are J. La Rue, senior policy analyst in the Community Transportation Planning Division of the State Department of Transportation (SDOT). One of your major responsibilities is to work with local communities in the state to help them assess their transportation needs and to make appropriate recommendations for action. At the top of your agenda is a request for assistance from the city manager of East Wallingford, a rapidly growing community of 45,000 people that has been plagued by chronic traffic congestion. As an ace cost-effectiveness analyst, your task in this exercise is to analyze East Wallingford's transportation situation and decide which of four main alternatives—a northern bypass, a southern bypass, street widening, or a bus-plus-perimeter-parking system—should be supported.

INSTRUCTIONS

Step One
Study the map of greater East Wallingford provided on Form 1 and familiarize yourself with the physical structure of the community.

Step Two
Read the "Preliminary Problem Analysis" memo (Form 2) prepared for you by your assistant, M. Ubahn. It provides important information about the dimensions of East Wallingford's traffic problem, including a discussion of certain political constraints. You may, if you wish, fill in the date of the memo with the current year.

Step Three
Complete Form 3, "Construction and Maintenance Cost Worksheet," by calculating the basic construction/acquisition and maintenance/operating costs of each alternative. Use the information provided on Form 4, "Cost Specifications," as a basis for your computations. Note that these costs represent costs to the state; for the purposes of this analysis, additional costs to be borne by other levels of government are ignored.

Step Four
Complete Form 5, "Environmental and Social Cost Worksheet." Note that you are to assign a cost figure, from 0 to 100, for each alternative. The figures represent your estimates of the *relative* costs of each of these strategies. It is not possible to put a price tag on environmental and social costs, but you can and should include these costs in your comparisons of the

advantages and disadvantages of the four alternatives. Arrive at reasonable estimates of relative costs based on your reading of the situation in East Wallingford. As the instructions on Form 5 indicate, take into consideration the likely environmental damage (air and water pollution, noise pollution, destruction of wildlife habitat, etc.) that will follow from each alternative. Social costs include dislocation and safety issues. Although your primary focus is on East Wallingford, as a state analyst you should also consider general issues, such as the likely effects on urban sprawl and the preservation of farmland.

Step Five
Complete Form 6, "Analytical Worksheet I." This form allows you to combine your cost calculations from Forms 3 and 5. Note that it is necessary to translate your costs from the "Construction and Maintenance Cost Worksheet" (Form 3) into terms compatible with a 100-point scale. You can do this easily by dividing your total for each alternative from Form 3 by 10,000. Note that you also have to decide on weights for each of the costs on Form 6. See the instructions on Form 6 for details.

Step Six
Complete Form 7, "Analytical Worksheet II." Refer again to Ubahn's memorandum, and calculate the cost per minute of reducing average trip times by following each of the outlined alternatives; for instance, Ubahn estimates that the Northway will reduce travel time from 30 minutes to 10 minutes; as you have already calculated the cost of constructing this highway, simply divide the cost by the minutes saved (20). These calculations provide you with a set of *cost–benefit ratios*, which you should use as a basis for deciding which alternative to recommend.

Step Seven
Based on the cost–benefit ratios you calculated on Form 7 and any other information you consider pertinent, choose an alternative. Use Form 8 to outline and justify your choice by composing a brief memorandum to your supervisor, the director of the Division of Community Transportation Planning of the SDOT.

Step Eight
Answer the questions on Form 9.

Map of East Wallingford

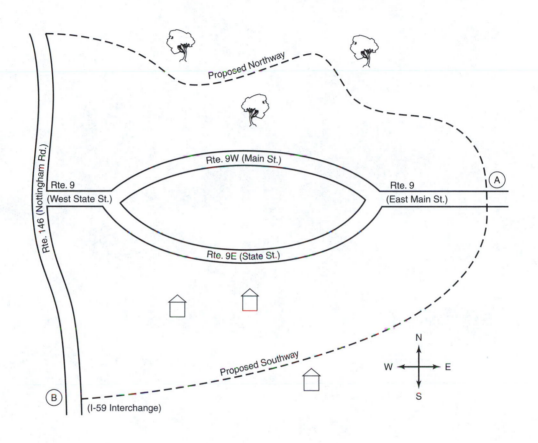

June 17, 20___

TO: J. La Rue
         Senior Policy Analyst
         Community Transportation Planning

FROM: M. Ubahn
         Junior Policy Analyst
         Community Transportation Planning

RE: Preliminary Problem Analysis, East Wallingford

In response to your request for a preliminary analysis of East Wallingford's traffic problems, I spent 3 days in East Wallingford last week, at which time I interviewed city officials and community leaders and initiated a traffic flow study. The city held public hearings to gauge public reaction to four alternative proposals identified by the study. My findings can be summarized as follows:

1. East Wallingford is served by two state highways. Route 146 (Nottingham Road), a north–south arterial, passes through the western side of the city. Route 9, an east–west arterial, passes through the center of East Wallingford and connects to Route 146, which is its western terminus. In the central business district, Route 9 is actually divided for 1.5 miles to allow for one-way traffic flows. Route 9E is known as State Street; Route 9W is known as Main Street.

2. Three miles south of the central business district on Route 146 is an interchange for Interstate 59.

3. Traffic flows are unacceptably heavy on Route 146 and on Main (Route 9W) and State (Route 9E) Streets. During peak travel hours (7:30 a.m. to 9:30 a.m. and 4:00 p.m. to 6:00 p.m.), average trip times are far below state standards for a community of this size. Trips between Point A and Point B in either direction (see map), a distance of 4.5 miles, require 30 minutes on average.

4. City officials want average trip time in this corridor to be reduced to 15 minutes. While this seems to be a reasonable goal, application of SDOT standards in this case suggest it should be seen as a target rather than as an absolute cutoff.

5. Federal highway money is available on a matching basis for highway construction, of course, but at the public hearings, people in the major residential districts south of the city opposed building a "Southway," a 4-mile-long link from

East Main Street to lower Nottingham Road near the Interstate interchange (projected trip time: 6 minutes).

6. On the other hand, local and state environmental groups interested in preserving the undeveloped streams and woodlands above East Wallingford have argued vociferously against a "Northway," a 5-mile-long stretch from East Main Street to upper Nottingham Road that would cut through the forest (projected trip time: 10 minutes).

7. Widening Main Street and State Street has received some support as an alternative, but local businesspeople have objected that this project (3 miles of street widening in total) would be disruptive for their trade in the short term (estimated two years of construction) and would probably cause them to lose valuable parking spaces in front of their stores in the long term (projected trip time: 16 minutes).

8. Perimeter parking, in conjunction with increased bus service, has been discussed as a fourth possibility, although it is not clear that this would alleviate the problem entirely. I estimate that the city (with state aid) would have to purchase five new buses and construct two 1-acre parking lots to relieve congestion to near-tolerable levels (projected trip time: 20 minutes).

Construction and Maintenance Cost Worksheet

Alternatives	Costs		
	Construction/Acquisition	Maintenance/Operating	Total
Southway			
Northway			
Street widening			
Perimeter parking			

Cost Specifications

Annualized Construction/Acquisition Costs*

Highways constructed mainly in residential areas $200,000/mile

Highways constructed mainly in undeveloped areas $100,000/mile

Street widening $100,000/mile

Parking lot construction $20,000/acre

Bus acquisition $70,000/bus

Maintenance/Operating Costs

Highway maintenance $10,000/mile/year

Additional maintenance for widened streets $10,000/mile/year

Parking lot maintenance $1,000/acre/year

Bus maintenance $1,000/bus/year

Bus operation $30,000/bus/year

*Although construction/acquisition expenditures are, in a sense, "onetime" costs, these figures represent annual costs to the state given the manner in which the investments would be financed. This allows you to sum construction/acquisition and maintenance/operating costs and to compare expenditures on an annual basis. Moreover, to simplify the analysis, these costs have already been standardized to account for the differential depreciation of these investments; thus the fact that buses need to be replaced more often than highways is already reflected in this cost structure. Finally, these figures represent costs to the state; additional costs borne by other levels of government are ignored in this exercise.

Environmental and Social Cost Worksheet

	Costs	
Alternatives	**Environmental**	**Social**
Southway		
Northway		
Street widening		
Perimeter parking		

Instructions: Review the map of East Wallingford, reread Ubahn's memorandum, and use any other resources you like to estimate the relative environmental and social costs of these four alternatives. Assign a number, from 0 to 100, to each alternative for each type of cost (0 = low cost; 100 = high cost). There is no one "correct" set of answers to these cost calculations. You should, however, try to assign *relative* costs that reflect the situation in East Wallingford as accurately as possible. The easiest way to do this (although not necessarily the most precise way) is to rank the alternatives against one another (1 through 4) on each dimension; then assign cost figures that reflect the ranking.

Analytical Worksheet I

Alternatives	Weighted Costs			
	Economic (Construction/ Acquisition & Maintenance) (EC) Weight =	Environmental (EN) Weight =	Social (S) Weight =	Total (TC)
Southway				
Northway				
Street widening				
Perimeter parking				

Instructions: This form allows you to combine your cost calculations from Forms 3 and 5. To complete this form, you must (1) translate your construction and maintenance costs into numbers compatible with a 100-point scale, and (2) assign weights to each of the three costs (EC, EN, and S) in this table.

To translate your construction and maintenance costs, simply divide each of the totals from Form 3 by 10,000. Do this now and make a note of your answers on a separate sheet of paper.

Now you must assign weights to each of the three costs in this table. To do this, first think about the relative importance of economic factors, environmental factors, and social factors in a decision of this kind. Are they equally important? Is one slightly more important than the other two? Is one far more important than the other two? Your answer will depend on your own (or your organization's) values. After you have thought about this, choose numbers that reflect your evaluation. For instance, if you think that economic factors are twice as important as environmental and social factors, assign a weight of 2 to EC and weights of 1 each to EN and S. If you think they are all equally important, assign weights of 1 to each. Feel free to use fractions: for example, you might weight EC at 1.5, EN at 1, and S at 1.25. Note the weights you have decided on in the appropriate spaces in the table columns. Then multiply the weight for each factor times the cost of that factor for each of the alternatives (from Forms 3 and 5) and enter the products in the table. Finally, add across the rows to determine the total costs (TC) of each alternative.

Analytical Worksheet II

Alternatives	Costs	
	Reduction in Trip Time (RTT)	Effectiveness (TC/RTT)
Southway		
Northway		
Street widening		
Perimeter parking		

Instructions: Calculate the effectiveness of each alternative by dividing the total cost (TC) (from Form 6) by the reduction in trip time (RTT) (from Ubahn's memo, Form 2). This cost–benefit ratio (TC/RTT) should then be used to guide your selection of the appropriate alternative. The lower the cost per mile, the more attractive the alternative—other things being equal.

FORM 8

Date:

TO: City Manager
        East Wallingford

CC: Director, Division of Community Transportation Planning,
        State Department of Transportation

FROM: J. La Rue
        State Department of Transportation

RE: Proposed Resolution of Traffic Congestion

Questions

1. Do you think that your decision about East Wallingford's transportation problem was rational or at least was made rationally? Why or why not?

2. Does this imply that the rejected alternatives should be considered irrational or nonrational? Elaborate.

3. What is the relationship between the values of the analyst and "objective" data in rational decision making? Is it possible to exclude your own biases entirely when making choices of this sort? Ideally, who should set the weights for a cost-effectiveness analysis?

4. Although it would seem from the facts presented in this case that none of the alternatives would satisfy all groups in East Wallingford, do you think that this is just an artifact of the exercise? That is, if you had more time and access to more information, do you believe an "optimal" solution to this problem could be found? In general, do most conflicts over public policy arise simply from misunderstanding and a lack of information such that good rational analysis will provide acceptable solutions?

Exercise 2

Policy Evaluation

THE IMPORTANCE OF POLICY EVALUATION

As far as most casual observers of American politics and public affairs are concerned, the policy process ends once a decision has been made—when a bill has been approved, a regulation promulgated, an executive order signed, and so forth. Those more familiar with the intricacies of policy implementation tend to be more skeptical and to wait until various administrative problems have been ironed out before they feel satisfied that the policy process has run its course.

Public policy is not an end in itself; it is a *means* to an end. Policies are designed, at least in theory, to accomplish goals or solve problems. Once a policy is in place, public administrators, as well as elected officials, must always ask themselves, What has the policy accomplished? Did we reach the goal we set forth? Has the problem the policy was designed to solve been ameliorated?

Questions such as these are central to *policy evaluation*, which may be formally defined as "the objective, systematic, empirical examination of the effects ongoing policies have on their targets in terms of the goals they are meant to achieve."[1] Policy evaluation is important for the very simple reason that it helps us know whether our policies have worked. Absent some effort to gauge the effects of public policy, we are not only throwing darts in the dark, we never even find out if we hit

the board.[2] And it is best if we have a clear idea of where we are aiming right from the start.

POLICY AS THEORY

A useful way to understand the problems (and importance) of policy evaluation is to think of a policy as a theory, or better, as a hypothesis or set of hypotheses derived from the theory. When we formulate a public policy, we are in a sense formulating a hypothesis. We are assuming that an action we take will have a specific and measurable effect: "If we do x, then y will happen" or "If we set the drinking age at 21, then highway fatalities will decline." This is exactly the logic that applies in a laboratory: "If we heat this metal to a temperature of 550 degrees Fahrenheit, then hydrogen gas will be emitted."

Although this analogy is sound logically, it can be challenging empirically. Working in a laboratory, we can often control conditions quite precisely. We can make sure that the gas we are looking for (and no other gas) has in fact been emitted; we can also take measures to ensure that other factors are not responsible for the presence of the gas (e.g., our lab assistant did not accidentally open a canister of hydrogen).

---

[1]David Nachmias, *Public Policy Evaluation: Approaches and Methods* (New York: St. Martin's, 1979), p. 4.

[2]A persuasive case can be made that many participants in the policy process, as well as most citizens, don't really care about the effects of public policy, at least not in the sense implied here. It can be argued that policy is to be understood mainly as a set of symbols, disseminated to engender popular acquiescence in the status quo; nothing fundamentally changes or is meant to change. For an elaboration of this argument, see Murray Edelman, *The Symbolic Uses of Politics* (Urbana: University of Illinois Press, 1964). For the purposes of this chapter, it will be assumed that policymakers do intend to achieve the effects stated in the policy.

This is not easy to do with public policy. Even when our policy (the *if* part of the hypothesis) is clear and unambiguous, it is often hard to know what sort of changes are going on (the *then* part of the hypothesis) out there in the real world. Not only do we often have difficulty measuring social effects in general, but also we can seldom be sure what is producing them.

To illustrate this point, suppose that your state has decided to try to stimulate urban redevelopment by designating a series of "enterprise zones" in the state's largest cities. The legislature has passed and the governor has signed a bill exempting businesses that locate within the zones from all state and local property taxes for a period of three years. The theory, of course, is that this sort of tax break will encourage investment in otherwise undesirable areas: "*If* we give businesses tax incentives, *then* they will invest in areas that need redevelopment."

A year or so passes, and the governor asks you to assess the effectiveness of this policy. How should you proceed? The laboratory model is not much help. You lack the rigorous controls and precise instruments available to experimental scientists. You can of course try to do before-and-after comparisons of income, employment, vacancy rates, gross sales, and so forth in the zones. But will such data be available? How reliable will they be? Anyway, what should you try to measure? The legislature spoke of "redevelopment." This seemed clear enough at the time, but what exactly does it mean? Does any kind of economic activity qualify as redevelopment? Is it important to look at income distribution as well as income in the aggregate? The odds are that if you go back and try to reconstruct the intent of the legislature by reading debates and committee reports, you will find more than one definition of redevelopment. That is, you will discover that there was something less than complete agreement on what the policy was and what it was intended to accomplish.

Moreover, even if you solve these preliminary problems and decide that redevelopment, by whatever definition, has indeed taken place within the enterprise zones, what inferences will you draw? It would be premature to conclude that the tax relief policy has worked. After all, is it not possible that other factors (e.g., general economic conditions, bank lending policies, interest rates, energy cost and availability, social attitudes, and spillovers from business activity outside the zones), alone or in combination, have produced the effect? Maybe the law had nothing to do with it. Indeed, maybe the redevelopment occurred *despite* the law and even more redevelopment would have taken place without it. That is not likely, perhaps, but it is possible. And it is important to know. If we just assume that the law was responsible, supporters of enterprise zones will undoubtedly use this evidence of "success" to justify similar actions in the future. If their theory is wrong, unnecessary social costs will have been incurred for no tangible benefits. But how can you make such causal inferences? The social world is not like a laboratory; everything else does not come to a dead stop while a policy is being implemented. Variables are many; constants are few.

None of this is to suggest that policy evaluation is impossible. Policy can and should be evaluated. The point is that evaluation is complicated. Good evaluation research requires a special sensitivity on the part of the evaluator. Great care must be taken in identifying and clarifying policy goals, adducing appropriate measures of success, collecting valid and reliable data, and drawing correct (and appropriately qualified) inferences.

EVALUATION PROCEDURES

For better or worse, though, there is no one policy evaluation technique that may be learned and applied in all circumstances. Because a policy is like a theory, all the methodologies and techniques available to test theoretical hypotheses may be brought to bear in policy evaluations. Controlled social experiments can be run; statistical analyses using historical or comparative data can be undertaken; mathematical models can be built; citizens and policymakers can be interviewed; qualitative assessments can be made. Which methodology or set of methodologies should be used will vary with the situation and with the time evaluators are given to do their job.

In the end, learning to do sound policy evaluations is the same as learning to do sound research. The trick lies in putting together a sensible research design, in asking the right questions in the right way.

But what does it mean to put together a sensible research design? From the foregoing discussion we can distill several steps:

1. *Identify clearly the policy to be evaluated.* This means understanding both the goal or intent of the policy and the instruments of policy. What was the policy supposed to accomplish? Precisely how was it to be done? Treat the policy as a theory and derive from it testable hypotheses. Use the "if, then" form to remind yourself of the hypothesized relationship between action and outcomes.

2. *Devise valid measures.* Restate policy goals and instruments in ways that can be measured. Remember that most policies—to attract support and minimize opposition—state goals only in very general terms that cannot be measured directly. You must translate broad aims like "urban redevelopment" into measurable variables, such as occupancy rates, employment, and income. In doing so, make sure that your measures are valid—that they measure what you think they measure.

3. *Collect empirical data.* For each of the measures of each of the variables in your policy hypothesis, collect the most reliable information you can find. This may mean sifting through government statistics or conducting interviews or other field research. Ideally, evaluation is anticipated when a policy is first implemented and data are collected at the beginning of a project or program (called "baseline data") so that before-and-after comparisons are possible.

4. *Analyze your data.* Does there appear to be a causal relationship between the independent variable (the policy) and the dependent variable(s) (the outcome)? That is, is a change in the former variable associated with a change in the latter?

5. *Consider competing theories.* This is actually part of step 4, but it is so important that it deserves special emphasis. In analyzing your data, consider whether the changes you observe could be attributed to other causes. Is the redevelopment we have seen a function of tax incentives or of something else? To answer this question, it will be necessary conceptually to start over at step 1 and follow all the procedures outlined. Before you can say that a policy has worked, you must be prepared to reject all plausible alternative explanations. This is not always easy to do. It requires controlling for (or

holding constant) some variables while you look at others. Absent experimental conditions, you will probably have to undertake some comparative research (e.g., look at similar neighborhoods *not* designated urban enterprise zones and see how they have fared) or otherwise try to isolate the policy from other effects.

6. *Look for unintended consequences.* Even though a policy may be aimed at one target, it may hit another accidentally. Urban enterprise zones may (or may not) stimulate economic activity, but they may (or may not) also displace poor people and contribute to the problem of homelessness, create new pockets of poverty as businesses shift areas of operation, reduce state and local revenues beyond levels anticipated, and so on. Sound policy evaluations look for unintended as well as intended consequences.

One final (and frustrating) question must be posed, however: what do we do with policy evaluations once we get them? If the "we" refers to American policymakers and various attentive publics in general, the answer is, unfortunately, "Not much." If they are executed well, policy evaluations can and should serve as valuable feedback to the policy system. We can learn what we are doing right and what we are doing wrong. But the feedback is sometimes ignored. Many people stop paying attention to a policy once the initial decision is made; some new issue or problem grabs the headlines and relegates the policy to the quiet recesses of the bureaucracy. Others ignore the fruits of evaluation research because they are less interested in policy outcomes than they are in the policy itself. Businesses that lobby for tax credits may bolster their arguments with rosy pictures of social benefits, for example. But it is the credits that count, not the benefits; once the tax concessions are obtained, systematic evaluation is likely to loom only as a threat.

This should remind us that policy and politics are inseparable. Policy evaluation is no more a neutral, value-free activity than any other administrative process. While public policies can, for analytical purposes, be treated like scientific hypotheses, they ultimately represent the codification of certain social values, which more often than not are in conflict with other social values. As long as people disagree about what government should do, people will disagree about what government has done. The questions that frame a policy evaluation will unavoidably reflect some values and ignore others, if only to the extent that some questions are never asked.

Consequently, it is not surprising that policy evaluators do not always find an eager and credulous audience. Those interested in policy evaluation may take some solace, though, from the fact that settled social consensuses do occasionally develop in particular policy areas. As that happens, as values converge, policy evaluations become more widely accepted. Moreover, as one well-regarded scholar of policy evaluation has put it:

> *Decision makers are not monoliths. . . . As time goes on, if confirming evidence piles up year after year on the failures of old approaches, if mounting data suggest new modes of intervention, this will percolate through the concerned publics. When the political climate veers toward the search for new initiatives, or if sudden crises arise and there is a scramble for effective policy mechanisms, some empirically grounded guidelines will be available.[3]*

FURTHER READING

Very useful texts are Carol H. Weiss, *Evaluation*, 2nd ed. (Upper Saddle River, NJ: Prentice-Hall, 1998); Eugene Bardach, *A Practical Guide for Policy Analysis: The Eightfold Plan to More Effective Problem Solving*, 3rd ed. (Washington,

DC: Congressional Quarterly Press, 2008); Peter H. Rossi, Mark W. Lipsey, and Howard E. Freeman, *Evaluation: A Systematic Approach*, 7th ed. (Newbury Park, CA: Sage, 2003); and David Royce, Bruce A. Thyer, and Deborah K. Padgett, *Program Evaluation: An Introduction*, 5th ed. (Florence, KY: Brooks Cole, 2009). Joseph Wholey, Harry Hatry, and Kathryn Newcomer, eds., *The Handbook of Practical Program Evaluation*, 2nd ed. (San Francisco: Jossey-Bass, 2004), contains 25 essays on designing, conducting, and using evaluation studies—all from a very practical perspective, as the title suggests.

On the Web

www.gao.gov The General Accountability Organization provides policy and program evaluations to the U.S. Congress. The nonpartisan agency produces sound, professional reports on a wide variety of current concerns.

Many of the state governments have legislative audit bureaus similar to the federal General Accountability Organization.

www.ignet.gov The Council of the Inspectors General on Integrity and Efficiency includes all the inspectors general of federal agencies. Inspectors general are internal watchdogs that provide program evaluations and analyses of waste, fraud, and abuse. The Council's website gives easy access to the reports of the inspectors general.

Overview of Exercise

In this exercise, you will design a strategy to evaluate the transportation policy chosen in Exercise 1. It will require you to think about the intent of the policy, devise appropriate measures of policy success or failure, and suggest ways that data might be gathered and analyzed.

INSTRUCTIONS

Step One
Review the material presented in Exercise 1, especially Forms 1 and 2, and generally refamiliarize yourself with the situation in East Wallingford.

Step Two
Identify the policy goal(s) articulated by East Wallingford and state officials. Working on the assumption that the alternative you recommended

---

[3]Carol H. Weiss, "Evaluation Research in the Political Context," in Elmer L. Struening and Marcia Guttentag, eds., *Handbook of Evaluation Research I* (Newbury Park, CA: Sage, 1975), p. 24.

in Exercise 1 was in fact adopted, briefly describe the policy itself. Record the information in the appropriate spaces on Form 10, "Design for Policy Evaluation."

Step Three

Describe how you might go about measuring the extent to which these policy goals have been met. What indicators of success would you use? Use Form 10 to record your comments.

Step Four

Given the indicators you described in Step Three, discuss how you would collect the necessary data. Feel free to use your imagination—but be sure to factor feasibility and cost into your recommendations. Use Form 10 to record your comments.

Step Five

Assume that you find some evidence that your policy goals have been met, in whole or in part. Outline some plausible competing explanations (reasons other than the policy you recommended) for the outcome, and describe how you might go about deciding which explanation ultimately to accept. Use Form 10 to record your comments.

Step Six

Answer the questions on Form 11.

Design for Policy Evaluation

Policy Adopted:

Policy Goal(s):

Measure(s) of Policy Success/Failure:

Data to Be Used in Evaluation:

Alternative Hypotheses:

Questions

1. Assume that you actually had to undertake the evaluation you designed for this exercise. How difficult do you think it would be to carry out? What would be the major difficulties?

2. What unintended consequences of this policy do you think it would be important to look for in your study? How would you go about it?

3. How much confidence would you have in the results of your study? How much confidence do you think others in East Wallingford or in the State Department of Transportation would have? Why?

Exercise 3

Designing Organizations

APPROACHING ORGANIZATION DESIGN

Not long ago, designing the structure of a new government organization—or a business organization, for that matter—was a fairly simple matter. Although people might disagree about things such as who should report to whom, how many layers there ought to be between the boss and the lowest-level worker, and whether it was better to organize around process or place or function, the basic template was seldom in dispute. The finished organization would resemble a pyramid, wide at the base and narrow at the top. And inside the pyramid, the sinews of the organization would reflect the military principles of command and control. Authority would emanate clearly and invariably from the top of the structure. Orders would cascade down the chain of command like water down a mountainside, from agency head to bureau chief to mid-level manager to frontline worker.

Although most organizations continue to use this hierarchical pyramid to some extent, designers of organizations have a much broader array of models from which to choose. Depending on their purpose and the inclinations of the individuals who devise and manage them, organizations and units within a general pyramid can be tall or flat or round—really any shape at all. Similarly, the authority systems that structure organizations can be as tight and centralized as the military or as loose and fragmented as a beach party.

THREE MODELS OF ORGANIZATION

Although there are many types of organization in contemporary public administration, most of them derive from one of three basic organizational designs. These are the *bureaucratic, matrix,* and *team* models of organization. Let us look at the structure of each in turn and consider their advantages and disadvantages.

Bureaucratic Model

The *bureaucratic model* has a traditional pyramidal form (see Figure 3.1). According to the great political sociologist Max Weber, bureaucracy is the organizational face of rational thought, the essence of modernity. Bureaucratic organization is hierarchical, highly specialized, governed by clear rules and procedures, and impersonal.[1]

Although examples of bureaucratic or at least quasi-bureaucratic organizations have been known for centuries, bureaucracy really came into its own in the late eighteenth and early nineteenth centuries with the blossoming of the industrial revolution and assembly-line technology. Organizing bureaucratically, with each worker responsible for one small task, proved to be far more efficient for large-scale manufacturing than traditional craft-style production. Adam Smith tells us, for instance, that one man responsible for all the operations that go into making a pin—drawing the wire, straightening the wire, cutting the wire, pointing the tip, grinding the head, and so forth—could, "with utmost industry, make one pin in a day, and certainly not more than twenty." But when

[1] See Max Weber, "Bureaucracy," in *From Max Weber: Essays in Sociology,* ed. and trans. H. H. Gerth and C. Wright Mills (London: Oxford University Press, 1946), reprinted in Jay M. Shafritz and Albert C. Hyde, eds., *Classics of Public Administration,* 4th ed. (Fort Worth, TX: Harcourt Brace, 1997), pp. 37–43.

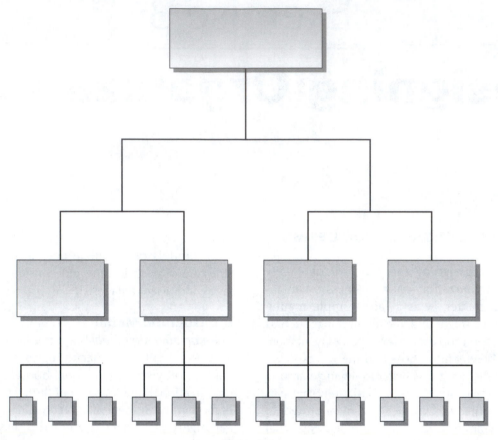

Figure 3.1
Bureaucratic Model of Organization

that man works as part of an assembly line, with clear division of labor and specialization of function, productivity soars: ten people working in such an arrangement "make among them upwards of forty-eight thousand pins in a day."[2]

Governments, too, have found bureaucratic organization useful. Just as in the private sector, bureaucracy in government affords relatively high levels of production—allowing more chickens to be inspected, more checks to be issued, more forms to be processed—than earlier, more casual methods of organization permitted. Bureaucracy has also proved to be a powerful tool in the fight against corruption, discrimination, patronage, and other types of organizational misbehavior. At least in principle, the color of your skin, whom you know, or which political party you support is

irrelevant in a bureaucratic organization structured by formal regulations and committed to impersonality. In a well-run bureaucracy, there are no surprises about what the organization does because employees follow prescribed rules. Control over outputs in turn simplifies democratic accountability. Citizens dissatisfied with public services can hold the elected officials who supervise the bureaucracy directly responsible for what the bureaucracy does.

It hardly needs to be said, however, that whatever its merits in theory, bureaucracy has disadvantages in practice. Indeed, the word *bureaucratic* has become a common pejorative, synonymous with "red tape." One prominent sociologist, Michel Crozier, even defines bureaucracy as organizational dysfunction.[3] Bureaucracies, public and private, are

[2]Adam Smith, *The Wealth of Nations* (1776), quoted in Jay M. Shafritz and J. Steven Ott, eds., *Classics of Organization Theory*, 2nd ed. (Chicago: The Dorsey Press, 1987), pp. 30–31.

[3]Michel Crozier, *The Bureaucratic Phenomenon* (Chicago: University of Chicago Press, 1964).

said to be by nature unresponsive, rule-bound, overly cautious, maladaptive, and even unproductive. Bureaucrats—now there is a real epithet!—are charged with caring only about procedures, not about goals. Lower-level workers in bureaucracies, in particular, are thought to be "dehumanized." Customers are treated like numbers, not like people.

Some critics argue that the problems of bureaucracy can be fixed either by modest changes in *structure* or by modifying organizational *processes.* Structural remedies generally entail making the bureaucracy flatter, reducing what are perceived as unnecessary layers of supervision. Process-related strategies typically focus on "human relations" and seek through training or other forms of organizational development to change the way people think and interact with one another in the workplace. Both such approaches hold considerable appeal for public managers because they are seen to address some of the major faults of bureaucracy without discarding its essential benefits.

Matrix Model

The *matrix model* of organization represents a sharp structural departure from traditional bureaucracy. In a matrix organization, specialists are arrayed in a functional structure (much like a traditional bureaucracy) for housekeeping purposes. The work that the organization accomplishes, however, is organized along project lines, which cut horizontally across the functional structure. The term *matrix* derives from the crosshatching created by these intersecting lines.

Figure 3.2 helps explain this idea. The lines running up and down connect each employee to a functional home—environmental engineering, biological sciences, licensing and inspection, and so forth. The lines running side to side connect each employee to a specific project—wetlands preservation, agricultural runoff mitigation, reforestation, and so on. Each employee is thus answerable in theory to two management structures. The functional structure represents, in effect, his or her permanent address, the place that issues the paycheck and provides

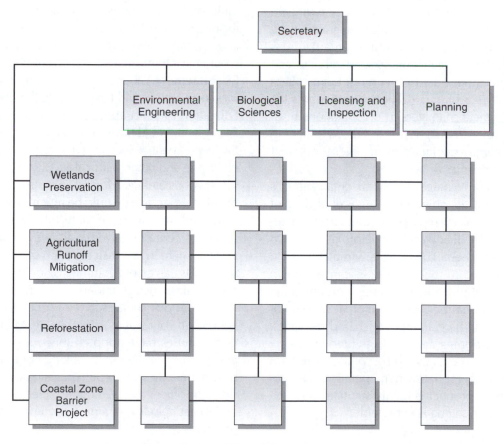

Figure 3.2
Matrix Model of Organization

administrative continuity. The project structure is where he or she lives at the moment—and in a matrix organization, one is almost always on the road. On a day-to-day basis, it is the project management structure that provides leadership and coordination.

Matrix organizations are still not widespread in government, but they are growing in popularity. They constitute a prime example of what organization theorist Henry Mintzberg terms *adhocracy.*[4] Indeed, the key advantage of the matrix organization is flexibility and fluidity. As problems come and go in an organization's environment, project structures can be created and dissolved to match them. Matrix organizations are especially suitable for bringing together groups of specialists to work intensively on well-defined, time-limited projects, like that covered in Exercise 7. In this situation, individuals within a hierarchically structured organization are assigned either for a specific period or for a percentage of their time to a particular project.

The concept of a matrix organization is the basis of outsourcing, which became a common practice of public and private enterprises in the late twentieth century. Instead of having a specialist integrated in the pyramid of a bureaucratic structure, organizations contract with that specialist for specific services and for specific time periods. In this model, specialists who are employees of organization A work under the direction of project managers in organizations B, C, D, etc. And project managers must direct and coordinate the efforts of specialists from several different contracting companies or agencies.

The chief disadvantage of a matrix organization is a mirror image of its chief advantage: dual lines of authority. Every matrix employee reports to two supervisors, one functional and one on the project to which he or she is attached. This clearly violates the old administrative maxim that no person can serve two masters. Certainly, life in the matrix organization demands an unusual degree of diplomacy, compromise, and delicate bargaining over shared resources. When these attributes are not in evidence, matrix organizations can be paralyzed by conflict. This form is generally not appropriate when operations are routine, a service or product is highly standardized, and the organizational setting is very stable.

[4]Henry Mintzberg, *The Structuring of Organization: A Synthesis of Research* (Englewood Cliffs, NJ: Prentice Hall, 1979).

Team Model

The third model is the *team approach* to organization, sometimes known as the *horizontal model* in recognition of its emphasis on decentralization. The team approach is integral to total quality management (TQM), which we will examine in detail in Exercise 6. More generally, though, this model of organization is built on the premise that small, integrated groups of people drawn from diverse disciplines but with a focus on a common *process* can most effectively deliver administrative services.

Figure 3.3 presents a chart of a team model of organization. In this particular example, the teams are drawn from several different departments; thus each of the five teams, designated by the five circles, has members from departments A, B, and C. It is also possible to assemble teams from within single departments or even from within single subunits of single departments.

To illustrate the advantages of the team model, imagine that you are an unemployed single mother and that you are trying mightily to remove yourself from the ranks of the unemployed and find a decent job. If all the organizations that might serve you were specialized and separate, here is the administrative trek that you would have to make: First, you would have to visit the Department of Labor to get information about openings; next, you would have to go to the Department of Education to learn about job training opportunities; finally, you would have to call various agencies within the Department of Social Services to try to get help with child care and other logistical support.

If your state has adopted the team model of organization, your quest would be much simpler. You can now walk into a single State Job Center, a facility staffed by representatives of all relevant state departments, where in one visit the team of complementary specialists can assess your needs, identify appropriate job openings, design a training program, and arrange for the various social service supports necessary to get you on your feet as an employee. Many states and communities have adopted this one-stop shopping approach for individuals seeking help and for businesses that otherwise would have to deal with several different offices to get required licenses and permits and to get help from training and financial assistance programs.

The team and matrix models are obviously similar in certain respects, especially in their essentially

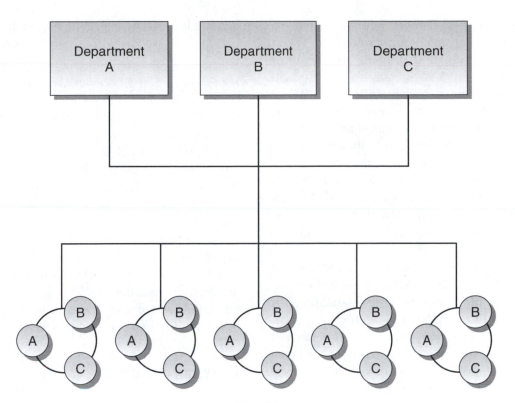

Figure 3.3
Team Model of Organization

antibureaucratic ethos. However, several key differences should be noted. First, the team model organizes around process, the matrix model around project. Teams are usually assembled to deliver ongoing services, while matrix projects generally have a specific time-limited mission to accomplish. A second difference between the team and matrix models is that official lines of authority remain functional in the team form of organization. The team member from the Department of Labor in the employment example continues officially to report to his or her supervisor in the Department of Labor. Although teams may designate leaders, there is no equivalent of a project manager to complicate reporting relationships under this mode of organization. Finally, as noted earlier, matrix organizations are by definition cross-functional. Teams may cross departmental lines or they may not. The key to a team model of organization is to identify the needs of a government's customers and to design administrative processes in ways that facilitate meeting those needs.

Team-based organizations require more than just rearranging boxes on an organizational chart. They require heavy investments in training to ensure that employees understand and are capable of accepting their new responsibilities and working with others. Team-based organizations also need to allow for a fair amount of "downtime," periods when team members are meeting and discussing team issues rather than serving customers, reviewing forms, or otherwise engaging in the actual work of the organization. Decentralizing authority sometimes means diffusing authority. Whenever a group rather than an individual is made responsible for an issue, it becomes more difficult to hold particular people to account when things go wrong.

WHICH MODEL IS BEST?

It is probably tempting to conclude that the matrix model or team-based model of organization is always better than the traditional bureaucratic form of organization. And if you were to browse the shelves of popular management books at your local bookstore, you'd find that there are a lot of titles in print that would support that conclusion—management theory tends to be rather faddish. But let us not be hasty.

Battered though it is, bureaucracy should not be counted out. In fact, many reputable organization theorists would suggest that there are plenty of circumstances when "bureaucracy" is still the right answer to the question, "Which model is best?"

The idea that different organizational designs are appropriate for different circumstances is called *contingency theory*. Contingency theory suggests that in some circumstances, traditional hierarchical organizations—or "mechanistic" organizations, to use the jargon of the field—work very well. At other times, in other circumstances, flatter and more "loosely coupled" organizations—or "organic" organizations—work better.

What are the times and circumstances when one is better than another? Actually, several contingency theories of organization are available, each emphasizing different factors—technology, size, environment, and so forth. This makes it difficult to generalize with full confidence. But here are some things one should take into consideration when thinking about organizational design:

- *Environmental stability.* Traditional bureaucracies are well suited to stable environments (e.g., a revenue department in a small city with an established population). Matrix organizations are well suited to unstable environments (e.g., a planning agency in a town experiencing explosive population growth). Teams can be used in either environment.
- *Control.* Traditional bureaucracies are the best choice when centralized control is paramount (e.g., the Department of Defense and decisions about the use of force). Team-based organizations are the best choice when on-the-spot decisions are needed (such as physician–nurse–rehabilitation therapist–social worker teams and long-term care programs for elderly outpatients). Matrix organizations are often the best choice when overall control of highly specialized but nonetheless intersecting projects is needed (e.g., NASA and the construction of the space station).
- *Nature of work.* Organic structures—matrix or team based—are generally more suited to highly trained specialists (e.g., researchers in the National Institutes of Health). Traditional bureaucratic structures *may* be more congenial for employees who engage in routine work (such as data entry clerks in an accounting department).

You should note that most organizations—public, not-for-profit, and private—have a basic bureaucratic structure, but within that structure and in relations with other agencies, one finds both matrix arrangements for projects and teams for serving customers. In addition, in the public sphere organizational structures frequently reflect political and policy priorities. A reorganization that splits an agency responsible for child and family issues from a general department concerned with social services may in part be a response to publicized cases of child abuse and neglect. A mayor who announces the establishment of a team combining parks, recreation, economic development, and streets may be signaling an emphasis on neighborhood revitalization. In short, organizational design can be symbolic as well as functional.

FURTHER READING

Books that promote a particular perspective on organizational theory—especially simplified, applied, management-in-five-easy-steps sorts of books—are legion and not particularly helpful. For collections of readings that provide general, balanced overviews of organizational theory and behavior, see Jay M. Shafritz, J. Steven Ott, and Yong Suk Jang eds., *Classics of Organization Theory*, 7th ed. (Belmont, CA: Wadsworth, 2010), and Mary Jo Hatch and Ann L. Cunliffe, *Organization Theory: Modern, Symbolic, and Post-Modern Perspectives* (New York: Oxford University Press, 2006). For more focused treatments of organizational design, see Harold F. Gortner, Kenneth L. Nichols, and Carolyn Ball, *Organization Theory: A Public and Nonprofit Perspective*, 3rd ed. (Belmont, CA: Wadsworth, 2007); and Karen Hult and Charles Walcott, *Governing Public Organizations: Politics, Structure, and Institutional Design* (Pacific Grove, CA: Brooks/Cove, 1990).

On the Web
www.aspa.net,org The American Society for Public Administration is the premier professional organization for public administrators and disseminates analyses and discussions of a wide variety of issues concerning organization and management in the public sector.

Overview of Exercise

This is an exercise in organizational design—or rather organizational *redesign.* Based on the models discussed in the text, you will be asked to review the structure of a state agency—the Department of Economic Development—and make some recommendations as to how it might be reconfigured.

INSTRUCTIONS

Step One
Read the background information presented on Form 12.

Step Two
Review the organization chart presented on Form 13.

Step Three
Redesign the structure of the Department of Economic Development so as better to serve the needs of the state's businesses. Use Form 14 to sketch your reconfigured organization chart. Everything is up for grabs in terms of structure. The only given is that the current missions, outlined briefly on the existing organization chart, must still somehow be performed.

Step Four
Answer the questions on Form 15.

Background on the
Department of Economic Development

For the past 20 years, the Department of Economic Development (DED) has been the state government's lead organization for stimulating exports, promoting the state to tourists, attracting new businesses to the state, and helping existing businesses grow. It has a total of 57 employees deployed across three main divisions: Business Development, Workforce Development, and Tourism. The DED's top staff, including the director, three associate directors, and two special assistants, are all exempt, non-civil service employees, meaning that they are essentially political appointees of the governor. Four of these five managers—the exception being the special assistant for communications, a young woman who had worked on the governor's last campaign—are former business executives. All other department employees are career members of the state merit system.

Despite the private-sector experience of its top leadership, the DED has been criticized in recent years for its unresponsiveness to the state's business community. Young entrepreneurs seeking assistance with loans, business development opportunities, employment problems, and other issues are, it has been said, "given the runaround": they are asked to fill out unnecessary paperwork, put on hold on the telephone for long periods of time, told to contact someone else (who turns out to be equally unhelpful), and so on.

Although he is proud of the state's economic growth during his first term, the governor is worried about his likely opponent labeling him "antibusiness" as he heads into his reelection campaign. Consequently, the governor has ordered the DED's director to shake the organization up and make it more responsive to its clientele by fundamentally redesigning its structure.

Organization Chart for the
Department of Economic Development

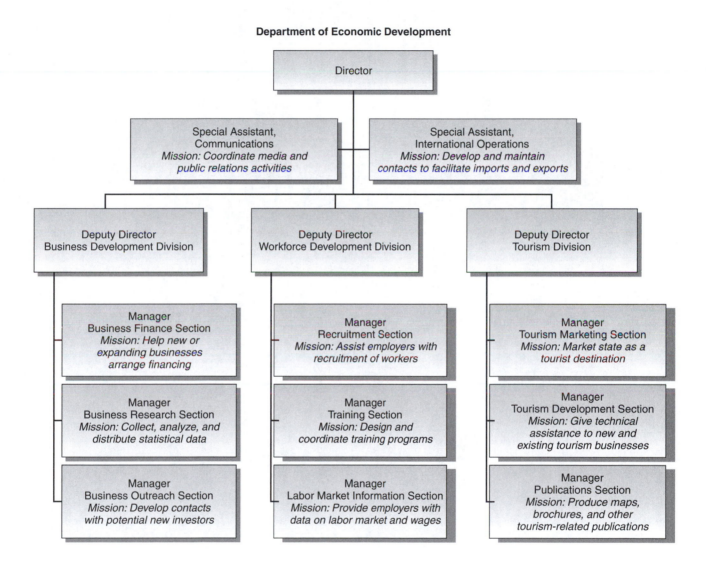

Department of Economic Development

Director

Special Assistant, Communications
Mission: Coordinate media and public relations activities

Special Assistant, International Operations
Mission: Develop and maintain contacts to facilitate imports and exports

Deputy Director Business Development Division

Deputy Director Workforce Development Division

Deputy Director Tourism Division

Manager Business Finance Section
Mission: Help new or expanding businesses arrange financing

Manager Recruitment Section
Mission: Assist employers with recruitment of workers

Manager Tourism Marketing Section
Mission: Market state as a tourist destination

Manager Business Research Section
Mission: Collect, analyze, and distribute statistical data

Manager Training Section
Mission: Design and coordinate training programs

Manager Tourism Development Section
Mission: Give technical assistance to new and existing tourism businesses

Manager Business Outreach Section
Mission: Develop contacts with potential new investors

Manager Labor Market Information Section
Mission: Provide employers with data on labor market and wages

Manager Publications Section
Mission: Produce maps, brochures, and other tourism-related publications

Reconfigured Organization Chart

Questions

1. How would you describe the organizational structure you created on Form 14? Is it a bureaucratic, matrix, or team model—or is it some new hybrid?

2. Why exactly did you design this structure? What impact do you expect it to have on the DED's effectiveness? Will the governor be pleased?

3. Would you like to work in this sort of structure? Why or why not? In general, which type of organization do you think you would find most congenial?

4. What sort of organizational structure do you in fact expect to work in when you graduate and take a professional job?

Exercise 4

Administrative Ethics

ETHICS AND AMERICAN GOVERNMENT

Kickbacks, bribes, no-bid contracts for major campaign contributions, revolving doors, secret meetings, lies, and misinformation—the dispiriting shorthand of today's newspaper headlines suggests that American government has been beset by a veritable plague of dishonesty, corruption, and malfeasance. Between "this-scam" and "that-gate" it is little wonder that citizens' confidence and trust in government has plummeted.

How much distrust is actually warranted is difficult to know, as bribes, payoffs, and other illicit behaviors are, by their nature, furtive. Although unethical behavior in government undoubtedly occurs—and likely always will, failing a basic change in human nature—the apparent epidemic of unethical behavior has mostly involved lobbyists, contractors, elected officials, and their political staffs and appointees. Since the 1990s, many of the ethical problems in government are related to campaign financing. With relatively few exceptions, the millions of men and women who work in the public sector do their jobs with honesty and integrity. But whether unethical behavior originates from a few politicians or a few administrators, it affects the lives and reputations of many.

WHAT ARE ETHICS?

The word *ethics* derives from *ethos*, the Greek term for the particular character or disposition of a people, society, or culture. In contemporary English usage, it refers, at least in the context that concerns us, to moral rules. To say that an act is ethical, therefore, is to say that it is morally defensible. In general, we make determinations about the morality of an act by holding it up to a general standard such as "Taking the life of another human being is wrong" or "You should never tell a lie." Some of these standards may be codified in civil or criminal law, in which case everyone in society is required to observe them. Other ethical standards may be rooted in general social mores, violations of which lead to disapprobation but not legal penalty. In American society, for instance, it is widely considered unethical to take advantage of someone in a business transaction, even when doing so is not strictly illegal. Still other ethical standards may pertain only to specific social groups; in some religious and moral traditions, for example, it is thought to be unethical to slaughter animals for food in other than a prescribed manner, while others disdain eating meat altogether.

Such group-specific ethics have also evolved in many established professions and occupations such as law, medicine, and journalism. Legal ethics, for instance, proscribe attorneys from representing someone involved in an adversarial proceeding with an individual who is already a client of that attorney. Medical ethics guide physicians' decisions on administering life-prolonging drugs to terminally ill patients. Professional ethics forbid journalists from revealing confidential news sources. In cases such as these, whatever sanctions there may be against violators of professional ethics are levied, at least in the first instance, by the profession itself.

Note that ethics and law are not identical. Although our public laws are, at least in theory, derived from general moral standards in society, many questions of ethics remain beyond the purview of the law, as clearly they must in a liberal, tolerant polity. This is an important point to remember, for in a society as law-oriented as ours, it is unfortunately easy to conclude, quite wrongly, that if something is legal, it must be ethical. Bear this warning in mind as you work through the case presented later in this exercise.

WHAT ARE ADMINISTRATIVE ETHICS?

When a highway administrator awards a paving contract in return for $10,000 in small, unmarked bills, most of us would agree that he or she has behaved unethically. So, too, would we think it unethical when the director of a state environmental agency puts his or her brother-in-law on the payroll for an essentially "no-show" job, uses public funds to build a new deck on his or her summer home, or runs a family business from his state office during work hours. These are easy cases, involving at a minimum bribery, theft, and nepotism.

But how about the highway administrator who accepts an unpaid speaking engagement before the monthly dinner meeting of the local Highway Contractors Association, which reimburses him for his carfare and feeds him chicken à la king? Should the highway administrator treat a contractor differently if company officials made campaign contributions to the governor? What about the agency director who hires her brother-in-law for a real job, uses public funds to cater a party at her summer home for a visiting delegation of foreign environmental officials, or charges the monthly rental on her personal cell phone, which she uses much of the time for public business, to her office account? These cases are less clear; certainly there appears to be no outright bribery or corruption involved. Any evaluation of the probity of these actions will probably start out with "Well, it depends. . . ." What are the agency rules about free meals from contractors? Was the brother-in-law the most qualified applicant? Was the catered party a matter of official business? Are the personal calls only incidental and infrequent?

Even answers to questions like these do not always provide clear resolutions of ethical dilemmas in the public service. Knowing what is ethical is not always easy. To be ethical is to do the right thing. But what is the right thing? As with law, medicine, and other professions, public

administration has developed ethical guidelines to help its practitioners deal with questions of this sort. One such set of guidelines is the code of ethics adopted by the American Society for Public Administration (ASPA) in 1981 (see box). As one would expect, the standards in this code stress the primacy of law, the importance of sound management, and the need to avoid conflicts of interest. The emphasis clearly reflects the traditional values of the profession and its historic sense of itself as a value-free instrument of public policy.

Yet, ASPA's code also makes pointed references to concepts such as "justice," "equity," "conscience," and "moral ambiguities" and gives a prominent place to the idea that public servants are ultimately responsible to the people. This suggests that ethical administrators sometimes have to make moral choices for themselves, that they cannot view themselves simply as order-taking technicians. And therein lies the major tension that underlies any discussion of ethics in public administration. How can a public administrator know what to do when ethical action is premised on both subservience to the law and a sense of individual conscience? What happens when obedience to those in lawfully authoritative positions requires actions that conflict with a person's own reasoned estimate of the demands of equity, justice, and the public interest? How should a person weigh the demands of an elected official against professional integrity and a careful, objective analysis? What is the ethical course for a state environmental official who believes that his agency's recent grant of a discharge permit to a large factory will have a subtle, though substantial, effect on groundwater pollution, and thereby increase cancer rates 10 or 20 years down the road? What is the responsibility of intelligence analysts when they hear public statements by top officials that conflict with information that has been given to these officials?

Sometimes the quandary is whether or not to participate in or to facilitate behavior that you consider wrong. There are also instances in which the issue is disclosing to the press or to legislative committees the unethical or illegal activities of others. Accountability and democratic discourse require information. But those who reveal evidence of fraud, corruption, and waste put themselves at risk. Even if the message is accurate, the messenger may get shot. And, of course, the message may be

---

A Code of Ethics for Public Administration

The American Society for Public Administration exists to advance the science, processes, and art of public administration. The Society affirms its responsibility to develop the spirit of professionalism within its membership and to increase public awareness of moral standards in public service by its example. To this end, we, the members of the Society, commit ourselves to the following principles:

1. Service to the public is beyond service to oneself.
2. The people are sovereign and those in public service are ultimately responsible to them.
3. Laws govern all actions of the public service. Where laws or regulations are ambiguous, leave discretion, or require change, we will seek to serve the best interests of the public.
4. Efficient and effective management is basic to public administration. Subversion through misuse of influence, fraud, waste, or abuse is intolerable. Employees who responsibly call attention to wrongdoing will be encouraged.

5. The merit system, equal opportunity, and affirmative action principles will be supported, implemented, and promoted.
6. Safeguarding the public trust is paramount. Conflicts of interest, bribes, gifts, or favors that subordinate public positions to private gains are unacceptable.
7. Service to the public creates demands for special sensitivity to the qualities of justice, courage, honesty, equity, competence, and compassion. We esteem these qualities, and we will actively promote them.
8. Conscience performs a critical role in choosing among courses of action. It takes into account the moral ambiguities of life and the necessity to examine value priorities: good ends never justify immoral means.
9. Public administrators are not engaged merely in preventing wrong, but in pursuing right through timely and energetic execution of their responsibilities.

Source: Adopted by the National Council of the American Society for Public Administration on December 6, 1981.

---

based on a misunderstanding or it may be false and intended to get a rival in trouble. To encourage responsible revelations of fraud, waste, and abuse, the federal government passed the Whistleblower Protection Act of 1989. Many states have similar laws. Those who go outside the chain of command to expose wrongdoing are protected from being fired, demoted, or otherwise disciplined while their charges are investigated. If the charges are found to be baseless, then the whistle-blower can be severely disciplined for being irresponsible. In short, whistle-blowing is valued and at least partially protected, but there still are risks.

The application of ethical guidelines is rarely clear and obvious. Consider this example: It is a widely accepted standard in public administration that it is unethical (as well as illegal) for an official to accept money or other gifts from individuals or groups who might materially benefit from a decision made by that official. Now, it is obvious that certain kinds of behaviors would clearly be out of bounds according to this rule. Certainly, an administrator would be in violation if he or she accepted, say, a gift box of gourmet coffee (much less $10,000 in small, unmarked bills) at Christmas from a contractor with whom he or she does business. But does that mean that the same administrator couldn't accept a cup or two of that same coffee from the contractor while visiting a job site? And if it is OK to accept the cup of coffee, what does that suggest about the principle? That it's all right to accept gifts as long as they have hot water added to them or are consumed immediately? Probably not. We could argue that what the principle really says is that an administrator shouldn't accept *valuable* gifts; that a cup of coffee worth $4.00 is allowable but a box of the beans from which the coffee is brewed is not. But then what is the cutoff in our definition of "valuable"? Would it be legitimate to accept a small packet of beans at Christmas worth $4.00? Again, probably not, so maybe we can avoid the problem by saying that the cup of coffee is not really a gift, that it is instead a common courtesy extended in normal social interaction; such courtesies, we might argue, are OK. But what are the bounds of common courtesies? In some circles, providing limousine service or an evening's entertainment falls under this heading. If you think those sound excessive, where would you draw the line? And doesn't drawing a line just put you back in the business of trying to define "valuable"?

In wrestling with these issues, it is important to acknowledge that the public sector has a set of standards and concerns that is different from the private sector. There is obviously nothing wrong with the owner of a private business hiring a relative. If that relative is so incompetent that he or she causes the company to lose money, that is unfortunate, but it is the risk the company took. If a private company wines and dines a customer or contractor, that is considered a legitimate business activity, and they may even deduct the expenses for tax purposes.

In the public sector, on the other hand, there is a need for public trust in the objectivity and integrity of government actions and decisions. Public-sector decision making in a democracy has to be open so that citizens can participate in the deliberations and monitor the behavior of their elected representatives. The concern for public trust in elected officials has focused on relations with lobbyists and on campaign finance. The current concern for public trust in administrators has generated the following general principles, which emphasize some of the principles in the ASPA code of ethics:

1. One should not use a public office for private gain.
2. The appearance of a conflict of interest is as unethical as the substance of a conflict of interest.
3. There is a responsibility to blow the whistle on instances of waste, fraud, and abuse.

These are weighty principles and, in some situations, call on public administrators to take courageous actions. These are also principles that have to be balanced against the need to be responsive to the direction from elected officials and are sometimes hard to apply in the inevitable ambiguities of specific situations. But risks and complexities do not excuse unethical actions or inactions.

FURTHER READING

A good place to begin further reading in this field is with Stephen Bailey's classic article "Ethics and the Public Service," *Public Administration Review* 24 (November–December 1964), 72–89. For important arguments on the relationship between constitutional values and administrative ethics, see two books by John Rohr: *Ethics for Bureaucrats: An Essay on Law and Values* (New York: Dekker, 1978); and *Public Service, Ethics, and Constitutional Practice* (Lawrence: University Press of Kansas, 1999). Albert Hirschman provides an especially pithy summary of the choices facing an administrator caught in an ethical quandary in *Exit, Voice and Loyalty* (Cambridge, MA: Harvard University Press, 1970). Another useful resource is Willa Bruce, *Classics of Administrative Ethics* (Boulder, CO: Westview Press, 2001).

In a 1980 article, "Whistle-Blowing in the Public Sector: An Overview of the Issues," *Review of the Public Personnel Administration*, James Bowman reviews the history of whistle-blowing and the legal protections available to administrators who take this step. Guy B. Adams and Danny L. Balfour provide a relevant book in *Unmasking Administrative Evil*, 3rd ed. (Armonk, NY: M.E. Sharpe, 2009). For a thorough study see C. Fred Alford, *Whistleblowers: Broken Lives and Organizational Power* (Ithaca, NY: Cornell University Press, 2002).

Terry L. Cooper has done a great deal of interesting work in the field of administrative ethics. His edited *Handbook of Administrative Ethics* (New York: Dekker, 1994) contains 29 essays on the subject that range from philosophical inquiries to comparative analysis. His book *The Responsible Administrator: An Approach to Ethics for the Administrative Role*, 5th ed. (San Francisco:

Jossey-Bass, 2006) discusses how people can remain ethical in an organizational environment. You will also find useful Michael S. Josephson, *Preserving the Public Trust: Five Principles of Public Service Ethics* (Bloomington, IN: Unlimited Publishing, 2005).

On the Web

www.ignet.gov Inspectors general in federal agencies are responsible for reporting on ethical concerns in the management of their respective organizations.

www.aspanet.org The American Society for Public Administration has a code of ethics for its members.

Overview of Exercise

In this exercise, you will read a case study describing the ethical dilemma confronted by a staff member in a county planning department. Your assignment is to analyze the situation from the staff member's perspective and to outline what you would do if you found yourself in these circumstances.

INSTRUCTIONS

Step One
Carefully read the case material presented on Form 16.

Step Two
Answer the discussion questions on Form 17.

The Case

THE SETTING

Windham County is one of the most rapidly growing areas in the United States. By almost any measure—employment, housing starts, population increase—it has experienced extraordinary development in recent years. Although its economy, as in many similar areas along the Eastern seaboard, was traditionally dependent on manufacturing, state and local officials worked hard to attract new service-based industries and have been successful in establishing Windham County as a major banking and insurance center. As a result, there has been a tremendous influx of white-collar workers, which has caused a boom in local residential and commercial construction. Consequently, pressures on Windham County's dwindling supply of vacant land are great. Roads that 5 years ago wound through quiet pastures and apple orchards are now clogged with cars making their way to and from the endless series of housing developments, shopping centers, and corporate plazas that line their tarmac. Demands for new water supplies, sewer lines, and other infrastructural improvements, as well as schools, medical facilities, and protective services, have multiplied apace. A Windham County version of Rip Van Winkle, awakening in the new millennium, would find his environs as foreign as the moon.

The entity mainly responsible for guiding this development is the county government. Although the county encompasses several small cities that bear responsibility for traditional urban services within their borders, most Windham County residents—and most of the county's land—are to be found in unincorporated areas. Thus, the county is in the business of providing many primary services, including police and fire protection. Moreover, under state law, county government exercises many county-wide functions, superseding the cities in such areas as transportation, libraries, health and social services, and land-use planning.

Windham County government is organized on a strong executive-council model. A county executive is elected on a county-wide basis for a term of 4 years; the executive is responsible for day-to-day administration, for appointing major administrative officers, and for preparing an annual budget. The county's legislative branch is a county council, the seven members of which are elected by district; they elect a chair from among themselves. Elections to all county offices are partisan and are usually hotly contested. Registration in the county is about evenly divided between Republicans and Democrats, and control of the executive and legislative offices has alternated between the two parties with considerable regularity.

Not surprisingly, development issues are central to county politics. In a jurisdiction where the names and faces of builders and bankers have become as famous—and occasionally infamous—as any politician's, candidates for office routinely stake out positions in favor of "responsible growth," suggesting vaguely that they will keep the fires of economic development stoked without buckling under to "undue pressures" from developers. The *Windham Journal*, the county's sole newspaper, regularly reports the development plans and deals, would-be and otherwise, that percolate through business and political circles and more than once has uncovered a distinctly malodorous transaction. Indeed, the whiff of corruption has never been far from development politics in Windham County, a fact that is not exactly dumbfounding given the tens of millions of dollars at stake in many of the deals. Developers and contractors are major contributors to campaign coffers. In the past 15 years, three elected officials have been indicted—two were convicted—for peddling their votes to developers. Two years ago, the director of planning resigned amid allegations that he had received consulting fees from an investment group with substantial land holdings in the county. Beyond these cases, if the rumor mills are to be believed, few top officials have maintained what one would consider a healthy distance between themselves and the contractors, builders, and real estate moguls who have transformed the face of the county.

THE ISSUE

For the past few years, the biggest story in local development circles has been Bluestone Golf Course, a facility owned and operated by the county. Situated on 200 acres of gently rolling hills, Bluestone is the last green space of any size in northeastern Windham County, an area known locally as Volvo Valley. Bounded on the east by the Windham River and on the west by a major state highway, this corridor, with the golf course at its center, presents, from a developer's perspective, eye-popping demographics: half the households within a 2-mile radius of the course have incomes of more than $180,000 a year; the average family consists of 1.8 professional wage earners and 1.1 children, owns 2.1 late-model foreign cars, and lives in an owner-occupied dwelling on 0.85 acre of land; moreover, 250,000 people live within a 15-minute drive of the golf course. What really makes the developers' pocket calculators smoke, though, is the fact that, as one put it, "the commercial potential of the corridor is under-realized." Roughly translated, this means that the upper-middle-class denizens of northeastern Windham County have to drive major distances to spend their money. Although the state highway that runs through the corridor, Windham Pike, is lined with seeming scores of strip developments, these are filled with grocery stores, insurance agencies, auto dealerships, chiropractors' offices, and the usual jarring array of fast-food outlets, muffler shops, gas stations, and all-night "convenience marts." The region's only major shopping mall is located just off an interstate highway in the center of Windham County, 20 to 30 minutes by car from Volvo Valley.

Three years ago, acting on a recommendation from the County Office of Economic Development, the County Council approved, in principle, a plan to "swap" with a developer the Bluestone land for a yet-to-be-specified parcel elsewhere and a yet-to-be-specified amount of money. The theory was that both parties would profit handsomely from the exchange. The county would receive a significant amount of cash immediately, plus property and sales tax revenues that eventually would amount to $50 to $75 million per year; golfers would be mollified, it was hoped, by using the new parcel for another course with even more attractive facilities. The developer would receive 200 acres of extraordinarily prime land on which a new mall—with major department stores, restaurants, boutiques, and movie theaters—could be built.

Since the council's approval-in-principle of the exchange, a bewildering variety of proposals has been floated, sunk, and refloated. Initially, five major developers presented formal prospectuses to the county executive's office. Although the submissions were theoretically confidential—in part to protect all parties from speculative effects on land values, in part to help the county get the best deal possible—at least the rough outlines of all the proposals made it into the press in short order. The opportunities for leaks were manifold. The proposals were seen by the county executive and her immediate staff, the directors of planning and of the Office of Economic Development and their top staffs, and all members of the council, who had resisted the suggestion that circulation of the proposals be restricted, for reasons of security, to a special committee. In any event, the net effect of the public disclosures was to make development politics in Windham County even more circuslike than usual. Citizen action groups sprouted like dandelions to stake out positions on the issue: The Bluestone Golf Association lobbied furiously to protect its "historic links"; the Windham River Committee formed to press the county to keep the Bluestone land but convert it to a park and nature preserve; the Emergency Housing Action Coalition insisted that any development include "affordable housing" to accommodate Windham County's "growing low-income and homeless population"; a group calling itself Concerned Homeowners of Northeast Valley opposed any development that would threaten the "unique social and environmental character" of the area; the Small Merchants Association worried that a new mall would siphon off trade and benefit only "big-money investors in London, New York, and Tokyo." Meanwhile, major business and civic leaders scurried around the county, painting glowing pictures of new jobs and other economic benefits that would spin off from one proposal or another.

In this atmosphere, firm decisions proved elusive. Each time county officials seemed close to some agreement, a leak would produce a newspaper story, complete with maps and artists' sketches, followed by the mobilization of anyone and everyone who had a stake in the issue. Charges would inevitably be made about who contributed what to whose campaign or which spouse or brother-in-law worked for which developer. Indeed, it was in the midst of this free-for-all that one council member was indicted for trying to "rent" his vote to one of the developers with a Bluestone proposal pending. Although the vote in question involved rezoning of another property, and although the developer cooperated with the prosecutor's office and allowed himself to be "wired" during a meeting at which money was to change hands, the affair further tainted the whole Bluestone affair.

After 3 years of commotion and indecision, the county executive and council agreed 6 months ago on a process that would, they believed, bring the matter to closure. According to Resolution 252, a final set of sealed proposals was to be submitted to the Office of the County Executive by October 1. A small team of county officials—the county executive, the planning and development directors, and the council president—would review the proposals, consulting only with their senior staffs, negotiate any changes with the developers, and recommend one to the full council by November 1. The council would have 2 months to hold public hearings and vote the proposal up or down.

THE PROBLEM

You have been observing this extended dispute from the vantage point of a desk in the County Planning Office, where you have been employed for 6 years as a planning analyst. You report directly to the chief of the Planning Analysis Division, one of the office's two operating divisions. Your division, which employs eight professional staff members, is responsible for the development and administration of the county's long-range (20-year) land-use and transportation plan, the mid-range (5-year) capital development plan, the annual county profile (a snapshot of demographic trends), and any special planning projects. The other, slightly smaller division of the planning office, Planning Services, deals with day-to-day zoning and assessment questions.

Given your responsibilities, you have dealt with one facet or another of the Bluestone issue almost continuously, although not exclusively, for the past few years. As a consequence, you are about as well informed as anyone else in the county when it comes to the various plans for the property. And with your professional training and experience, you are well equipped to assess the costs and consequences of the various proposals. In general, you have grown weary of the whole affair. While you see genuine benefits accruing to the public if a Bluestone exchange goes through, you have begun to wonder whether development has gotten totally out of control in the county. Sometimes it seems that the 20-year plan might as well be written on an Etch-a-Sketch, the way planned green space regularly gets nibbled away in rezoning applications. It might not be so bad, you think, if the process were more orderly, if people stopped and thought about what they were doing and made more rational decisions. That's what you learned in your courses in school. But that's not how the process works. There's too much money at stake. Otherwise sensible people start acting like hogs at a trough.

For years, though, you've stuck it out, keeping your head down and doing the best job you could. For various Bluestone schemes alone, you've dutifully completed three transportation flow analyses, put together a county recreational needs assessment, and coordinated impact studies with the county's Water Resource Agency. Although you've gotten the impression that most of your work might as well have been chucked into a black hole—the politicians seem already to know the answers they want and are just looking for ways to rationalize them—you've always figured that your job was to analyze facts, not to set policy. No one—at least no one in a position of authority—has asked for your considered opinion about what to do with that golf course, and it's unlikely anyone will. Sure, you've heard the rumors about palms being greased and silent partnerships being arranged; no one who lives in Windham County, much less who works in the County Building, can avoid them. But you've never actually seen any hard evidence of corruption yourself, so you've decided to let the district attorney and the feds worry about it.

At least that was the situation until last week. On Wednesday, 6 days ago, your boss called you to his office and asked you to sit down. After a warm greeting and preliminary chitchat about your family, he indicated that the Bluestone Review Committee, as the small county team had become known, was nearing a decision on a development proposal. Although he (your boss) wasn't a member of the committee, he had, he said, been consulted frequently, particularly on technical planning questions. "Now we need your help," he smiled. He picked up a manila folder from his desk and withdrew a thin sheaf of papers that he passed across to you, indicating, with a wave of his hand, that you should look it over. You recognized it immediately as one of your transportation flow analyses—the one triggered by TriState's proposal for a sprawling, 200-store, multilevel mall at Bluestone. You flip through it perfunctorily and raise an eyebrow at your boss, as if to say, What of it? This was an easy one as far as you were concerned. The study showed conclusively—about a year ago—that even with improvements, Windham Pike could not begin to handle the volume of traffic generated by a project of that size; it wasn't even close. Why bring it up now, you wonder?

"There seems to be a problem with some of the numbers in that report," your boss continued, still smiling. "Nothing serious—and certainly no reflection on your work. It's just that the volume estimates are high and some of the destination data need cleaning up. I wonder if you could take a look at it this afternoon and fix it up. I've got to report back to the committee tomorrow."

You agree to check it over, although you doubt that there is anything wrong with it, and after a few more minutes of personal banter with your boss, you return to your office and pull out the files containing the supporting documentation for the report. After 3 hours of poring over the original demographic projections, trip studies, and transportation flow models, you lean back in your chair and rub your eyes. No errors here, you think. Sure, there's some room for judgment—after all, we're dealing with assumptions piled on top of assumptions. But how can we just reduce the volume estimates? And why should we? If anything, the new demographics bolster the original conclusions. You call your boss, but he's left for the day. So you position yourself in front of your computer and send him an e-mail message that says, in essence, the report as written stands as far as you're concerned. You grab your coat, head for home, and forget the whole thing.

Two days later, on Friday afternoon, you run into a casual acquaintance, an administrator from Economic Development, down by the vending machines in the basement. He gives you a playful poke in the ribs and says, "Hey, I hear it's gonna be TriState. You heard anything?"

"What?" you ask, never paying much attention to this fellow.

"You know, Bluestone. I hear the committee's coming out with an endorsement of the big TriState project. But it's still hush-hush. Keep it under your hat." He gives you a conspiratorial wink and walks away.

You're puzzled but are distracted enough by other problems not to give it too much thought. Later, though, your boss stops by the office and says something you find peculiar: "Sorry I didn't see you yesterday. I was tied up in meetings all day. You know, I think this Bluestone thing is finally going to be off our neck. I can't say anything more now, of course, but a deal is in the wind. Anyway, I got your e-mail and wanted to let you know I appreciate the time you spent checking over that report. Some of the estimates were still a little off, but fortunately we got some revised numbers from Fogarty at the State Department of Transportation. Listen, have a good weekend."

New numbers from Fogarty? What new numbers? Why would the state transportation department have generated any new numbers? You make a note to call Fogarty on Monday.

MONDAY

Your call to Anne Fogarty has not been enlightening. Although you'd worked with her a fair amount in the past, today she seemed distant, even evasive. Yes, she said, her office had reassessed their flow projections in the northeastern corridor of Windham County. Just a routine adjustment based on some "revised assumptions." And no, she couldn't be more specific about the assumptions just now. She really didn't have the time today. There were a lot of things to wrap up around the office. You knew, didn't you, that she was leaving at the end of the week? Three weeks of accumulated vacation, then off to a new job in the private sector. Oh, really? With who? TriState Development, she said, and then rang off.

Now your stomach begins to hurt, and you really don't want to think about why. After staring out the window for half an hour, you decide to go down the hall and speak to your boss.

His office door is open. After he motions you in, his usual broad smile seems to fade a bit as you mention that you had been chatting with Fogarty. You are curious, you say, about the changed assumptions in the Windham Pike projections.

"Just a technical adjustment," he says. "DOT initiated it."

"But they don't seem to jibe with any of the other data we have," you point out.

"Look," says your boss. "You know how these things work. The assumptions in these models are always up for grabs, anybody's guess. DOT made the call; we accepted it. Now, I think it would be best if we didn't pursue this any further."

"I understand," you say. "But you know, I've heard some rumors that the TriState proposal is alive again. I know you can't talk about it, but ..."

"That's right. I can't talk about it, and you shouldn't talk about it either."

"But just hypothetically ... if those numbers are used ..."

"Life is full of ifs," he says, cutting you off again. "Just like mathematical models." Then, with his smile completely gone, his eyes lock onto yours. "Let me be clear about this," he says. "This project has been in the works for 3 years. We've seen things get screwed up time and time again. Now it finally looks as if we're making progress. A lot of people have invested a lot of time and a lot of money. The political balance here is very delicate. No one is going to appreciate anyone who does anything to upset that balance. Your flow projections were estimates. DOT's flow projections were estimates. I have decided, and the rest of the committee has agreed, to go with the DOT's estimates. As an associate director of this office, that is my judgment to make. Now, do we understand each other?"

You nod your head vaguely and walk back to your office. Once at your desk, you reach for your telephone ... but you are not sure whose number you are going to dial.

Questions

1. What should you, the young planner in this case, do now? Is it necessary or appropriate to report your suspicions to anyone? If so, to whom? Whose number should you dial?

2. If you fail to report your suspicions in this case, are you guilty of an ethical violation? If so, why? Should a person who fails to report such information be subject to any sort of penalty? If you don't think that you, as the planner in this circumstance, have an obligation to pursue the matter, what are your reasons?

3. What would the ASPA code of ethics advise you to do?

4. Assume that there is someone you trust at the *Windham Journal.* Would it be a good idea to leak your suspicions to the press and let them investigate? What would be the consequences?

5. Do you think you should be able to make a report about your suspicions anonymously?

6. Assuming that you decide to report something to someone, what exactly will you report? Would you say something just about your boss, just about Fogarty, or about both of them? Why?

7. Is there anything that can be done to avoid, or at least minimize, unethical behavior in public administration in general? How about in this case in particular?

PART II
Public Management

WHAT IS PUBLIC MANAGEMENT?

The millions of men and women who comprise the public sector in the United States represent an extraordinary variety of skills and occupations, from architecture to zoology. Indeed, it is difficult to imagine an occupation that does not have a few of its practitioners laboring away in one corridor or another of American government. One consequence of this diversity is that the terms we commonly apply to their collective activities—*public administration* or *public management*—are not as descriptive as we might like. Even if we reserve our usage of *public manager* (as we probably should) for those who exercise some supervisory or discretionary authority, we can still encounter difficulties. Although they are all public administrators by this definition, a virologist at the National Institutes of Health, for instance, will likely not feel a close kinship with either an air transportation safety specialist at the Federal Aviation Administration or a regional administrator for the U.S. Department of Housing and Urban Development. As we shall see in Part III, our rank-in-job personnel system, which nicely accommodates technical specialists while frustrating administrative generalists, is largely responsible for this phenomenon.

But while the day-to-day work of public managers does vary tremendously in substance, there are important similarities in how they do what they do, similarities that mark them both as managers (as opposed to nonmanagers) and as public managers (as opposed to private managers). In what is perhaps the best-known formulation of the tasks of an executive, Luther Gulick and Tyndall Urwick offered the mnemonic acronym POSDCORB: planning, organizing, staffing, directing, coordinating, reporting, and budgeting. Other theorists—and most textbook authors—have compiled similar lists.

For our purposes in *The Public Administration Workbook*, we will go beyond these general theories and focus on a key skill, that is, communicating within an organization, and on five types of challenges faced by managers in the public sector, each requiring a distinct approach to marshalling the resources and talents in an organization to achieve public goals:

1. Operational management—providing ongoing services and programs.
2. Project management—completing a task that is not ongoing, but has a specific beginning and end.
3. Contract management—negotiating and monitoring agreements with private businesses and not-for-profit organizations.
4. Regulatory management—promulgating administrative rules and ensuring compliance with them.
5. Emergency management—responding to disasters, whether from natural forces, human error, or intentional attacks.

FURTHER READING

Two classic attempts to define public administration and public management are Woodrow Wilson "The Study of Administration," *Political Science Quarterly* 2 (June 1887), 35–51; and Dwight Waldo, "What Is Public Administration?," in Waldo, *The Study of Administration* (New York: Random House, 1955), both of which have been reprinted in Jay M. Shafritz and Albert C. Hyde, eds., *Classics of Public Administration*, 6th ed.

(Florence, KY: Wadsworth, 2008). A good essay articulating the unique values of public agencies is Charles Goodsell, *The Case for Bureaucracy: A Public Administration Polemic* (Washington, DC: CQ Press, 2004). For a discussion of the differences between public and private management, see Graham T. Allison, "Public and Private Management: Are They Fundamentally Alike in All Unimportant Respects?," *Proceedings for the Public Management Research Conference*, November 19–20, 1979 (Washington, DC: Office of Personnel Management, OPM Document 127-53-1, February 1980), also reprinted in Shafritz and Hyde.

On the Web

www.sec.gov/pdf/handbook.pdf Believe it or not . . . a widely used guide to good writing in government was produced by the federal Securities and Exchange Commission: *A Plain English Handbook: How to Create Clear SEC Disclosure Documents.*

Exercise 5

The Administrative Memo

AN IMPORTANT TELEPHONE CONVERSATION

Professor Jones is sitting at his desk grading term papers and rubbing his forehead when the telephone rings:

PROFESSOR JONES: Hello?

PERSONNEL OFFICER: Professor Jones? This is Molly MacIntyre from the Department of the Interior in Washington. I hope I'm not interrupting you.

PROFESSOR JONES: No, no, not at all. What can I do for you?

PERSONNEL OFFICER: Well, I'm calling to follow up on a letter of recommendation you wrote last fall for a young man named Jeff Stone. Do you remember Jeff?

PROFESSOR JONES: Yes, of course. He took . . . let me think . . . two courses with me. That's right—he took my introductory undergraduate public administration course and later my course in organization theory.

PERSONNEL OFFICER: Good. Well, Jeff has applied for a position as an entry-level analyst in our budget office. He is one of the finalists for the job, and now I'm trying to get a little more information to help us make the decision.

PROFESSOR JONES: I'll be happy to help. Jeff is a very bright fellow.

PERSONNEL OFFICER: Yes, he seems to have quite a strong record. And in the initial interview we had with him, he came across very well. Very articulate and personable.

PROFESSOR JONES: I recall using similar adjectives in my letter.

PERSONNEL OFFICER: Yes, you did. But there is one thing that troubles us.

PROFESSOR JONES: What's that?

PERSONNEL OFFICER: His writing.

PROFESSOR JONES: Ah.

PERSONNEL OFFICER: Yes, you know, on the recommendation form you filled out for Jeff, you checked "excellent" for all the characteristics except writing.

PROFESSOR JONES: Jeff is a really bright guy. He has great problem-solving abilities. He works well with other people. And he's motivated.

PERSONNEL OFFICER: But his writing?

PROFESSOR JONES: I also remember that he made a terrific oral presentation to the class.

PERSONNEL OFFICER: But he can write?

We will cease our eavesdropping here, as Professor Jones tries to frame a response that is both honest and fair to Jeff. How the conversation ends in this particular case doesn't really concern us anyhow. What is important is that similar exchanges occur all the time. When you graduate and begin applying for your first professional job, you will need to provide references from professors or other people who know your work. They will be asked to evaluate, among other things, your analytical skills, your motivation, your maturity, and, very importantly, your ability to write. You will no doubt have to write something as part of your application. Public agencies—and private-sector employers—want to hire people who can write well. You may be a

69

natural leader and as sharp as a tack, but if you can't write, you will be at a tremendous disadvantage.

In some respects, the idea of good administrative writing may seem to be a contradiction in terms. Certainly we are all painfully familiar with examples of "bureaucratese," that bloated form of prose that seems designed to obfuscate rather than communicate, where *kill* becomes "terminate with extreme prejudice" and *to be fired* is rendered as "subjected to involuntary outplacement." Breathes there a person who has not been confounded from time to time by the "EZ" instructions for Form 1040 or by the baleful opacity of insurance policies? Probably not, for as Max Weber noted long ago, bureaucracies—public and private—hide behind language, and bureaucracies are ubiquitous.

These tendencies notwithstanding, the ability to write well is an important administrative skill. What sort of things will you have to write? Memoranda, annual reports, budget narratives, personnel evaluations, policy proposals, legislative testimony, and press releases are all examples.

Writing is a skill like any other. It is honed through practice. No single course, much less any single exercise in a book of this sort, can magically turn you into a good writer. It can, however, help you learn some of the fundamentals. And you *can* learn them.

THE ABCs OF GOOD ADMINISTRATIVE WRITING: ACCURACY, BREVITY, AND CLARITY

Accuracy
Good writing is accurate writing. This is true in two senses. First, the statements that you make in your writing—the facts on which you rely—should be true. If you are writing a report for the county office of social services and you note that last year its social workers had an average case load of 75 clients each, make sure that is a correct figure. Everyone makes mistakes occasionally; good writers minimize them. Nothing causes the credibility of an administrator to plummet as quickly as a reputation for error.

Accuracy is important in a second sense as well: Your spelling, punctuation, and grammar all should be correct. There is an old saying: "You can't expect anyone to take your writing more seriously than you appear to take it yourself." If you draft a memo or prepare a report that is sloppy, filled with

---

The U.S. General Accountability Office: A Paragon of Accuracy

The United States General Accountability Office, often called the investigative arm of Congress, is an independent federal agency responsible for evaluating the performance of federal programs and agencies. You may have seen some of its blue-covered reports on such topics as "Medical Waste Regulations: Health and Environmental Risks Need to Be Fully Assessed" and "Navy Ships: Status of SSN–21 Ship Construction Program." Because it almost always serves as a critic of bureaucratic performance, it has to get its facts right to maintain its credibility—and it does. Over the years, GAO staffers have developed an intricate system of fact checking and report verification that is unrivaled in thoroughness. As a report reaches its final stages of drafting, a GAO employee marks it up with a red pencil, cross-referencing every assertion, phrase, and number in the manuscript to a set of supporting documents in GAO files, creating, in effect, hundreds, even thousands, of invisible footnotes!

---

run-on sentences or misspelled words, you clearly have not taken your writing seriously. Others will treat it accordingly.

This rule is not hard to follow. One clearly does not need to have "natural writing talent" to be careful in the use of facts or to use a dictionary.

Brevity
The best administrative writing is short and to the point. Administrators are busy people. So are the legislators, contractors, customers, and others with whom they interact. Almost no one has the time or patience to wade through a memo that runs on like a Norse saga. In many offices, the rule is that if a document is longer than three or four pages, it must have an "executive summary" attached to the front for interested parties to scan quickly. You need to exercise judgment in following this rule of brevity, of course. If your assignment is to write an evaluation of a major agency program, you likely will need to say more than "This program has failed to meet its objectives."

<table>
<tr><td>

A Brief Poem on Brevity

In general those who have nothing to say
    Contrive to spend the longest time in doing it,
They turn and vary it in every way,
    Hashing it, stewing it, mincing it, *ragouting* it.
             —James Russell Lowell,
             An Oriental Apologue, Stanza 15

</td><td>

A Writing Checklist

1. Know your main point, state it at the outset, and build the rest of your writing around it.
2. Verify your facts.
3. Check your spelling and grammar.
4. Eliminate unnecessary words and phrases.
5. Use the active voice.
6. Keep it short, simple, and to the point.

</td></tr>
</table>

Clarity

Good writing is clear writing. It is writing that takes the work—and the guesswork—out of reading. When you write clearly, your audience knows exactly what you mean, and that should be your primary goal.

To keep it clear, keep it simple. Too many people knit their words together as if they were weaving an oriental carpet, producing awesomely intricate and ornamented patterns of prose. Even if you think your readers enjoyed diagraming sentences in tenth-grade English (a doubtful proposition, by the way), don't construct your sentences as if they were puzzles to be solved. For those who aspire to clear writing, there is no better friend than the simple declarative sentence, arranged in subject-verb-object form (e.g., "The Department of Transportation [subject] awarded [verb] 300 contracts [object]").

Avoid unnecessary jargon and fancy words. Although you may be justly proud that you have mastered the foreign language of your profession (Pentagon-speak, legalese, accountingish, or whatever), don't assume that all your readers are equally adept. As the great essayist E. B. White wrote more than 40 years ago, "Do not be tempted by a twenty-dollar word when there is a ten-center handy, ready and able."[1]

Clarity does not come cheap. In fact, there is an inverse relationship between the ease of reading and the ease of writing. As Hemingway put it, "Easy writing makes hard reading."[2] Thus, it is a good guess that the crisper and clearer the sentence, the longer it took to write. The key is to rewrite, and then rewrite some more.

FURTHER READING

William Strunk Jr. and E. B. White, *The Elements of Style*, 50th Anniversary Edition (New York: Longman, 2008), is one of the pithiest and most useful volumes on good writing. Margaret D. Shertzer, *The Elements of Grammar* (New York: Longman, 1996), provides a solid grounding in the rules of our language. A good guide specific to public administration is Catherine F. Smith, *Writing Public Policy: A Practical Guide to Communicating in the Policy-Making Process* (New York: Oxford University Press, 2005). Probably the best advice for someone who wants to write well is this: read a lot of good writing. No one ever learned to write a snappy sentence by watching television.

Overview of Exercise

This exercise has two parts. First, you will read a short memorandum drafted for the signature of your boss by one of your coworkers and make any corrections you deem necessary. Next, you will write a brief memorandum on a subject as specifically assigned by your instructor or as outlined in Step Two of the instructions.

INSTRUCTIONS

Step One

You are J. Wilson, a staff assistant to A. Babcock, Secretary of the Department of Environmental Protection. Secretary Babcock has sent you a brief note asking you to review—and revise as necessary—a

---

[1]William Strunk, Jr. and E. B. White, *The Elements of Style*, 50th Anniversary Edition (New York: Longman, 2008), p. 63.

[2]Quoted in Samuel Putnam, *Paris Was Our Mistress: Memoirs of a Lost and Found Generation* (New York: Viking, 1947).

memo drafted for his signature by someone else in the department. Read Babcock's note to you (Form 18) and the draft of the memo (Form 19). Bearing in mind the ABCs of good writing (summarized in a memo on Form 22) and the points in Babcock's note, rewrite the memo on Form 20.

Step Two

You are the student representative on the college or university committee charged with making recommendations for improving parking, registration, or food service (pick one) on your campus. Use Form 21 to write a brief memorandum (no more than one page) setting forth your views to the other members of the committee, all of whom are either faculty members or administrators. Use a situation on your own campus as the basis of your memo.

Office of the Secretary
Department of Environmental Protection

April 1, 20__

J——

Please read and fix the attached. It's supposed to be a brief cover memo to our field staff officially informing them of our new responsibilities under the Wetlands Protection Act. Because we'll be attaching copies of Titles II and III, you can keep it short. Just summarize the main points, which I hope you can ferret out of this mess. And please send a note to the folks down in personnel and ask them to tighten up our screening for writing ability.

Thanks,
A.B.

April 1, 20__

TO: Field Personnel

FROM: A. Babcock, Secretary
         Department of Enviromental Protection

SUBJECT: Wetlands Conservation Act of 2007

Being that the Wetlands Protection Act, which was passed finally into law last year in 2010 and signed by the Governor has many ramifications and implications for personnel who work in this Department. I am writing to all field personnel to bring them to their attention. First I will exactly explain the purposes and previsions of the law. The first part of the law, which is called Title I, sets forth the purposes of the Act, which was to protect the wetlands and to generally improve the quality of life. The second part of the law, which is called Title 2 and also called "Wetland Protection" assigns to this Department the authority to issue rules and also the State Transportation and Agriculture Departments. A copy of which is attached.

Briefly it says that it is the responsibility of this Department to survey and catalog wetlands in the State and propose rules about proper uses, where to for fines would be levied, which we would propose, when violated. Finally, the last part concludes with Title III which is also called the "Wetland Support Program" which provides grants and loans to private citizens which own lands which have been designated wetlands which need to be protected. A copy of this title, too, is attached, the information which it contains within may be dissembled by you to interested partys.

Funding for all parts of program have been recomended by the Administration. The amount of funding which has been recomended by the Administration is $144 million dollars for the next fiscal year which is expected to increase. But not more than ten percent. Which would mean that expenditures would be about $260 million the year after that. Some of this money, which would be dedicated, or about half, would be in a special loan fund, at low interest rates, which be available and paid back by farmers and private citizens who own lands which have been designated wetlands over twenty years to prevent unnecessary destruction.

As further information becomes available which is revelant to your role in the program it will be made available to you.

January 1, 20__

TO: Student Readers

FROM: Dennis L. Dresang, Author, *The Public Administration Workbook*

SUBJECT: Hints on Writing a Good Memo

To begin a memo, tell the persons to whom you are writing why you are writing to them.

    A good memo redeems the promise made in the first sentence or two by making a lucid, concise, and logically ordered set of points. Bear in mind the ABCs of good writing:

1. *Accuracy.* Make sure that your writing is correct in both form and substance. Check your facts as well as your spelling, punctuation, and grammar.
2. *Brevity.* Keep your memo short and to the point.
3. *Clarity.* Make your meaning clear by using appropriate language arranged in intelligible sentences and logical paragraphs.

Exercise 6

Process Management: Techniques for Total Quality Management

TOWARD QUALITY IN PUBLIC ADMINISTRATION

"Hey, Al," said Pete, pointing with his paintbrush. "You missed a spot in that corner."

"Aw," responded Al, "it's close enough for government work."

Close enough for government work. Now there's a telling phrase that everyone has heard and most of us have used at one time or another. What we mean when we say this is: "It's not that important. There's no penalty for doing a less-than-perfect job—just like in government."

Although tales of government inefficiency have always been exaggerated, it was probably true that not so long ago, quality of work received less than systematic attention in many government agencies. Government, after all, is a monopoly. It has no competitors nipping at its heels, keeping it on its toes. Managers may become complacent. Good performance may go unrecognized, poor performance unpunished. Without the discipline of the marketplace, innovation may be discouraged, with results subordinated to rules.

However much this used to be true, times have changed. A fundamental transformation in the character of public management has been under way in the United States for the past 25 years. Beginning in quiet corners of state and local government in the 1980s and spreading outward and upward in the 1990s, public agencies have increasingly been "reinvented." Out have gone traditional, knee-jerk bureaucratic, rule-bound remedies to every problem. In have come ideas that are innovative, entrepreneurial, and "outside the box." David Osborne and Ted Gaebler, the chief chroniclers and advocates of this movement, outline the core principles of reinvented government as follows:[1]

- Promote *competition* between service providers.
- Focus on *outcomes,* not inputs.
- Be driven by *missions,* not by rules and regulations.
- Treat clients like *customers,* giving them meaningful choices.
- *Prevent* problems before they emerge, rather than waiting to solve them.
- *Decentralize* authority and embrace participatory management.
- Prefer *market* mechanisms to bureaucratic mechanisms.
- *Catalyze* all sectors—public, private, voluntary— to address community problems.

What sparked this revolution? No one single event was responsible. Declining public confidence in government in the aftermath of Vietnam and Watergate set the stage. The fiscal crisis that hit the public sector—epitomized by California's Proposition 13 in 1978—gave added impetus. The success that some large corporations seemed to have reinventing themselves in the face of mounting global competition in the late 1970s and early 1980s provided a tantalizing model for government leaders. The momentum of this period has carried forth through the first decades of the twenty-first century.

[1]Adapted from David Osborne and Ted Gaebler, *Reinventing Government: How the Entrepreneurial Spirit Is Transforming the Public Sector* (Reading, MA: Addison-Wesley, 1992), pp. 19–20.

Whatever the cause of the reinvention revolution, the thread that ties all of its elements together is *quality*. Reinventing government is about making government work better. It is about relegating the line "close enough for government work" to the dustbin of history.

As you might guess by looking at Osborne and Gaebler's list of principles, governments use many different methods to try to improve the quality of their services. Not all of them are new. Some of them—management by objectives (MBO), planning programming budgeting system (PPBS), and zero-base budgeting (ZBB)—we will consider in other exercises. In this exercise, we will focus on what has become one of the most widespread and accepted of the quality-in-government initiatives applied to those agencies that provide ongoing services, such as delivering the mail, processing income tax returns, and licensing new drivers: total quality management (TQM).

TOTAL QUALITY MANAGEMENT

Like many of the other techniques that may be considered under the broad heading of "reinventing government," TQM has been borrowed from the private sector, where it has been used to great effect in corporations such as Kodak, Honda, Federal Express, IBM, Delta Airlines, and Citicorp. Industrial engineers have developed specific analytical tools and training programs, such as Lean Six Sigma, that have their foundation in TQM. In essence, TQM involves reorienting the culture of an organization toward quality and relying on customers to define quality. To that end, TQM requires a high degree of communication with customers, employee participation in decision making, careful measurement of performance, and the relentless pursuit of "continuous improvement" in organizational processes.

Although the roots of TQM stretch all the way back to Frederick Taylor's scientific management approach to management and subsequent efforts to develop statistically based quality control systems in industry, the real credit for TQM is generally accorded to W. Edwards Deming (1900–1993), an American engineer and physicist who played a key role in helping rebuild Japanese industry after World War II under the auspices of General MacArthur's occupation command. The work of Deming and his colleagues—some American and some Japanese—helped shape the economic miracle of postwar Japan. Deming is probably best known for his "14 points for management," which distilled his philosophy into a relatively simple list of directives (e.g., point 7 is "Adopt and institute leadership"), and for his plan-do-check-act (PDCA) cycle. As shown in Figure 6.1, the PDCA cycle is a reminder that quality is a continuous commitment to planning, doing, checking (reviewing), and acting, not a linear path with a beginning and an end. Successful quality management requires unceasing planning, doing, checking, and acting. A major difference between Deming's total quality management and Taylor's scientific management is that while the latter assumes a person can discover the single best way of doing something, TQM assumes that there is always room for improvement. Note that in both approaches these are assumptions—it is not possible to prove that there is a single best method or that there is always room for improvement.

What exactly does TQM require beyond these philosophical abstractions? The short answer is, a lot of hard—although often fun—work. TQM implementation is complex and time-consuming; it is anything but a "quick fix" to an organization's problems. Because it entails nothing less than a wholesale change in organizational culture, TQM generally

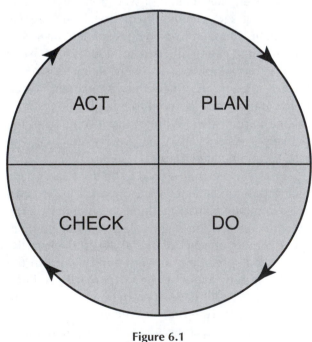

Figure 6.1
PDCA Cycle

necessitates both an initial intervention by consultants trained in a program like Lean Six Sigma and a commitment by top management to ongoing training of employees (and of themselves). This exercise serves as an introduction to the perspectives and techniques of quality management. It is not meant to be a substitute for courses and full training in the field.

With that caveat, it may be said that TQM implementation consists of six basic steps:

1. *Create teams* of employees whose work intersects to deliver a product or service.

2. *Establish incentive systems* so that team members can realize the benefits of increased productivity and offer suggestions for improvements in quality without anxiety or fear.

3. *Identify how customers*—both those outside the organization (the final or "external" customers) and those inside the organization (the intermediate or "internal" customers)—*define quality.*

4. *Map existing work processes* of each team and each employee. All teams should ask how they might improve processes better to help meet customer needs.

5. *Measure performance.* Develop baseline and benchmark measures for all aspects of work. The aim should be continuous improvement.

6. Identify suppliers and subcontractors whose work bears on the final product or service. *Forge partnerships* to ensure that suppliers and subcontractors provide quality service and products that suit your needs rather than some general standard specifications.

Although some observers suggest that TQM is not as well suited to the public sector as it is to the private sector,[2] it is clear that governments all across

America have moved ahead with one variant or another of TQM. The federal government, most state governments, and many city, county, and other local governments adopted TQM practices in the 1990s and have continued to use them, although sometimes with different labels, such as "quality management" and "continuous improvement."

TQM TECHNIQUES

Implementation of a full-scale TQM program necessitates the use of a wide array of specific administrative technologies and managerial techniques. These range from simple questionnaires that can be administered to vendors and customers to sophisticated strategies of leadership and team building. Somewhere in between are the tools that allow managers and workers to measure and track their performance. Such tools are essential if defects in products or service are to be minimized and quality is to be maximized—the real goal of TQM.

Six especially useful TQM tools, which can easily be mastered, are cause-and-effect diagrams, flowcharts, Pareto charts, run charts, histograms, and scatter diagrams. Each of these tools is designed to display information visually in a way that is simple but powerful. Managers (and workers) who use these charts and diagrams are often able to gain insight into the sources of production or service delivery problems that would otherwise elude them—and thus to strive for continuous improvement. In the next few pages, you will learn about each of these techniques as we build a set of charts aimed at solving the following illustrative problem: Why am I not getting better grades? After reading through this section, you will be asked in the exercise that follows to apply what you have learned and chart some data from a case study.

Cause-and-Effect Diagrams
The cause-and-effect diagram is sometimes called a "fishbone diagram" because of its distinctive shape and sometimes an "Ishikawa diagram" in honor of its creator, Kaoru Ishikawa, a prominent Japanese quality control engineer. Whatever its name, the purpose of this chart is the same: to stimulate thinking about the factors that enhance or impeded quality.

---

[2]They argue, for instance, that although some government agencies may have unambiguous customers that they can aim to please, many do not. The National Park Service will never be able to make all of its "customers"—tourists, vendors, nearby businesses and industries, and so on—happy at the same time. And can we really expect the "customers" of the IRS to be "delighted"—the frequent measure of success cited by TQM advocates? Would we *want* the "customers" of various regulatory agencies—the Security and Exchange Commission, the Federal Communications Commission, and so forth—to be really pleased with the fruits of their labor? Perhaps not, although it should be noted that TQM emphasizes that customers should define quality, not necessarily that customers should be happy. For an elaboration of these arguments, see James E. Swiss, "Adapting Total Quality Management (TQM) to Government," *Public Administration Review* 52:4 (July–August 1992): 356–362.

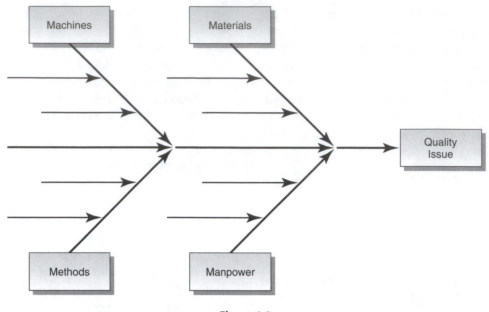

Figure 6.2
Cause-and-Effect Diagram

As is shown in Figure 6.2, each of the lines angling into the main axis of this diagram represents a major category of quality-affecting factors. "Machines," "Materials," "Methods," and "Manpower" are the four categories used most commonly in TQM exercises, although you should feel free to use whatever categories best reflect the needs or practices of an organization. Each of the shorter lines shooting off from the major category lines marks a related, subordinate potential factor.

It is important to stress that we don't need to know for certain what the cause of a problem is before producing this sort of chart. In fact, cause-and-effect diagrams are usually created at an early stage of problem solving, to assist brainstorming and to get people actively involved in thinking an issue through. It is also important to note that cause-and-effect diagrams can be constructed for any sort of problem, from the simplest to the most complex.

To illustrate, let us take the problem of your grades in your college classes. And by the way, before you object that you have no problems with your grades because you are a good (or even excellent) student, remember that this is a chapter on total quality management, with an emphasis on continuous improvement: The assumption is that every student, no matter how good, can get better.

Ideally, we would begin by sitting down in a brainstorming session with you and a group of people who know you well—friends, family, room-mates, teachers. Looking at the bare skeleton of a cause-and-effect diagram, we would try to list all of the possible things—a hectic schedule, inadequate study time, cutting classes, noisy roommates, an outmoded computer, and so forth—that interfere with you doing your best, labeling the bones as we went along. Ultimately, we might produce the sort of creature shown in Figure 6.3.

Note that no one solution necessarily jumps out of this (or any such) diagram. In and of itself, the chart in Figure 6.3 does not tell us if your primary problem is, in fact, inadequate time with your books or too much time with noisy roommates. Instead, the chart serves to focus discussion and to initiate a process whereby possible causes can be weighed and remedies identified.

Flowcharts

In general, a flowchart is a visual description of a *process*. Where cause-and-effect diagrams provide a schematic overview of possible sources of problems, flowcharts seek to depict the sequence of events in some operation that is of interest. For instance, the flowchart in Figure 6.4 indicates that a "no" at gateway 1 requires a detour through activity A, whereas a "yes" leads directly to gateway 2. Although symbols vary from flowchart to flowchart, in general, it is useful to distinguish between gateways

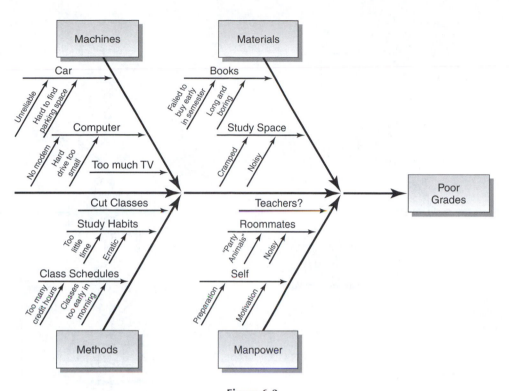

Figure 6.3

Cause-and-Effect Diagram for Poor-Grades Problem

or yes–no decision points on the one hand and activities that result from particular yes–no decisions on the other. A gateway in a flowchart serves as a sort of sentry, checking ID before allowing us to pass the guardhouse: has step *x* in the process been completed? If yes, do *a;* if no, do *b.*

Professionals in many different fields—computer science and engineering prominent among them—use flowcharts to try to put into systematic form on paper what may be a complex series of interdependent activities. TQM uses flowcharts to depict the process of work in an organization. The idea is that by representing work processes graphically, one can begin to identify areas susceptible to improvement. Effective flowcharts do not have to be sophisticated. The point is to try to capture all of the elements that go into a finished product or service.

Let's say we decide, based on our "fishbone diagram," that one of the root causes of your less than perfect GPA is your propensity to procrastinate when it comes to tackling term papers and other writing projects. We could then sit down and sketch a flowchart that links all the events and activities that optimally ought to take place

between the announcement of the assignment and your turning in the final draft of the paper, as in Figure 6.5.

Note that we have also included in the chart alternative flows of events that take place when the optimal path isn't followed. TQM cognoscenti sometimes call these alternative flows "no loops." In effect, the "yes" path constitutes the normative ideal; the "no loops" are drawn from an honest appraisal of real-life behavior. A good flowchart identifies "no loops" as a first step in the battle to improve performance; indeed, honesty in flowcharting is essential to addressing shortcomings in quality. In this case, we know we need to eliminate the "no loops" of not hearing about the assignment in a timely fashion, failing to consult the instructor, not undertaking careful background research, and so on.

Pareto Charts

A Pareto chart displays data on the types and frequency of problems in the delivery of a product or service (see Figure 6.6). A good Pareto chart gives a clear idea of what factors are most responsible for product or service defects and thus what to work on first. Pareto charts stimulated the so-called 80–20 rule

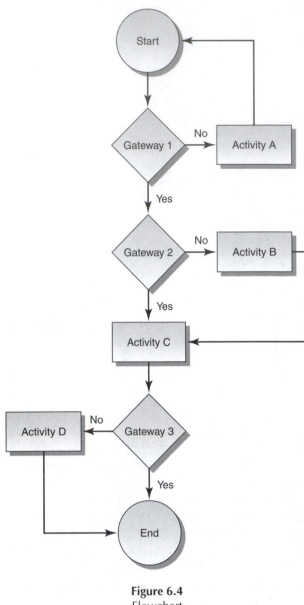

Figure 6.4
Flowchart

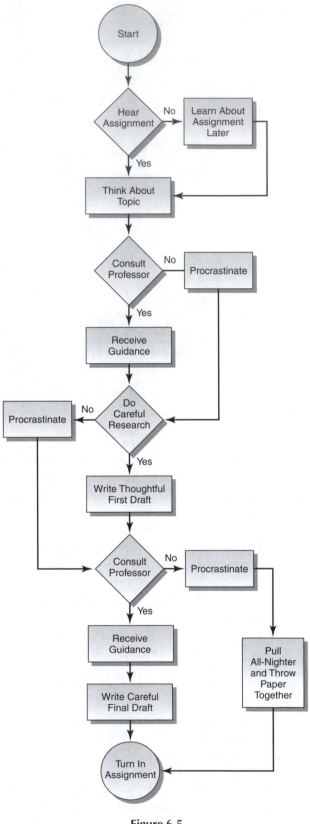

Figure 6.5
Term Paper Flowchart

in TQM: 80 percent of an organization's problems stem from only 20 percent of the causes. With a clear idea of which items are most responsible for compromising quality, a manager can, at least in the near term, focus like a laser beam, ignoring factors that are relatively trivial.

A good use of Pareto charting in our effort to improve your grades would be to compile written comments from all of your instructors on all of your papers. This would allow us to count and compare the frequencies of each type of criticism. As we can see in our hypothetical illustration in Figure 6.7, grammatical errors were cited far more often than

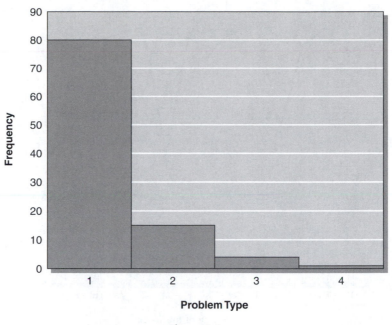

Figure 6.6
Pareto Chart

any other problem in your writing. This suggests that spending a few hours each week with a tutor in the university's writing center would be the best investment of your time and energy—even more useful than investing in a new spellchecker, poring through the library or using Google on the Internet for an extra fact or two, or learning a new system of footnoting (although the logic of continuous improvement would suggest that sooner or later you'll have to address these matters too).

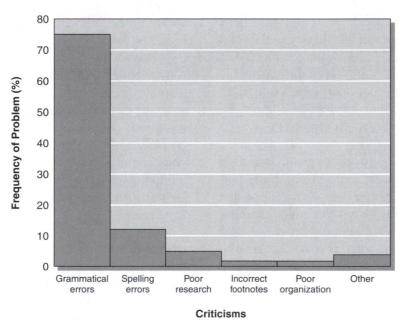

Figure 6.7
Pareto Chart of Criticisms of Writing Assignments

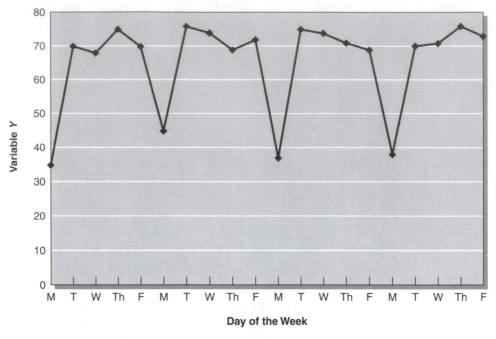

Figure 6.8
Run Chart

Run Charts

A run chart is simply a graphic display of some variable over time. For that reason, run charts are also often called "trend charts." Figure 6.8 shows a simple run chart that plots some variable (production defects? the Dow Jones average? hospital admissions?) over four weeks of time. Run charts allow managers to glance at this display of data and get a sense of pattern—if there is any. If these data were charting defects on an automobile assembly line, for instance, the production supervisor might want to investigate what kind of condition the workers are in on Monday mornings and to try to do something about it.

As you will have guessed, we could use a set of run charts to deal with some of our grade performance problems. For instance, let's assume that after going through the cause-and-effect exercise, you have decided, sensibly enough, to set aside a certain amount of time each day to study. Because of other obligations—such as a part-time job, sports, and social life—the amount of time you budget varies from day to day. It might be two hours on Monday; three hours on Tuesday, Wednesday, and Thursday; only an hour on Friday; and so on. In any event, you decide (like a

good TQM analyst) to keep careful track of how close you are to the budgeted mark each day over a four-week period. You are then able to produce a run chart that displays, day by day, the discrepancy between the amount of time you planned to study (in your search for continuous improvement) and the amount of time you actually studied (see Figure 6.9).

Of what use is such a chart? If, in fact, you were to see the sort of pattern that this set of charts displays, you would know that you have some serious problems focusing on schoolwork during weekends (assuming you budgeted your time properly in the first place). It may be time to adjust your social schedule, watch one or two fewer football games, limit your time on Facebook and Twitter, or get up before noon on Saturday and Sunday.

Histograms

Although a histogram may sound like something unpleasant that your doctor prescribes, actually it is nothing more than a chart that displays the frequency with which something occurs. Typically, a histogram takes the form of a bar chart, with frequency measured along the y-axis and the levels

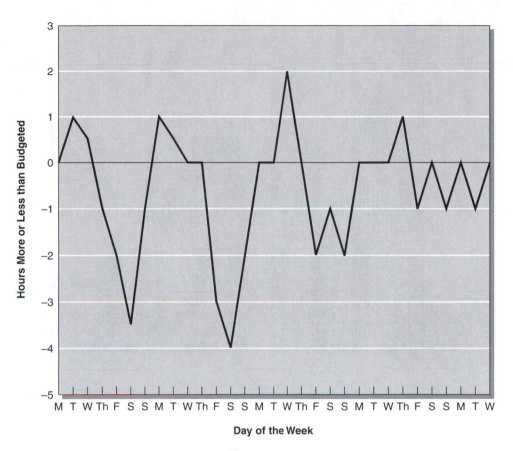

Figure 6.9
Run Chart of Study Times

of occurrence (expressed in "bins") measured along the x-axis, as in Figure 6.10.

Although histograms may resemble Pareto charts on the surface, in fact they measure different sorts of things. Where a Pareto chart uses vertical bars to compare the relative frequency of different types of phenomena (apples vs. oranges vs. bananas), histograms use vertical bars to show the frequency with which a single phenomenon occurs at different levels or intensities (small apples vs. medium apples vs. big apples).

Histograms are useful in many different circumstances. For instance, a college admissions office might create a histogram to chart how often students with various SAT scores apply to that college. A police chief might use a histogram to display emergency response times. A hospital administrator could use a histogram to show how many multiple-bypass patients spend 10 days in the hospital, as opposed to 12, 14, or 16 days.

And you can use histograms to improve your academic performance. How? Let's assume that one of your problems is that you seldom get all of your reading done on time. Let's further assume that at least part of the reason for this is that you simply don't do a very good job estimating how long it will take to plow through your various assignments. You sort of eyeball that novel from Brit Lit 101 or that textbook chapter from Physics 200, guess that you'll have to spend an hour with each—which you are sure you can do the night before the classes—and proceed to head out to a party with your friends.

Let's say that for a few weeks you kept track of how many minutes it took you to read each of the various chapters of text you were assigned (51, 23, 46, 65, etc.). This would allow you to produce the sort of histogram displayed in Figure 6.11, which, in turn, would tell you that it generally takes you 45 to 65 minutes to read each chapter of text. Only very infrequently does it take you less than

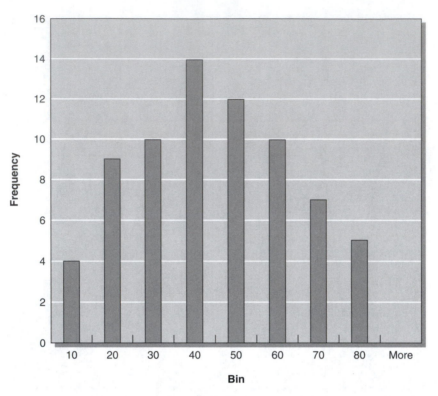

Figure 6.10
Histogram

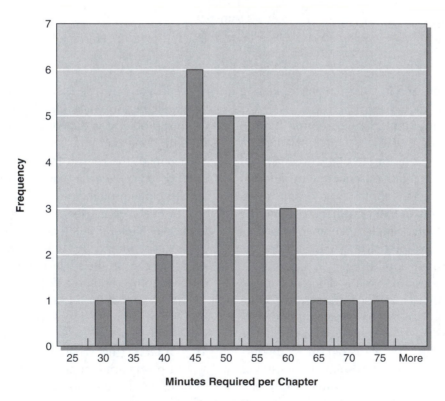

Figure 6.11
Histogram of Reading Times

40 minutes or as much as 70 minutes or more. Knowing this about yourself, you could add up the number of chapters you had to get through each week and budget a realistic amount of time to get your work done.

Scatter Diagrams

Except for cause-and-effect diagrams and flowcharts, which are, by design, only tentative approximations of reality, the graphic displays that we have discussed so far have dealt only with the relative frequency of discrete variables. At most, they have told us that x happened this often and y happened that often. They have not really told us anything about the relationship between x and y. Probing such relationships is the point of a scatter diagram. In a scatter diagram, two variables are plotted against one another on the same chart, as is illustrated in Figure 6.12.

In the scatter diagram shown in Figure 6.12, it appears to be the case—just by eyeballing things— that an increase in variable x tends to be associated with an increase in variable y. We do not know from these data if the relationship is causal—does x cause y? does y cause x?—nor do we know how strong the relationship is; these and related questions require more sophisticated statistical tools.

But knowing that there appears to be *some* relationship is useful. If this scatter diagram were displaying data on the number of broken windows (x) versus the number of serious crimes committed (y) in a particular area, for instance, then a police department might want to explore deploying more resources in deterring quality-of-life or nuisance crimes. Similarly, if this scatter diagram were plotting the length of time it took welfare recipients to find employment (x) against distance in minutes from a major public transit line (y), then a social service manager might want to consider stimulating alternative transportation programs for welfare-to-work candidates. Again, in neither case (or in others that we might imagine) can we be sure that there is, in fact, a causal relationship between these variables. Such a diagram does serve as a starting point for further analysis, however. It may even provide a reasonable basis for action, if the two variables are closely related logically as well as empirically. For instance, if this scatter diagram were representing number of hours worked (x) and the number of errors made by keyboard operators (y), it would probably not be unreasonable for a manager to hire additional keyboard operators rather than to encourage existing employees to work a lot of overtime.

One obvious candidate for a scatter diagram in our academic improvement program may be found in Figure 6.13. Here, we have carefully plotted grades received on a series of quizzes against the amount of time you invested in studying for each quiz.

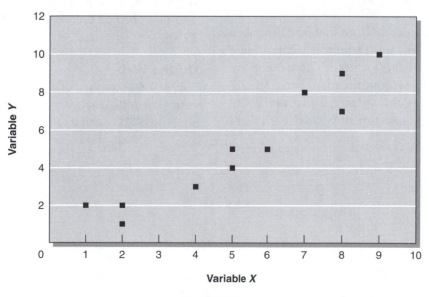

Figure 6.12
Scatter Diagram

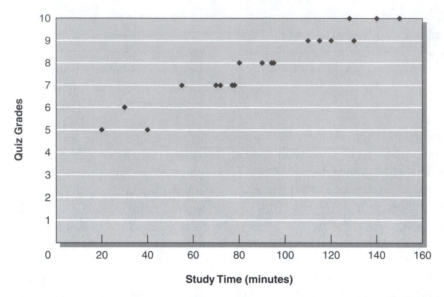

Figure 6.13
Scatter Diagram of Quiz Scores and Study Time

Not surprisingly, this scatter diagram suggests a pretty strong relationship between the two variables. Although we can't know for sure which way the causal arrow runs—or even if there is a causal arrow—it seems pretty likely that the more time you spend studying for a quiz, the better the grade you will receive.

FURTHER READING

The book by the founder of TQM that best describes the approach is W. Edwards Demming, *Out of Crisis* (Cambridge, MA: MIT Press, 2000). There are many guidebooks to TQM written for managers. Among the most useful and most accessible are Mary Walton, *The Deming Management Method* (New York:

Perigee Books, 1988); and James R. Evans and Philip B. Crosby, *The Management and Control of Quality*, 6th ed. (Cincinnati, OH: SouthWestern Publishing, 2010). For a description of the application of TQM in the public sector, see Max Travers, *The New Bureaucracy: Quality Assurance and Its Critics* (San Francisco: Policy Press, 2007). A good example of a major analytical approach based on TQM is Mark O. George, *The Lean Six Sigma Guide To Doing More With Less: Cut Costs, Reduce Waste and Lower Your Overhead* (Hoboken, NJ: Wiley, 2010).

On the Web
There are a number of software and training programs for total quality management and Six Sigma advertised and available on the Web.

Overview of Exercise

This exercise allows you to practice the six common TQM techniques—cause-and-effect diagrams, flow-charts, Pareto charts, run charts, histograms, and scatter diagrams—described in the narrative portion of this exercise. You will read a brief case study about the state Department of Motor Vehicles (DMV) and, working in TQM teams, use the information provided to produce the required charts and diagrams.

INSTRUCTIONS

Step One
Read the case study provided on Form 23.

Step Two
Form in TQM groups as directed by your instructor.

Step Three
Brainstorm within your group, and use Form 24 to sketch a cause-and-effect diagram of the DMV's slow processing problem.

Step Four
Use Form 25 to flowchart the registration process at the DMV. Include the extra steps someone registering for the first time must take. Be prepared to discuss the "no loops" that you have identified and how to eliminate them.

Step Five
Use Form 26 to translate the raw complaints data contained in the case study (see Box 1 on Form 23) into a Pareto chart. Be prepared to discuss which problems seem to be serious and which relatively trivial. Do these data conform to the 80–20 rule?

Step Six
Construct a run chart on Form 27 using the average processing time and days of the month data from the case study (see Box 2 on Form 23). Is there a discernible pattern here? Assume that the first Monday was the first of the month. Does this suggest a pattern? Based on your run chart, how might the DMV management address this problem?

Step Seven
Create a histogram on Form 28 using the processing time data from Box 3 on Form 23. For the purposes of this step, ignore the third column, the times-of-day data. Your y-axis will display frequency; your x-axis will designate discrete sets of time, measured in minutes. In constructing the x-axis, pick an interval (a "bin," to use the technical term) that is neither too wide (0–50, 51–100, etc.) nor too narrow (0–2, 2–4, 4–8, etc.). What do we learn from this chart?

Step Eight
Use Form 29 to produce a scatter diagram that plots processing time against time of day. All the data necessary may be found in Box 3 on Form 23. Plot the time of day along the x-axis and the minutes in processing time along the y-axis. What does this scatter diagram suggest? What remedial actions might management take?

Step Nine
Answer the questions on Form 30.

Case Study

The Department of Motor Vehicles (DMV) is a state agency responsible for titling, licensing, and inspecting cars, trucks, and motorcycles and for testing and licensing drivers. In most respects, the DMV's operations are the epitome of bureaucratic routine. In each of the state's 17 counties, there is a DMV inspection and licensing center staffed with lower-level civil servants who check headlights and windshield wipers, scrutinize proof of liability insurance, administer driving tests, collect fees, stamp forms, and otherwise push paper for the 4 million owners and operators of motor vehicles in the state.

Despite some administrative improvements in recent years, the DMV remains almost every citizen's worst governmental nightmare. Once every 5 years, each licensed driver must report to the local DMV center for license renewal, a process that involves standing in seemingly interminable lines for pictures to be taken, vision to be checked, forms to be completed, and fees to be paid. Even worse, once a year the owner of every motor vehicle—car, truck, bus, van, RV, motorcycle, and so on—must report to the center for vehicle relicensing, a process that is even more complex and time-consuming. Discontent with DMV procedures has become so widespread that it has become an issue in state politics. The chairman of the state assembly's transportation committee has even introduced legislation that would contract with a private business to do the work of the DMV, a move vigorously opposed by the civil service employees' union and viewed skeptically by other legislators. Other proposals have included opening more centers, mandating the use of computer technology and online services, moving to biennial or even triennial inspections and relicensing via mail-in renewals.

The DMV's single biggest problem is the time it takes for vehicles to be inspected and licensed. On average, it takes 75 minutes from the time a driver pulls into one of the vehicle inspection lanes to the time he or she walks out the door of the processing center with a new license plate or sticker. The crawl through the inspection lane is almost always painfully slow but is at its worst during the lunch hour (when the DMV is at half-staff) and on the 15th and 30th of each month (when tags expire). Once a driver has made the start-and-stop journey from the end of the line to the inspection bay, a state employee checks headlights (high and low beams), taillights, turn signals, horn, windshield wipers, emergency flashers, emissions, and brakes. The inspection itself takes only 5 minutes or so. Vehicles that fail the inspection are given 48 hours to remedy the problem and return for a reinspection.

Once a vehicle has passed inspection, the driver parks it in a lot and walks into the processing center with all of the necessary relicensing paperwork. This includes (1) the form from the vehicle inspector stating that the vehicle passed all safety and emissions tests, (2) a current "insurance card" from a state-approved insurance company attesting to the fact that the driver carries appropriate liability insurance, and (3) the current vehicle registration. Vehicles being registered for the first time also have to present (4) proof of title and (5) a notarized bill of sale specifying the price paid for the vehicle. Most of these forms must be checked against a computer database and then stamped by a DMV employee, a set of operations that requires the driver to stand in three or four separate lines—one for each form other than the bill of sale.

The final stop for reregistering and the penultimate stop for newly registering is a cashier, who collects the stamped documents and receives payment for the registration. The cashier also collects a 4 percent motor vehicle excise tax on all vehicles, new or used, being registered for the first time. Separate checks are required for registration (payable to the DMV) and for the excise tax (payable to the Division of Revenue); credit cards are not accepted. After payment has been received, the cashier gives the driver two small stickers bearing a four-digit month–year code that are to be applied to the bottom right-hand corner of the front and rear license plates. The driver who is registering for the first time has to go to yet one more station and stand in yet one more line—to receive a set of vehicular license plates.

As noted, even when this process works smoothly, it is aggravatingly time-consuming for the DMV's customer-clients. And unfortunately, the process doesn't always work smoothly. Massive traffic jams occasionally plague the inspection lanes when one of the four bays has to be closed—when a machine breaks or a staff shortage arises—and the scores of drivers who had been in that lane try to squeeze into one of the other crowded lanes, already filled with exasperated drivers. Drivers may or may not remember to bring their registration with them as they go through the lanes, and without this document (which contains the previous odometer reading), inspectors are unable to test a vehicle—necessitating a return trip. The inspection itself offers myriad opportunities for failure—a headlight slightly misaligned, brakes that pull slightly to one side or another, an obscure bulb burnt out, and so forth.

Once inside the building, having the proper documents becomes even more important. A missing or out-of-date insurance card, a forgotten checkbook, or an improperly written or unnotarized bill of sale are just a few of the problems that can derail the process. Given the possibilities for fraud and other forms of corruption, employees are not permitted to deviate from published procedures. Consequently, pleas to accept photocopies of documents or to "call my insurance company—they'll tell you I'm properly covered" fall on deaf ears.

In an effort to address some of these problems, the governor announced 6 months ago the appointment of a new DMV director. The director, in turn, immediately announced that she had contracted with a major outside consulting firm to diagnose DMV problems and to make recommendations for reform. Preliminary data from the consulting firm's studies have already started to come in. Box 1 presents partial findings from a survey of the state's drivers.

Box 1 presents a breakdown of the complaints about DMV's registration process. Box 2 provides raw data on the processing times experienced by 100 different drivers randomly selected over a month-long period. Box 3 tracks processing times for 50 drivers at various times of the day.

Box 1
Survey Results: Driver Complaints about DMV Registration Process

Complaint	Number
Number of inspection lanes is insufficient	17
Employees are rude or discourteous	6
Process is too slow	187
Inspection procedures are unfair	8
Rules are inflexible	22
Business hours are inadequate	18

Box 2
Mean Processing Time (to the Nearest 10 Minutes) for a 4-Week Period

Day	Mean Processing Time
Monday	90
Tuesday	80
Wednesday	70
Thursday	70
Friday	50
Monday	50
Tuesday	60
Wednesday	50
Thursday	60
Friday	90
Monday	100
Tuesday	90
Wednesday	70
Thursday	70
Friday	70
Monday	60
Tuesday	80
Wednesday	70
Thursday	70
Friday	80

Box 3
Processing Times for 50 Customers at Various Times of the Day

Customer	Time in Minutes	Time of Day (Start)	Customer	Time in Minutes	Time of Day (Start)
1	95	12:38	26	50	14:25
2	72	12:35	27	70	14:45
3	41	9:15	28	60	15:33
4	85	11:55	29	36	9:37
5	60	14:20	30	41	10:05
6	71	11:20	31	52	10:02
7	87	12:18	32	38	10:20
8	33	9:05	33	49	11:02
9	48	10:50	34	83	12:47
10	61	10:42	35	84	13:05
11	92	12:45	36	81	13:10
12	77	11:49	37	91	13:25
13	70	13:35	38	102	13:00
14	52	10:55	39	81	13:55
15	88	12:40	40	90	13:39
16	56	11:10	41	43	14:55
17	75	12:05	42	50	15:15
18	86	12:10	43	75	15:47
19	65	11:31	44	62	15:44
20	70	14:10	45	77	16:02
21	68	12:00	46	82	16:15
22	90	13:14	47	91	16:22
23	100	12:30	48	97	16:27
24	31	9:10	49	96	16:44
25	46	9:45	50	102	16:38

Cause-and-Effect Diagram of Slow Processing Times

Flowchart of Registration Process

Pareto Chart of Complaint Types

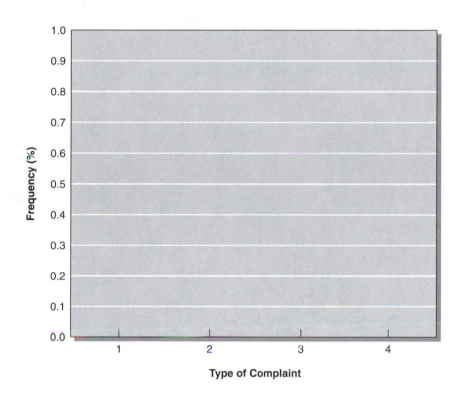

Run Chart of Weekly Processing Times

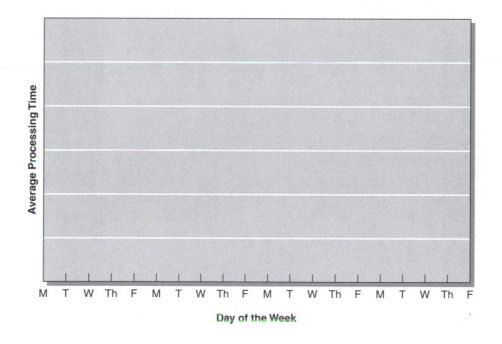

Day of the Week

Histogram of Processing Times

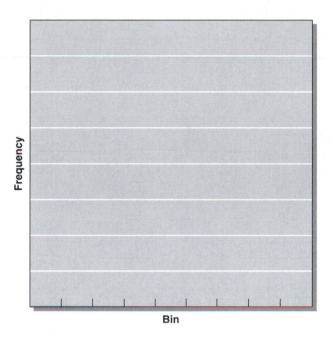

Scatter Diagram of Processing Times and Times of Day

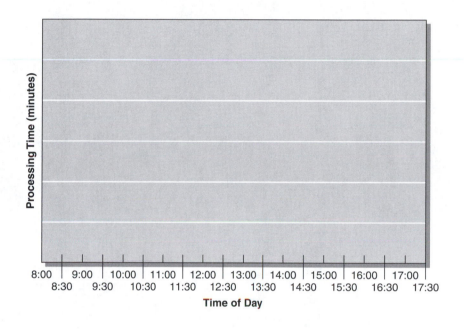

Questions

1. How useful are the various TQM techniques?

2. What would it take to get various members of an organization to use these techniques and otherwise to engage in a process of "continuous improvement"? Do you believe that the DMV can turn things around using these methods? Why or why not?

3. Is government in general more or less suited to TQM techniques than the private sector—or the same? Explain your answer.

4. What can citizens do to encourage political leaders to pursue quality in public management? Do citizens really care enough about quality to pursue the issue?

Exercise 7

Project Management: Critical Path Method

WHAT IS SPECIAL ABOUT MANAGING PROJECTS?

Total quality management is appropriate primarily when dealing with the processes for administering ongoing programs and services or, in the private sector, for producing goods such as automobiles, computers, and cameras. But sometimes the implementation of a public policy involves the successful completion of a project. Projects have a beginning and an end. The requirements of project management are to marshall and coordinate the resources necessary to complete the project on time and in a way that is efficient and that accomplishes all the goals of the project. Completing the construction of a bridge or a road, holding a conference, and training employees or volunteers are examples of projects.

Because projects are so important and so common, special approaches and techniques have evolved that are now considered the essential ingredients of project management:

1. *Project manager.* A specialty among administrators, both public and private sectors, is to focus on projects. There are individuals, especially in the construction industry and in event planning and execution, that go from one project to another, sometimes providing direction over several projects simultaneously. In some public organizations, the responsibility for managing a project may be an occasional assignment that becomes part of one's job.

2. *Matrix organization.* Often, but not always, projects require the cooperation of several agencies or organizations and so the matrix type of organization, described in Exercise 3, is typical in project management. A project manager responsible for a conference may, for example, need the cooperation of an agency in charge of facilities, a food service, a hotel for conference participants, a travel agency, program experts, and a financial administration bureau. The manager will probably need to have at least one representative from each of these organizations on a committee to plan, coordinate, and monitor all the activities and services needed for the conference. These representatives will probably have to spend some of their time on this project, and they will have to report to their regular supervisor as well as to the project manager for the duration of the project. This, as you recall from Exercise 3, is the essence of matrix organizations.

3. *Project management techniques.* There are several approaches to management tasks that are especially appropriate for projects. The most common and central of these techniques is *critical path method* (CPM), sometimes called *network analysis* or *PERT charting.*[1] CPM provides a way of representing graphically, in an easy-to-grasp form, the steps required to implement a decision. This technique is especially appropriate for projects, which have specific beginning and end points. As two exponents of CPM have put it, this method "facilitates logical thought by permitting the administrator . . . to recognize more fully the relationships of the parts to the whole." Through a simple system of circles and arrows, a project planner can depict the flow of policy and predict likely impediments

---

[1]PERT, an acronym for performance evaluation review technique, was a management system developed in the 1950s for the U.S. Navy as part of the Polaris submarine program.

to smooth implementation "before they actually occur."[2] Internet links listed for this exercise include CPM software that is available.

CRITICAL PATH METHOD

Part of the appeal of CPM is its simplicity. CPM networks are composed of just two elements: *events* (represented by circles) and *activities* (represented by arrows). An event is defined as the start or completion of a task; events consume no resources and simply mark time in a CPM network. Activities represent the flow of tasks themselves; activities, by definition, consume resources—invariably including time. To create a CPM network, the analyst identifies the set of events that must occur to complete a project and links them together in the proper sequence with activity arrows. Each activity arrow represents the amount of time (or other resources) that must be consumed to produce an event.

Figure 7.1 represents a simple three-event, two-activity CPM network. This network indicates that beginning with event A, activity 1 must be completed to reach event B; activity 2 must be completed to reach event C. Moreover, you cannot get to C without finishing B and thus must graph the sequence of going from A to B and then to C.

To use a less abstract illustration, let's assume that a club on campus has decided to hold a food drive to make sure the local Food Pantry has enough to help needy families celebrate Thanksgiving. You are in charge. As a first step in the planning process, you decide, very sensibly, to make a list of the things that need to be done:

1. Contact the Food Pantry about what items are needed.
2. Brainstorm about drop-off points to use.

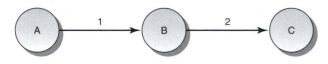

Figure 7.1
Basic Critical Path Model

3. Get permission to have students and faculty leave their donations at events and places on campus.
4. Publicize the drive.
5. Pick up the donations and get them to Food Pantry.

You next ask yourself, in what order do we need to do these things? You could just run around and try to accomplish them randomly, but it seems that a certain order would be appropriate. After all, you don't want to publicize the drive before you know what kinds of food are needed. And you need to let people know where they can leave their donations, so you had better get drop-off sites identified and authorized before you develop publicity. So you need to work out a sequence of activities that makes sense. Figure 7.2 provides a CPM network that does exactly that. Each of the activities is represented by one of the arrows. The events (circles) designate the beginning or end of an activity.

What exactly does the CPM network of Figure 7.2 tell you? Frankly, not much at this point. All it really does is represent schematically what you plan to do. The real utility of CPM lies in taking the additional step of estimating the amount of time it will take to complete each activity and produce the next event. This allows the analyst to anticipate the flow of action and manage resources as efficiently as possible.[3] The time estimates are obtained simply by making reasonable judgments about each activity. The analyst figures out (or asks a knowledgeable observer) how long an activity is likely to take. Time estimates are often expressed in ranges, with a minimum, a most likely, and a maximum number of days.

The main purpose of CPM is to identify the *longest* path that connects your starting point with your destination. Because you will walk all these paths simultaneously (a difficult feat in a real forest), the time required to complete the longest path is equal to the time required to complete the total project. The longest path in a CPM network is called the *critical path*. This is because timely completion of the entire project hinges on the successful execution

[2]Anthony J. Catanese and Alan W. Steiss, "Programming for Governmental Operations: The Critical Path Approach," in Richard D. Bingham and Marcus E. Ethridge, eds., *Reaching Decisions in Public Policy and Administration: Methods and Applications* (New York: Longman, 1982), p. 388. Originally published in *Public Administration Review* 28 (March–April 1968).

[3]Normally, three separate time estimates are made for each sequence of activities: (1) the most *optimistic* time (t_o), (2) the most *pessimistic* time (t_p), and (3) the *most likely* time (t_m). The mean of these three times then is used as the *average expected time* (t_e) for the activity.

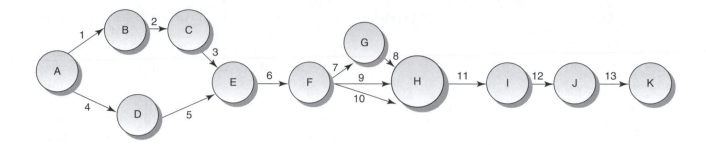

Events

A – Decision to hold food drive
B – Drop-off points identified
C – Drop-off points authorized
D – List of needed food items
E – Necessary information secured
F – Decision on message
G – Posters designed
H – Publicity distributed
I – Drop-off points prepared
J – Donations collected
K – Donations brought to Food Pantry

Activities

1 – Identify preferred drop-off points
2 – Get permission for drop-off points
3 – List drop-off points
4 – Consult with Food Pantry about needs
5 – List needed items
6 – Develop message for publicity
7 – Design posters
8 – Distribute posters
9 – Post on Facebook
10 – Twitter
11 – Bring barrels & boxes to drop-off points
12 – Pick up donations from drop-off points
13 – Bring donations to Food Pantry

Figure 7.2
Critical Path Method for Food Drive Planning

of this sequence of activities as scheduled; any delays along the path will necessarily delay the project. Thus, it is critical that these activities proceed expeditiously and that activities that are not on the critical path be completed in accordance with the schedule on the critical path. In our food drive example, the activities to identify potential drop-off points and get permission to use these points can and should take place simultaneous to the activities to develop a list of needed food items. If it takes longer to set up the drop-off points than to develop the food list, then those responsible for the list do not have to get started right away or work as quickly as those working on the drop-off points. But, the list must be done by the time the drop-off points are set. Otherwise, the work on the publicity will be delayed and that may mean the food drive may not be completed in time for Thanksgiving.

The term used to describe the excess time available on the noncritical paths is *slack*. The amount of slack on any path is equal to the amount of time consumed by the critical path minus the amount of time consumed by the path in question. In the most carefully planned projects, administrators arrange activities to obtain the maximum use of resources,

allowing as little "down" or idle time as possible. The identification of slack time can be as valuable as the mapping of events and activities to determine the critical path. Typically, a project requires the participation of several different agencies. Clearly, if your agency is on the critical path, you know that the success of the project depends on you completing your assigned tasks without delay. If you are the head of an agency that is not on the critical path, CPM tells you how much time you can devote to responsibilities other than this particular project and still meet the needs of the project. Slack time, in other words, is not necessarily down time. Rather, it provides important information that allows for the efficient use of time and resources in everything that agencies do. Good project management means that all deadlines are met and no one has to wait for someone else to finish their work before getting started on a task. It also means that those involved in the project know when they have to get jobs done on your project and when they are able to work on other things.

Armed with this information, let us turn again to the food drive. The time needed to complete each activity is listed in Figure 7.3. To simplify this

Activity	Time Estimates (days)
1 – Identify preferred drop-off points	1
2 – Get permission for drop-off points	5
3 – List drop-off points	1
4 – Consult with Food Pantry about needs	2
5 – List needed items	1
6 – Develop message for publicity	2
7 – Design posters	3
8 – Distribute posters	1
9 – Post on Facebook	1
10 – Twitter	1
11 – Bring barrels & boxes to drop-off points	1
12 – Pick up donations from drop-off points	1
13 – Bring donations to Food Pantry	1

Figure 7.3
Activities with Time Estimates

illustration, the most likely amount of time needed for each activity is used, rather than a range.

The critical path in this network is A-B-C-E-F-G-H-I-J-K (Figure 7.2). Again, this is because it is the longest path in the network. The expected time of completion for this project is 16 days, the length of the critical path. Thus, if you want to get the donations to Food Pantry one week before Thanksgiving, you need to get started—and stay on schedule—16 days prior to that date.

Note that there are two sets of activities where there is slack. Path A-D-E takes four days less than A-B-C-E. Similarly, F-G-H (designing, producing, and distributing posters) is three days shorter than F-H (posting on Facebook and Twitter). You can now set deadlines for those in charge of getting a list of needed food items and those who will be posting publicity on Facebook and Twitter, and let them know that they will have some wiggle room to schedule other activities and still contribute successfully to the food drive project.

While you will find it useful to construct a critical path chart to plan a food drive, this methodology is essential when managing a complex project. Consider, for instance, the avian influenza problem outlined in Exercise 1. No matter which alternative state agriculture department officials choose to pursue (quarantine, limited inspection, flock destruction), implementation will be far smoother and the success of the policy far more assured if the multitude of discrete activities necessary to bring it to completion is carefully planned and coordinated. If a quarantine is

chosen, for example, it will be necessary to write and publicize regulations; identify and monitor target areas; hire and train new enforcement staff; procure additional field equipment, including vehicles; contract or otherwise arrange for fowl testing with state or private laboratories; coordinate activities with adjacent states and with other agencies within the state; and perhaps establish a compensation program for farmers. The other two alternatives would entail equally complex planning. Because many of the steps are interdependent, such that a failure to complete one will cause delays all down the line, use of the critical path technique could save valuable time and resources. Indeed, it would be hard to imagine a program this complex achieving its objectives without such systematic implementation planning.

The critical path method is appropriate for the implementation of projects, which have a beginning and an end. This technique is not useful when implementing an ongoing program of services or regulation. Instead, one should use an approach like total quality management, which was presented in Exercise 6.

FURTHER READING

One of the technical articles on the critical path method most useful for students of public administration is Anthony J. Catanese and Alan W. Steiss, "Programming for Governmental Operations: The Critical Path Approach," *Public Administration Review* 28 (March–April 1968), 47–60; it has been reprinted in Richard D. Bingham and Marcus E. Ethridge, eds., *Reaching Decisions in Public Policy and Administration: Methods and Applications* (New York: Longman, 1982). Two useful books explaining CPM are Ted Klastorin, *Project Management: Tools and Trade-offs*, 3rd ed. (Hoboken, NJ: Wiley, 2003) and Harold Kerzner, *Project Management: A Systems Approach to Planning, Scheduling, and Controlling*, 10th ed. (Hoboken, NJ: Wiley, 2009).

On the Web
There are a number of software and training programs for critical path method advertised and available on the Web.

Overview of Exercise

In this exercise, you reassume your role as J. La Rue, senior policy analyst in the State Department of Transportation. After considering your recommendations (from Exercise 1), the city of East Wallingford has decided to construct the Northway. Although preliminary approval has been granted by the state, final authorization to proceed with construction will not be given until a series of hurdles has been cleared.

Your job is to coordinate the initial implementation of the Northway decision. In particular, you are to undertake a critical path analysis of the steps leading up to the start of Northway construction. In so doing, you will design a critical path network, calculate the time of completion of various sequences of activities, identify the critical path, and estimate the amount of slack in noncritical paths.

INSTRUCTIONS

Step One

Study the memorandum (Form 31) prepared by M. Ubahn, your assistant. It contains all the information you need to design a CPM network for the Northway project. Use Form 32 to draw your network. Remember that the first event (circle) in your network should be the Northway decision; the last should be the beginning of construction. You will find that there are two distinct phases of the implementation process, and each one has its own critical path.

Step Two

Complete Form 33 by calculating the estimated time of completion of each event, identifying the critical path for each phase, and computing the amount of slack in the noncritical paths.

Step Three

Answer the questions on Form 34.

September 15, 20__

TO: J. La Rue
           Senior Policy Analyst
           Community Transportation Planning

FROM: M. Ubahn
           Junior Policy Analyst
           Community Transportation Planning

RE: Northway Preconstruction Planning

Per your instructions, I have assembled the data necessary to produce a CPM implementation analysis of the Northway project. Herewith is a summary:

1. Preliminary highway design, required for all subsequent action, should require 45 days.

2. Preparation of a draft Environmental Impact Statement (EIS) will require 60 days.

3. Following release of the EIS, 2 days of public hearings must be scheduled prior to submission of documentation to the Environmental Protection Agency (EPA). An additional 3 days will be necessary to pull together all paperwork after the hearings.

4. EPA approval will require approximately 60 days.

5. Formal approval of the preliminary design by our highway counterparts in SDOT [State Department of Transportation] should require only 5 days from submission. They don't need to wait for the EPA results, of course.

6. Because of the new state Agricultural Lands Preservation statute, we'll need to clear the preliminary design with DOA [State Department of Agriculture]. It will take approximately 30 days to prepare the paperwork after the preliminary design is completed for the DOA submission. An additional 30 days will be required for DOA consideration, interagency coordination, and approval.

7. Following EPA, DOA, and SDOT responses to the preliminary design, 60 days will be necessary to make modifications and prepare the final highway design. This includes the time necessary to clear any changes with the interested agencies.

(*continued*)

8. Once the final highway design has been prepared and approved, two further activities can commence: land acquisition and contract preparation and bidding. These activities can proceed independent of one another. It will require 90 days to acquire the necessary land and 65 days to prepare and award construction contracts.

9. Once all necessary land has been acquired, SDOT surveyors will require 14 days to complete their work.

10. After all contracts have been prepared and bid, 21 days will be required to certify and award contracts.

11. Construction can begin once contracts have been certified and awarded and once the survey work is completed.

CPM Network for Northway Planning

CPM Calculations

1. Identify below the amount of time it will take to complete each event in your CPM network. You can determine this by summing the time consumed by all the necessary activities preceding the event.

Event   Expected Time of Completion

2. Identify the *critical path* for each of the two phases in your CPM network. How long will it take to begin construction?

3. Identify the *noncritical paths* in your CPM network, and calculate the amount of *slack* in each.

Questions

1. What are the advantages of creating CPM networks?

2. What limitations, if any, does CPM have?

3. What resources, other than time, might usefully be represented by activity arrows in CPM networks for the purposes of planning projects?

Exercise 8

Contract Management: Privatization

DEVELOPMENT OF CONTRACTING

Governments in the United States provide life and sustenance to businesses and not-for-profit organizations. Public agencies contract with private agencies (both for-profit and not-for-profit) to do work for which the public agency is responsible. A fundamental part of public administration is contracting or outsourcing—the major form of privatization (i.e., using private sector firms and organizations to accomplish the work of the public sector). Some private companies are in existence primarily because of government business. One of the most visible examples of this was when the giant aircraft company McDonnell-Douglas folded when it failed to get a contract from the Defense Department for a Joint Strike Fighter. Similarly, some local companies providing emergency paramedical services, not-for-profit organizations administering welfare programs, and consultants completing various evaluations depend on government contracts for their sustenance.

Local governments have the longest and most extensive history of contracting for services. Cities, villages, counties, and school boards have used private vendors to pick up garbage, fill in potholes, construct buildings, test drinking water, maintain parks, transport schoolchildren, and clean public buildings. In the 1950s, the federal government developed a management policy of avoiding competition with private firms that offered goods and services similar to those that might be offered by federal agencies. This policy was set forth in Office of Management and Budget Circular A-76, "Performance of Commercial Activities." President Reagan launched an initiative that went further and identified activities done by federal workers that could be privatized. Presidents Bill Clinton and, especially, George W. Bush pursued this policy extensively. One study estimated that the number of workers on federal contracts is more than four times the number of federal employees.[1] In 2001, the federal government spent more than $200 billion on contracts and either awarded or modified contracts more than 560,000 times.[2]

State administrative agencies expanded their use of contracts primarily in the 1990s. In addition to the traditional use of private companies for building and maintaining roads and highways, states turned to businesses and not-for-profits for running prisons, training employees, providing welfare services, and monitoring campers in state parks and forests. The pervasiveness and some of the concerns of government contracting provided the story line for the Tony award–winning musical, *Urinetown.* This musical satire depicts what happens when a private company gets a contract to provide public toilets in a community and then uses its influence to force everyone to use only these toilets and pay the set fees. Ideally, public agencies negotiate good deals and hold contractors accountable for quality services, rather than letting vendors manipulate government for private gains.

WHY CONTRACT?

There are both ideological and practical reasons for public administrators to use contracts. If you believe that government is inherently inefficient and that private organizations provide the highest quality at

[1]B. Guy Peters and John Pierre, "Governance without Government? Rethinking Public Administration," *Journal of Public Administration Research and Theory* 8 (1998): 223–254.
[2]Federal Procurement Data Center, www.fpds.gov.

the lowest price, then contracting is the obvious way to go. If, on the other hand, you think the profit motive of businesses leads to cutting corners and getting away with whatever you can, you will place your trust in government. These ideological assumptions converge with current partisan positions, with Republicans tending to favor reliance on businesses and Democrats on the public sector.

Ideology quite aside, there are practical reasons for contracting. These include:

1. *Temporary needs.* It makes little sense to create a permanent bureaucratic agency to conduct a study, construct a bridge, or fulfill some other short-term need.
2. *Technical expertise.* A village that needs to test its drinking water every six months has an ongoing need, but it is likely to be more cost effective to contract with a private-sector expert than to employ someone and continually provide training so they can stay current with scientific developments.
3. *Economies of scale.* Large firms that specialize in a particular service or product often benefit from bulk discount purchasing and organizational efficiencies that give them advantage over public agencies that are smaller or multifunctional. An example of this is a regional or national concession firm that might operate food services and equipment rentals in public parks.
4. *Labor.* Significant savings can be achieved by contracting with profit and not-for-profit organizations that hire workers at low levels of wages and benefits and might even use some volunteers, rather than compensate individuals at levels paid to most public employees.
5. *Accountability.* Some argue that it is easier to hold someone accountable by severing or not renewing a contract than it is to fire a public employee or to change the direction of a public agency. Ironically, the George W. Bush administration sent mixed messages on this point when in response to the attacks of September 11, 2001, it replaced all the contracts with private vendors for airport security with a new federal agency, the Transportation Security Agency. In contrast, the administration used multibillion-dollar contracts with private companies to provide security and support services in Iraq and Afghanistan rather than using military personnel.

CONCERNS WITH CONTRACTING

General imperfections in the market and pressures generated by electoral politics—especially the financing of campaigns—have raised some concerns about the practice of contracting by public agencies:

1. *Lack of competition.* The assumption that taxpayers and public agencies benefit from the competitive process that awards contracts does not apply to all contracts. Some contracts—including the multibillion-dollar ones used in Iraq and Afghanistan—are no-bid contracts. There is no competition among vendors. Instead, there is negotiation between the government and a particular vendor. In some communities, there simply are not multiple companies to compete for the contract to bus schoolchildren or to fill in potholes or to plow snow. In these situations, there aren't the pressures to ensure that contracts are awarded to get the best-quality service at the lowest prices.
2. *Accountability.* Governments often lack the capacity to monitor contracts to be sure that vendors are complying with the agreements, in letter and in spirit. If you peruse the websites of Inspectors General in federal agencies, you will find a long list of cases in which contractors have overbilled or not delivered. These cases, like those at the state and local levels, are typically found after the fact, if at all. Monitoring contracts takes considerable resources and may nullify any savings that an agency hopes to get by contracting.
3. *Patronage.* Contracts are the most recent form of political patronage. Campaign contributions—and sometimes bribes and kickbacks adding to a politician's personal bank account—seem, at times, to be a prerequisite to getting a government contract. This applies to not-for-profits as well as private businesses. The quid-pro-quo of campaign contributions for advantage in contracting is referred to as "pay-to-play" and applies across the political spectrum and to all levels of government.
4. *Union busting.* Public employee unions have resisted outsourcing as a way of reducing their numbers and limiting workers' rights. Unions that represent government employees do not also cover those who work for government

contractors. Contract employees are usually not unionized. An attraction of contracting can be to avoid the higher labor costs available under collective bargaining agreements. This is especially true for work that is relatively low skilled, like cleaning services. Unions concerned about threats from outsourcing have negotiated provisions that require that they have to agree—or at least be notified—when a contract eliminates union jobs.

5. *Goal displacement.* The allure of cash has significantly altered the mission and goals of some not-for-profit organizations and some businesses. A community organization that was established to work with young people can have the energies of its volunteers and other resources diverted from a variety of activities to a midnight basketball program that must be run because of a government contract. Goodwill Industries, the Salvation Army, Boys and Girls Clubs, the YMCA, the YWCA, and churches have successfully competed in some states to administer welfare programs, operate homeless shelters, and run gang diversion programs. While these contracts are usually related to the general mission and goals of the organizations and while the money is certainly welcome, the contract commitments require changes that sometimes sacrifice traditional programs and identities.

Contracting or outsourcing is neither a panacea nor a monster. This is but one approach to public administration and it has potential advantages and disadvantages. It is an approach that can be appropriate in some cases and inappropriate in others. It certainly is a major and common instrument in the toolkit of public administrators, and thus needs to be understood and used correctly.

THE PROCESS OF CONTRACTING

Assume that instead of doing everything to manage the food drive described in Exercise 7, you decided to spend that time doing extra reading for your public administration class. You decide to outsource to a nonprofit organization in your community. For a fee, they will conduct the food drive and publicize it as a partnership with your campus club so you can get some credit for doing good things.

To bid or not to bid—that is the question. You could randomly select an organization from the list kept by an umbrella association like United Way, you could work with an organization headed by a good friend, or you could contact several organizations to compare what they would do for the fee that you are offering. Each government has its own rules on when it is necessary to invite vendors to compete for a contract. Typically, the rule assumes that there must be competitive bidding and provides exceptions for low-cost (e.g., below $50,000) contracts or for emergencies (e.g., immediate needs after a hurricane).

Whether a contract is put out for bid or negotiated with a single vendor, the administrative agency must specify what it expects. You need to make clear to the potential organization "partnering" with you for the food drive:

1. *What you want.* For example, (a) food items specified by Food Pantry and (b) solicitation of all students and faculty.
2. *How much you want.* This depends on whether the food drive is just for Thanksgiving or an opportunity to stock the Food Pantry shelves as full as possible, despite the focus on Thanksgiving.
3. *When you want it.* In this case, the project is to be completed in time for needy families to get food for Thanksgiving.
4. *Payment.* The "partner" organization may want some money up front. You will probably want to make some or all of the payment dependent on satisfactory service.

Similarly, contracts between public agencies and private or not-for-profit vendors include the following:

- *Deliverables*—what goods or services the public agency wants. There may be quality standards set here.
- *Schedule*—when the goods or services will be provided. This may include benchmarks for completing a project and when the benchmarks will be reached.
- *Payment*—when payments will be made. These might be tied to benchmarks, if any. Some contracts pay for the vendor's costs and then an agreed-on profit. These are known as *cost-plus contracts.*

- *Liquidated damages*—when a contract specifies penalties. Some contracts include penalties to be levied on the vendor if standards or schedules are not met.
- *Dispute resolution*—how differences over how to interpret contract provisions will be settled. This process anticipates the possibility of disagreements after the contract is signed.
- *Additional work authorizations*—addendums to the contract can be agreed to when the agency decides it wants the vendor to complete tasks related to but additional to the original contract.

If a contract is to be bid, the administrative agency notifies organizations and firms that might be interested. This step, often called a *request for proposals (RFP)*, usually includes notices in trade publications and in government announcements made in official documents and on websites. To minimize collusion among potential bidders and to encourage vendors to offer their lowest prices and best services, an RFP may require the submission of *sealed* (final and confidential) bids, due by a specified date. RFPs can also provide for a process where discussions and negotiations occur between the agency and vendors after initial bids are submitted.

A common practice is for the RFP to explain the criteria for deciding the winning bid. One approach is to award up to a certain number of points for each part of the contract. The RFP to the organizations interested in conducting the food drive might, for example, explain that bidders will be awarded points in accordance with how they intend to achieve the following:

- Quantity of food donated—up to 50 points (This is, after all, of highest importance!)
- Diversity of food items—up to 5 points
- Nutritional value (lack of junk food)—up to 15 points
- Quality of publicity—up to 30 points

The assignment of points to each proposal usually involves some judgment, thus a committee goes through the bids.

There is a presumption that the bidder with the most points will be offered the contract. In some jurisdictions, the presumption is that the lowest cost bid will win the contract. Typically, procurement policies allow for the consideration of creativity and special circumstances among the bidders. Ideally, available discretion does not include political patronage or favoritism.

ADMINISTERING CONTRACTS

Once a contract is awarded, it must be administered. Someone needs to monitor whether the list of food items was developed and the publicity went out. Public administrators need to certify that benchmarks were reached on schedule and whether deliverables met quality standards. Payments should then be made or penalties imposed.

Smooth contract implementation occurs when all provisions have been met and there has been no need to utilize the clauses for dealing with disagreements and conflicts. Clear RFPs and contracts help make implementation go smoothly. Even when there aren't schedule delays and disagreements, however, there may be a need for authorizing additional work. It is hard to anticipate all problems and all opportunities. Almost inevitably it is better to have a contractor do additional work than it is to have them come back or to go through another bidding process.

FURTHER READING

One of the first statements promoting a major increase in contracting was E. S. Savas, *Privatization: The Key to Better Government* (Chatham, NJ: Chatham House, 1987). An influential book that boosted privatization is David Osborne and Ted Gaebler, *Reinventing Government: How the Entrepreneurial Spirit Is Transforming the Public Sector* (New York: Plume, 1993); and academic reviews of this trend were provided by Paul Light, *The True Size of Government* (Washington, DC: Brookings, 1999); and Phillip J. Cooper, "Government Contracts in Public Administration: The Role and Environment of the Contracting Officers," *Public Administration Review* 40 (1988): 457–469. A good collection of essays is in Arie Halachmi and

Kenneth L. Nichols, eds. *Enterprise Government: Franchising and Cross-Servicing for Administrative Support* (Burke, VA: Chatelaine Press, 1997). Important reviews of the role of not-for-profit organizations are Nicole Marwell, "Privatizing the Welfare State: Nonprofit Community-based Organizations as Political Actors," *American Sociological Review* 69 (2004): 265–291; and Stephen Oster, "Nonprofit Organizations in a Franchise Age," *Nonprofit Management and Leadership* 2 (1992): 223–238.

On the Web

www.acquisition.gov is a good central source of information for contracting with the federal government. For state and local governments, this information is often available through the website of governors, mayors, and other chief executives.

www.acq.osd.mil/osbp/doing_business/Government %20Contracting%20052006.pdf The Department of Defense has produced a useful document providing information and guidelines for getting contracts with the military.

Overview of Exercise

In this exercise, you will assume that the debate over whether or not to contract has been resolved in favor of contracting. You will simulate a competitive bidding process to establish a contract between a public agency and a private company. First, a group of you will play the role of a panel that must review and complete a draft request for proposals. Then other groups in the class will act as vendors and submit sealed bids. These bids will be submitted to and reviewed by the first group, who will decide which contractor to recommend for the project.

INSTRUCTIONS

Step One

As in Exercise 7, assume that the Northway was selected as a result of the analyses and decision making done in Exercise 1. The State Department of Transportation (SDOT) has determined that it needs to contract with someone to complete a land survey of the route for the Northway project. Your instructor will appoint some of you to act as the SDOT committee to issue a RFP and to evaluate the bids that are submitted. The charge to the SDOT committee is presented in Form 35. A draft RFP is Form 36.

Step Two

The final RFP developed by the committee should be distributed to students assigned to play the role of vendors (individually or in teams). Vendors should review the fact sheet (Form 37) and prepare bids. Remember, you want to make money on this contract. You can be creative in what you include in your bid, but it obviously should be guided by the RFP. Submit your bids as sealed (final) to the Survey Contracting Committee by the deadline set by your instructor. You may use Form 38 for your bid.

Step Three

The Survey Contracting Committee considers the proposals. The first step should be to award points to each bidder based on how well they met each of the criteria. Then the proposals should be rank ordered based on total points. Make any changes in the ranking that seem necessary and explain why the changes were made. Write a brief memo with your recommendation and the ranking of all proposals (Form 39)

Step Four

Answer the questions on Form 40.

FORM 35

September 15, 20___

TO: Members, Survey Contracting Committee

FROM: U. Gotit

         Deputy Secretary
         State Department of Transportation

RE: Northway Preconstruction Survey

Thank you for agreeing to add service on the Survey Contracting Committee to your already busy schedules. As you know, East Wallingford is going to construct a bypass going north of the community in order to reduce traffic time for drivers going through the area.

Obviously, before construction can start, we need to complete a survey of the land on the route. Because we do not have surveyors currently on our staff, we will have to contract for these services. I have provided you with a draft of a Request for Proposals to solicit bids from vendors interested in doing this for us (Form 36). Please review and revise this as necessary. You will note that I have not assigned points for the various criteria that we will use in reviewing bids. Please be sure to assign the potential points for each category, giving the most points, of course, for the most important factors.

Also, please set the deadline by which bids must be submitted. We are using the process where bids are sealed, that is, final. We want to encourage a competitive process rather than engage in negotiations with vendors. You might want to consider including some kind of penalty for not completing the work on time.

Your final task will be to review the bids that are submitted and to recommend which vendor we should select. Please rank order the other bids. The Secretary and I expect you to be guided by the point system you develop, but you should feel free to go beyond a strict addition of points. If you do recommend a ranking other than what would be dictated by point totals, we need you to explain your thinking.

Your supervisor/instructor will let you know when we need your recommendations.

Request for Proposals (Draft)

The State Department of Transportation seeks proposals for the completion of a professional survey to be used in the construction of a bypass north of East Wallingford. The planned road will have four lanes (two in each direction and divided by a 30-foot green space). It includes a bike and walking path, approximately 35 yards wide, running parallel on the north side of the road. The road will be 5 miles long and stretch from East Main Street to upper Nottingham Road, running through what is currently an area that is undeveloped woodlands, with several streams.

The survey must be completed within 14 calendar days after the contract is signed by the parties and no longer than 21 calendar days after the State Department of Transportation notifies the winning bidder by certified mail. The deliverable report must meet the needs of civil engineers.

The criteria for selecting the vendor with whom to contract is as follows, with specified maximum points to be awarded for each consideration. The selection will be guided by point totals, but the successful bid may not necessarily have the highest number of points.

Factor	Maximum Points
Cost	
Professional qualifications of personnel	
Experience with similar projects	
Local or regional firm	

Fact Sheet

1. Certified surveyors earn $175 to $200 per hour. Support personnel earn $65 per hour. Those preparing final reports for civil engineering projects earn $95 per hour.

2. A team of one surveyor and three support staff generally can finish work on 1 mile of wooded land in 2 to 4 working days. A report meeting the specifications for a civil engineering project takes 3 days to complete.

3. There are three certified surveyors living in the East Wallingford area. Each of them is freelancing.

Proposal for Preconstruction Survey for Northway Project, East Wallingford

Name of Company:

Address:

Proposal:

TO: Deputy Secretary U. Gotit

FROM: Survey Contracting Committee

RE: Northway Preconstruction Survey

Based on our review of proposals for completing a survey to be used in constructing the Northway project for East Wallingford, we recommend that the State Department of Transportation contract with

Questions

1. What issues did you have to consider and resolve to establish the point system in the request for proposals? How closely did the committee follow the point totals in rank ordering the bids?

2. Were there ways in which the vendors could have colluded to get around the sealed bid process? Are there alternative processes that you can think of that might be more effective in ensuring competitive bids?

3. Was this an appropriate situation for a public agency to contract with a private company? Are there activities or responsibilities that governments have for which contracting would be inappropriate?

Exercise 9

Regulatory Management: Administrative Law

WHAT IS ADMINISTRATIVE LAW?

In addition to services and projects, public agencies are responsible for enforcing government regulations. While private and not-for-profit organizations, like government agencies, have programs, projects, and outsourcing, the public sector uniquely has the authority to enforce regulations. Regulatory management is the substance of administrative law. The federal Administrative Procedures Act of 1946, which has been amended only a few times since its passage, is the most important single codification of administrative law. Most, but not all, states have a law similar to the federal one. However, administrative law is tucked away in many different places—in federal and state constitutions, statutes, executive orders, signing statements, administrative rules, waivers, treaties, and court decisions. All of these things taken together as they affect public administration constitute administrative law.

WHY IS ADMINISTRATIVE LAW IMPORTANT?

The traditional theory of public administration held that elected officials make policy and administrators implement it. Whether this neat distinction ever applied in practice is doubtful. Certainly it does not apply today. The scope of modern government is so vast and the issues government confronts are so technically complex that elected officials can attend directly only to a minute proportion of the items on the public agenda. Consequently, much of the day-to-day responsibility for making public policy is delegated—formally or informally—to public administrators. This is what is meant by the concept of the *administrative state*. Public administrators, not legislators, are the ones who, for example, determine safety standards for oil drilling, set the specific requirements for health insurance companies, define what can be classified as organic food, and decide thousands of other questions, large and small. General laws are passed and administrators fill in the details—and the devil is in the details!

Administrative law sets forth the extent to which agencies are allowed to fill in the details, the procedures that must be used in doing so, and the rights of those affected by agency actions to appeal administrative decisions. Administrative law is grounded in the basic separation of powers doctrine incorporated into governance in the United States. Agencies have important inherent powers, but these powers are limited by the respective powers of legislatures and courts.

STATUS OF ADMINISTRATIVE LAW

Whenever a legislative body passes a law, it specifies which executive branch agency (existing or new) has the authority for making detailed rules to describe what the affected individuals and organizations must do to comply with the law. And the limits of an agency's authority are set by the legislature as well. State legislatures, for example, have passed laws that require drivers of cars to have a license based on requirements to ensure safety. These laws establish an agency to license drivers. That agency then determines what kinds of written tests, eye examinations, and performance tests applicants must pass to get a driver's license. The agency, however, does not have statutory authority to venture into other areas, such as selling shirts or encouraging the consumption of ice cream. This agency, in fact, does not even have authority over other issues involving highway safety, such as setting speed limits. There is another agency that has authority over that.

If the driver's licensing agency did something that the state legislature did not like, the legislature could pass a law directing it to do something differently. Statutes trump administrative rules. It is rare that a legislature changes the regulatory decisions of an administrative agency and it is important to know that those decisions have the force of law.

If the agency did something that exceeded its authority (sold shirts) or violated its own rules (singled out you to have a higher exam score on a drivers test than was normally considered passing), then the courts are available to check the agency. Courts generally confine themselves in administrative law to procedural and jurisdictional issues. They do not substitute the wisdom of judges for the wisdom of administrators. A court would not second-guess the agency administering drivers' licenses on the content of examinations or what constitutes a passing score.

THE ADMINISTRATIVE PROCEDURES ACT

The federal Administrative Procedures Act (APA) was a response to the confusion caused when there were no standard guidelines for when and how an agency should promulgate rules to implement laws and for how, if at all, someone might appeal administrative actions. The American Bar Association played a major role in drafting standards that would apply to all federal agencies. In a few cases, Congress will set a different standard or procedure for a particular agency. The basic structure of the APA was set in 1946 and has been amended only a few times since then. Two major amendments that you may be familiar with are the Freedom of Information Act and the Privacy Act. The Freedom of Information Act (section 552 of the APA) requires federal agencies to make various documents and records available to the public. The Privacy Act (section 552a of the APA) prohibits agencies from disclosing information about individuals without their consent and gives individuals the right to inspect records maintained on them. If you've ever asked a professor to fill out a letter of recommendation for you, you may have noticed a

Privacy Act disclaimer—a place on the form that asks if you wish to waive your right of access to the letter so as to keep it confidential.

The heart of the APA, though, deals with rule making and the adjudication of disputes. A *rule* is an action taken by an administrative agency that describes how a law will be interpreted and applied by the agency. For example, the Federal Aviation Administration (FAA) has issued a rule if it adopts a policy requiring all aircraft flying within a certain distance of major airports (class B airspace) to have onboard radio equipment (a mode C transponder) that automatically provides air traffic controllers with information about aircraft altitude. The APA provides for a court-like process for resolving disagreements over how administrative rules are applied in specific cases. If the FAA revokes the license of John Smith, a pilot who flew through the Philadelphia class B airspace on April 15, 2009, without a mode C transponder, Mr. Smith will have the opportunity to challenge the FAA action before an administrative law judge (ALJ).

Administrative rules have the force of law, and violators can be fined or their license to operate a business or service can be withdrawn. A full treatment of APA requirements for rule making and adjudication is beyond the scope of this chapter. Suffice it to say that the APA recognizes several different types of rules and rule making and a range of adjudicatory procedures. The most rigorous rule-making requirements are imposed on agencies that propose *substantive rules* under *formal rule-making procedures*. When establishing new rules, agencies must follow very strict guidelines, publish proposed rules in the *Federal Register* (www.gpoaccess.gov/fr), hear testimony from all affected parties, and issue the rule based on "substantial evidence" in the written record. Another process, which applies to clarifying how existing rules will be applied, does not require a hearing, but does stipulate that the proposed clarifications be published in the *Federal Register* to invite public comment before the clarifications apply.

The same variation applies to adjudicatory procedures. Some actions simply require a notice of charges and an opportunity for the affected party to present his or her side of the story. Other actions require far more detailed safeguards of due process rights with the adjudicatory procedure resembling in its structure a full-blown trial complete with attorneys, cross-examination, rules of evidentiary disclosure, and so forth. What set of procedures must be followed depends, in general, on the seriousness of the interests involved and the costs of making a mistake. Courts have found that a student challenging a suspension from school is entitled to considerably less protection, for instance, than a person whose disability benefits are about to be terminated.

Although the provisions of the APA sound complex—and in many ways they are—the general principle of the statute is simple: If agencies follow correct procedures, the public interest will be protected. This process orientation reflects the belief, fundamental to American society in general and to American jurisprudence in particular, that if everyone's rights are respected and due process is observed, justice will have been done and outcomes will take care of themselves. The tricky part with respect to public administration is striking a balance between this precept and the need for administrative efficiency. Governance in the modern state without administrative discretion is inconceivable. Administrative discretion without constraint would be unbearable. Administrative law, properly applied, constrains the discretion of administrative regulators without destroying it.

Some federal and state agencies have specialized, independent employees called ALJs who serve as hearing officers and judges in disputes arising between an agency and those affected by the agency. Certain agencies also have elaborate procedures for making decisions or promulgating rules and regulations, procedures that are intended to guarantee fairness and due process. This is especially true of regulatory agencies such as the Federal Trade Commission (FTC), Federal Communications Commission (FCC), Interstate Commerce Commission (ICC), and Securities and Exchange Commission (SEC), among others, which are charged with quasi-legislative or quasi-judicial functions.

Courts generally insist that the administrative appeal process be used before someone takes a dispute into the courtroom. Courts confine any review of the decisions of ALJs to the question of whether the ALJ followed proper procedures and kept the scope of decisions within his or her area of authority. Courts do not second-guess the substantive decisions of ALJs.

FURTHER READING

A good text on administrative law is Steven J. Cann, *Administrative Law*, 4th ed. (Thousand Oaks, CA: Sage, 2005). See also, William F. Funk and Richard H. Seamon, *Administrative Law. Examples and Explanations,* 3rd ed. (New York: Aspen Publishers, 2009).

Good essays on some of the issues in American administrative law can be found in Peter Schuck, ed., *Foundations of Administrative Law* (New York: Oxford University Press, 1994); Phillip J. Cooper and Chester A. Newland, eds., *Handbook of Public Law and Administration* (San Francisco: Jossey-Bass, 1997); and David Rosenbloom and David H. Rosenbloom *Administrative Law for Public Managers* (New York: Westview, 2003). State-level concerns—and an analysis of the Model State Administrative Procedures Act—form the core of Michael Asimow, Arthur Earl Bonfield, and Ronald M. Levin, *State and Federal Administrative Law*, 2nd ed. (Eagan, MN: Thomas West, 2007).

For discussions of the rule-making process, see Cornelius M. Kerwin, *Rulemaking: How Government Agencies Write Law and Make Policy*, 3rd ed. (Washington, DC: Congressional Quarterly Press, 2003) and Cindy Skrycki, *The Regulators: Anonymous Power Brokers in American Politics* (Lanham, MD: Rowman and Littlefield, 2003).

On the Web

www.gpoaccess.gov/fr As presented above, the *Federal Register* is the source for proposed and approved regulations. Publication in the *Federal Register* is a key, required part in the process for establishing administrative law.

Most states have processes similar to that of federal government.

Overview of Exercise

This role play illustrates the issues of interpreting a statute, applying administrative rules based on that statute, and resolving disputes that occur in this application. The substance of the role play is Title IX of the 1972 Amendment to the Education Act, which mandates gender equity in athletics, including intercollegiate athletics. The role play begins with the parties presenting their cases and making their arguments. It ends with a ruling by an administrative law judge (or, if your instructor so chooses, a panel of administrative law judges).

Your instructor may want to supplement this role play with one in which you make rules. If so, the same documents and facts will be used, but instead of adjudicating a dispute, the focus will be on drafting new rules to define and achieve gender equity in intercollegiate athletics. This role play will not include an administrative law judge, but there will still be interested and affected parties and an administrative agency.

INSTRUCTIONS

Step One

Your instructor will assign you to one of the following roles:

> Attorney for Women's Water Polo Club at College of Mine (plaintiff)
>
> Attorney for College of Mine (codefendant)
>
> Regional Director of Office for Civil Rights (codefendant)
>
> Administrative law judge in federal Department of Education

All participants should read the role information provided in Forms 41 through 44.

Step Two

All participants should read the background information, the administrative rule, and the clarification presented on Forms 45, 46, and 47.

Step Three

Plaintiff's attorney should prepare and present an oral argument to the administrative law judge

seeking a ruling that College of Mine must upgrade women's water polo to a varsity sport.

Step Four

College of Mine attorney should prepare and present an oral argument to the administrative law judge denying plaintiff's request and finding the college in compliance with Title IX.

Step Five

Office for Civil Rights regional director should prepare and present an oral argument to the administrative law judge upholding the finding of noncompliance for College of Mine and denying plaintiff's request.

Step Six (optional)

The administrative law judge allows each party to present a rebuttal and closing argument.

Step Seven

The administrative law judge reaches and announces a decision, explaining the rationale to the contending parties.

Step Eight

Answer the questions on Form 48

INSTRUCTIONS FOR OPTIONAL EXERCISE IN RULE MAKING

Step One

Your instructor will assign the administrative law judge from the previous exercise to a new role. The regional Office for Civil Rights will be reconstituted as the national Office for Civil Rights in the federal Department of Education. Other role assignments continue.

Step Two

The Office for Civil Rights drafts revisions to the rules in Forms 45 and 46. The revisions should address the issues raised in the previous exercise adjudicating the dispute between the College of

Mine and the women's water polo club. Make the changes on Form 45 and/or Form 46 and distribute the draft revisions to the rest of the class.

Step Three

The Office for Civil Rights holds a hearing and receives testimony on the draft revisions. Those presenting testimony should be as specific as possible about the features that they like and dislike. Requests for changes in the draft should be specific and in writing.

Step Four

The Office for Civil Rights considers whether or not to make any changes in its draft and issues a final rule. Again, incorporate the changes on Form 45 and/or Form 46.

Step Five

Answer the questions on Form 48.

Role Information: Attorney for Women's Water Polo Club

Working with any other students assigned by the instructor to this role, you must review carefully the administrative rule and clarification (Forms 45 and 46) and the background and facts in Form 47 and prepare a statement to the administrative law judge.

Your instructor may allow you to include additional evidence as part of your case. If so, you may want to produce documents that help substantiate your case. You must give the codefendants adequate notice of the nature of any evidence you plan to introduce and, if they ask, allow them to examine that evidence. Failure to observe this rule may lead to your evidence being ruled inadmissible by the administrative law judge.

Present a clear and convincing oral presentation of your case to the administrative law judge. You may have to respond to questions posed by the judge, and you may (depending on directions from your instructor) have an opportunity to rebut the case made by the codefendants.

Role Information: Attorney
for College of Mine

Working with any other students assigned by the instructor to this role, you must review carefully the administrative rule and clarification (Forms 45 and 46) and the background and facts in Form 47 and prepare a statement to the administrative law judge. Although you have a codefendant, you should remember that you do not share a common position or set of interests with your codefendant.

Your instructor may allow you to include additional evidence as part of your case. If so, you may want to produce documents that help substantiate your case. You must give the plaintiff and codefendant adequate notice of the nature of any evidence you plan to introduce and, if they ask, allow them to examine that evidence. Failure to observe this rule may lead to your evidence being ruled inadmissible by the administrative law judge.

Present a clear and convincing oral presentation of your case to the administrative law judge. You may have to respond to questions posed by the judge, and you may (depending on directions from your instructor) have an opportunity to rebut the case made by the codefendant.

Role Information: Regional Director of the Office for Civil Rights

Working with any other students assigned by the instructor to this role, you must review carefully the administrative rule and clarification (Forms 45 and 46) and the background and facts in Form 47 and prepare a statement to the administrative law judge. Although you have a codefendant, you should remember that you do not share a common position or set of interests with your codefendant.

Your instructor may allow you to include additional evidence as part of your case. If so, you may want to produce documents that help substantiate your case. You must give the plaintiff and codefendant adequate notice of the nature of any evidence you plan to introduce and, if they ask, allow them to examine that evidence. Failure to observe this rule may lead to your evidence being ruled inadmissible by the administrative law judge.

Present a clear and convincing oral presentation of your case to the administrative law judge. You may have to respond to questions posed by the judge, and you may (depending on directions from your instructor) have an opportunity to rebut the case made by the codefendant.

Role Information: Administrative Law Judge

Working with any other students who may be assigned to this role by the instructor, your job is to hear the presentations by the attorneys and the Regional Director of the Office for Civil Rights, to weigh all arguments and evidence, and to come to a conclusion.

It is your responsibility to ensure that proper procedures are followed and that evidence is presented fully and fairly. If your instructor permits additional evidence to be generated, you have the right to rule on the admissibility of individual pieces of evidence, and you should be sure that each party has an opportunity to examine whatever evidence is introduced. You should bear in mind that evidentiary rules are somewhat relaxed in administrative law cases. Hearsay evidence, for instance, is generally allowed, although it is typically not given as much weight as direct evidence. When the presentations are made, it is expected that you take an active role and ask questions whenever you feel a need to probe.

It is critical that your conclusion be clear and definitive. You can accept, reject, or modify the ruling of the Regional Director of the Office for Civil Rights. But you are to resolve the case. You may not, in other words, create an order that has contingencies that would require you or someone else to evaluate whether the conditions have been met. Assume that you will never again have to consider the issues of water polo or Title IX compliance at College of Mine.

Office for Civil Rights Administrative Rule on Gender Equity in Athletics

106.41 Athletics.

a. *General.* No person shall, on the basis of sex, be excluded from participation in, be denied the benefits of, be treated differently from another person or otherwise be discriminated against in any interscholastic, intercollegiate, club or intramural athletics offered by a recipient, and no recipient shall provide any such athletics separately on such basis.

b. *Separate teams.* Notwithstanding the requirements of paragraph (a) of this section, a recipient may operate or sponsor separate teams for members of each sex where selection for such teams is based upon competitive skill or the activity involved is a contact sport. However, where a recipient operates or sponsors a team in a particular sport for members of one sex but operates or sponsors no such team for members of the other sex, and athletic opportunities for members of that sex have previously been limited, members of the excluded sex must be allowed to try out for the team offered unless the sport involved is a contact sport. For the purposes of this part, contact sports include boxing, wrestling, rugby, ice hockey, football, basketball and other sports the purpose or major activity of which involves bodily contact.

c. *Equal opportunity.* A recipient which operates or sponsors interscholastic, intercollegiate, club or intramural athletics shall provide equal athletic opportunity for members of both sexes. In determining whether equal opportunities are available the Director will consider, among other factors:

    (1) Whether the selection of sports and levels of competition effectively accommodate the interests and abilities of members of both sexes;

    (2) The provision of equipment and supplies;

    (3) Scheduling of games and practice time;

    (4) Travel and per diem allowance;

    (5) Opportunity to receive coaching and academic tutoring;

    (6) Assignment and compensation of coaches and tutors;

    (7) Provision of locker rooms, practice and competitive facilities;

    (8) Provision of medical and training facilities and services;

    (9) Provision of housing and dining facilities and services;

    (10) Publicity.

Unequal aggregate expenditures for members of each sex or unequal expenditures for male and female teams if a recipient operates or sponsors separate teams will not constitute noncompliance with this section, but the Assistant Secretary may consider the failure to provide necessary funds for teams for one sex in assessing equality of opportunity for members of each sex.

d. *Adjustment period.* A recipient which operates or sponsors interscholastic, intercollegiate, club or intramural athletics at the elementary school level shall comply fully with this section as expeditiously as possible but in no event later than one year from the effective date of this regulation. A recipient which operates or sponsors interscholastic, intercollegiate, club or intramural athletics at the secondary or post-secondary school level shall comply fully with this section as expeditiously as possible but in no event later than three years from the effective date of this regulation.

(Authority: Secs. 901, 902, Education Amendments of 1972, 86 Stat. 373, 374; 20 U.S.C. 1681, 1682; and Sec. 844, Education Amendments of 1974, Pub. L. 93–380, 88 Stat. 484)

Office for Civil Rights 1997 Clarification on Gender Equity Participation

5. Application of the Policy—Levels of Competition.

In effectively accommodating the interests and abilities of male and female athletes, institutions must provide both the opportunity for individuals of each sex to participate in intercollegiate competition, and for athletes of each sex to have competitive team schedules which equally reflect their abilities.

a. Compliance will be assessed in any one of the following ways:

1. Whether intercollegiate level participation opportunities for male and female students are provided in numbers substantially proportionate to their respective enrollments; or

2. Where the members of one sex have been and are underrepresented among intercollegiate athletes, whether the institution can show a history and continuing practice of program expansion which is demonstrably responsive to the developing interest and abilities of the members of that sex; or

3. Where the members of one sex are underrepresented among intercollegiate athletes, and the institution cannot show a continuing practice of program expansion such as that cited above, whether it can be demonstrated that the interests and abilities of the members of that sex have been fully and effectively accommodated by the present program.

b. Compliance with this provision of the regulation will also be assessed by examining the following:

1. Whether the competitive schedules for men's and women's teams, on a program-wide basis, afford proportionally similar numbers of male and female athletes equivalently advanced competitive opportunities; or

2. Whether the institution can demonstrate a history and continuing practice of upgrading the competitive opportunities available to the historically disadvantaged sex as warranted by developing abilities among the athletes of that sex.

c. Institutions are not required to upgrade teams to intercollegiate status or otherwise develop intercollegiate sports absent a reasonable expectation that intercollegiate competition in that sport will be available within the institution's normal competitive regions. Institutions may be required by the Title IX regulation to actively encourage the development of such competition, however, when overall athletic opportunities within that region have been historically limited for the members of one sex.

Background Information

In 1972 Congress and the president mandated that all colleges and universities receiving federal funds provide athletic opportunities for women and men at equivalent levels. The law—known as "Title IX" because it added this title or section to the Education Act—authorized the Office for Civil Rights in the federal Department of Education to define how that general principle would be met and to enforce its application. The sanction for not complying with the law and the administrative rules specifying its application was to withdraw all federal funds from the offending college or university. Note that it is highly unusual for any federal funds to go to an intercollegiate athletic program. Thus, the funds that would be withdrawn would actually affect departments and programs in the university that were not related at all to athletics.

The Office for Civil Rights has a central office in Washington, D.C., and regional offices throughout the country. The regional offices deal directly with the colleges and universities in their respective areas. These offices apply the administrative rules that have been promulgated, receive complaints against specific universities, conduct investigations in response to those complaints, and make rulings regarding whether or not a university is in compliance with the rules. The regional offices also provide information and advice regarding Title IX.

Title IX provides "standing" to anyone to file a complaint. In other words, a person does not have to meet the usual standard of demonstrating that he or she has been or is in danger of personally being harmed by someone's action or inaction in order to initiate legal action.

College of Mine has a Division I program in the National Collegiate Athletic Association. That means it recruits student-athletes for its teams, provides scholarships to them, and hires coaches. Like other Division I programs, there are club sports, which are formed by students at the college, and although they compete against club teams from other colleges, there are no scholarships and the college does not hire coaches for these teams. Among the club sports at College of Mine is women's water polo.

Mine women's water polo petitioned the college's athletic department to be upgraded to a varsity sport. The Athletic Director, supported by Mine Chancellor, denied the request, citing expenses and a lack of competitive opportunities. If the college were to have a varsity women's water polo team, it would have to spend $7.5 million to construct a regulation-sized pool or spend $5.9 million to upgrade the existing pool on campus. In addition, there would be an annual expense of $625,000 for scholarships, coaches, travel, and uniforms. In the last 4 years, Mine has added women's soccer and volleyball to its varsity sports and claims it cannot afford the additional costs of water polo. Mine argued that it should be credited for having had a history of expanding opportunities for women student-athletes. Moreover, Mine is a member of the Middle Eight athletic conference. Only two colleges in the conference currently have a women's water polo team, so there are not enough teams for conference competition.

The women have secured the services of an attorney. The attorney filed a Title IX complaint with the Office for Civil Rights. The complaint notes that College of Mine has an undergraduate student population that is 51 percent female, yet the student-athletes on varsity teams is only 39 percent female. Obviously, the women on the club water polo team demonstrate interest and ability in the sport and argue the College, which is currently not in compliance with Title IX, is obliged to add this sport.

The Regional Office for Civil Rights (OCR) conducted an investigation in response to the complaint that was filed and confirmed the facts provided both by the college administration and by the club team. It ruled that indeed College of Mine was not in compliance with Title IX. OCR noted that 7 years ago, Mine eliminated women's fencing as a varsity sport, supposedly for budgetary reasons and a lack of interest, and thus could not be considered as having a history of expanding athletic opportunities for its female students. However, OCR did not find that Mine had to add women's water polo in order to come into compliance with Title IX.

The water polo players want to make a big splash. They have asked their attorney to appeal the decision of College of Mine and the ruling of the Office for Civil Rights. The attorney has decided that the best course of action is to bring the matter before an administrative law judge in the Department of Education.

Questions

1. Do the rules found in Forms 45 and 46 allow any discretion to the Office for Civil Rights?
2. Do agencies have too much power to set and then adjudicate administrative rules? Is this power an inevitable outcome given the complexity of issues and the dynamics of legislating?
3. What are the differences between administrative law on the one hand and court proceedings for civil and criminal cases on the other?

Exercise 10

Emergency Management: Tabletop Exercise

THE SPECIAL CONCERNS OF EMERGENCY MANAGEMENT

When Hurricane Katrina hit land on August 29, 2005, it not only devastated New Orleans and the Gulf Coast region, it also made visible the importance of emergency management. Even though storm trackers provided a four-day warning, government agencies responsible for dealing with emergencies were inept and uncoordinated. Obviously, some of the property damage from winds and floods could not have been prevented. Just as clearly, hundreds of lives—especially of poor and vulnerable people—could have been saved. Survivors could have been served more effectively.[1] The problem was a dramatic failure in governance and public administration.

Emergencies do not occur only from storms and floods. The attacks on the Pentagon and New York's World Trade Center on September 11, 2001, were conscious acts of terrorism. Shootings on campuses and in elementary and high schools are the results of anger and mental illness. Human error and insufficient attention to safety measures led to the explosion of the oil drilling operation of BP in 2010 that killed 11 workers and wreaked havoc on the environment and economy of the Gulf Coast. Whatever the precise causes, emergencies are unusual and unanticipated events that require quick responses to mitigate damage.

Emergency management is in stark contrast to the principles of organization and administration that are critical to the principles covered in Exercise 3 and that are fundamental to the types of management discussed in Exercises 5 through 9.

Emergency management is, by definition, a quick, immediate response to a single, unusual event and does not have the kind of existing structures and processes that we associate with most organizations. In fact, one of the fundamental impediments to effective and timely responses to Hurricane Katrina was adherence to the established organizational structures and decision rules of the agencies involved. When firefighters from around the country volunteered to help with rescue operations, for example, the Federal Emergency Management Agency insisted that they first complete a standard two-day training program on sexual harassment in Atlanta, Georgia. While the firefighters were told how to treat one another in a way that did not subject individuals to hostility and harassment because of their gender, desperate people in New Orleans were—not always successfully—seeking to avoid being swept away by flood waters.

THE BASIC CHARACTERISTICS OF EMERGENCY MANAGEMENT

Almost inevitably, responses to emergencies require the expertise, resources, and cooperation of more than one agency. Typically, police departments, fire departments, and health agencies are involved. It is not unusual for several local governments, one or more state governments, and the federal government to participate. Private companies and not-for-profit organizations help. As the 2010 explosion of an oil drilling rig demonstrated, sometimes the equipment and expertise needed to handle a crisis are solely in the hands of a private company, rather than a public agency. When the company with the required

[1]See the series of articles chronicling the storm and its aftermath in the *New Orleans Times-Picayune,* August 27–September 30, 2005.

resources is also the company responsible for the crisis, there can be complications to the appearance, if not the substance, of an effective response.

Emergencies require the establishment of an ad hoc organization that brings together all the agencies and companies that need to be involved. The team of responders will be different for each emergency. Once the crisis has passed, there may be a continued organization for recovery and rebuilding, but the first responders (e.g., police and firefighters) will probably no longer be needed.

Another characteristic of emergencies is uncertainty. Police, firefighters, and medical personnel responding to reports of a campus or school shooting must act promptly, even though they probably will not know who is shooting or why, what weapons are being used, who the targets and/or victims are, what kinds of injuries exist, or what, if any, plans have been made by the shooter(s). Has the shooter or shooters planted explosives? Are they suicidal? Even with satellite photos, when Hurricane Katrina hit, no one could tell for sure exactly which communities would be hit the hardest, how long the rain and winds would last, what infrastructure would be damaged, or what public health hazards would emerge. Oil spills may be the result of human error or accident, but the damage, as is the case with hurricanes, depends heavily on unpredictable and uncontrollable currents, winds, and weather. Nonetheless, decisions have to be made, and agencies have to act quickly. Someone has to set priorities and address situations where lives are at stake first and then stabilize the situation to minimize harm and to begin recovery.

The importance of having a central commander—referred to as an incident commander—in emergency management cannot be stressed too much. The combination of having multiple agencies responding and high levels of uncertainty begs for someone to take control. Most emergencies occur without warning, and this can complicate the identification and acceptance of a single commander. However, even when there were the warnings that Hurricane Katrina would strike the Gulf Coast, no one took charge. Despite the knowledge that the storm would be Category 5 (the most severe) and would affect a

multistate area (Louisiana, Mississippi, and Alabama), the federal Department of Homeland Security did not use its authority to declare an emergency of "national significance" and coordinate the efforts of state, local, and federal agencies. Even though New Orleans was in the direct path of the hurricane, no one at the state or local levels assumed control.

No one ordered an evacuation of the city until it was too late. Two years before Hurricane Katrina, city planners had estimated it would take three days to evacuate the area. Mayor Ray Nagin followed the advice of lawyers, who warned that the city would be liable for declines in the tourist businesses if there was an evacuation and the storm missed the city. Mandatory evacuation was not declared until the day before Katrina hit. People, especially in the poorer areas, were stranded and many perished. The chaos that occurs when there is no effective leadership and coordination inevitably makes a bad situation worse.

Because emergencies affect specific communities and need immediate responses, state and local governments have always had the primary responsibility for emergency management. The federal government has been a source of disaster relief and more recently has played a role in emergency planning and preparedness. In 1979, President Jimmy Carter consolidated more than 100 programs and units and established the Federal Emergency Management Agency (FEMA). The primary concern of FEMA has been preparedness and relief for natural disasters. In 1997, Congress passed PL 104–201, known after its primary sponsors as the Nunn-Lugar-Domenici Act, which directed the federal government to work with state and local governments to be prepared for disasters caused by weapons of mass destruction. In the aftermath of 9/11, FEMA was placed in the new Department of Homeland Security and directed to prepare for disasters due to terrorism as well as natural causes and accidents.[2] FEMA was harshly criticized for its role in responding to Hurricane Katrina and has

[2]GWU Institute for Crisis, Disaster, and Risk Management, "Statutory Authority: Disaster Management in the 21st Century," *EMSE* 232, p. 2, ch. 3, http://www.seas.gwu.edu/-emse232/emse232book3.

been rebuilt with new leadership, organization, and oversight.[3]

The federal government has provided assistance and funding to local governments to conduct tabletop exercises, which are simulations of emergencies, to prepare for emergencies. These exercises recognize that the first responders to a disaster are inevitably local police, fire, and health agencies. Tabletop exercises provide an opportunity to practice the establishment of ad hoc organizations in reaction to specific situations.

KEY STEPS IN EMERGENCY MANAGEMENT

Although emergency management is necessarily ad hoc and specific to each situation, there are some key steps that must be taken to maximize the chances of an effective response:

1. *Designate an incident commander.* Most states have designated the chief of the community fire department as the incident commander in emergencies, although the public health officer is the incident commander if the emergency is bioterrorism or is fundamentally a biological threat. The most important point is that someone needs to take responsibility as the one in charge.

2. *Establish a command center.* The command center is in part a place where agencies, private organizations, volunteers, the media, and others can go to get information and instructions. The command center is also a steering committee that consists of representatives of key, relevant organizations and serves to advise and work with the incident commander.

3. *Communicate*
   a. *Internally.* The agencies and volunteers participating in the response need both the technology and the organization to facilitate communication with the incident commander and with each other. Communication must be clear and allow for immediate reception of urgent messages.
   b. *Externally.* The public generally and the individuals most affected need to be kept informed. It is generally useful to have a mayor, governor, or some other elected political official talk with the media, even though this official is not the actual incident commander.

4. *Contain the problem.* A fundamental responsibility of police departments is to cordon off an area, both to keep a problem from spreading and to restrict access to those who need to provide relief. Public health crises may require a quarantine of affected individuals.

5. *If relevant, apprehend perpetrators.* Another responsibility of the police is to issue alerts, conduct investigations, and apprehend those responsible for disasters. Besides holding these people responsible for their acts, there is a concern about repeated incidents.

6. *Rescue and treat victims.* Treatment can be obvious first aid for those affected by a disaster. Treatment may also require careful diagnosis and then a prescription for what needs to be done. Where there is uncertainty and the need for medium- to long-term treatment, it is essential to identify and contain victims.

7. *Provide immediate relief.* Individuals who have lost their homes, cannot return to their jobs, or are separated from their family are examples of cases in which there is a need for immediate relief. FEMA has resources and authority for distributing limited immediate relief. The Red Cross is federally chartered to provide emergency shelter and provisions.

8. *Restore basic infrastructure and services.* Individuals and communities are heavily dependent on electricity, water, transportation, and the like. If these services and facilities are disrupted, it is essential to restore them as quickly as possible. This can affect rescue operations as well as recovery efforts.

9. *Clean up.* Once the height of the crisis is past, it is important both functionally and symbolically that the disaster area be cleaned of hazards and debris. In the case of an oil spill or other crisis involving hazardous waste, the cleanup phase may take years and may require supervising the activities of the private company responsible for the incident.

[3] *A Failure of Initiative: The Final Report of the Select Bipartisan Committee to Investigate the Preparation for and Response to Hurricane Katrina*, U.S. House of Representatives, February 15, 2006. www.katrina.house.gov and *Hurricane Katrina: Ineffective FEMA Oversight of Housing Maintenance Contracts in Mississippi Resulted in Millions of Dollars of Waste and Potential Fraud*, General Accountability Office, November, 2007.

10. *Plan recovery.* Near- and long-term recovery typically requires the resources and expertise of several agencies, not-for-profit organizations, and companies. The development of a recovery plan may also require an ad hoc organization, although not necessarily the same one as the structure established for dealing with the emergency.

11. *Keep records.* Records of what happened and who was affected are critical. There is often a need to share this information with the families of victims or suspected victims. In addition, this information is important to relief agencies and insurance companies so they can be sure to serve the right people. Issues of legal liability and criminal prosecution also require good records.

12. *Evaluate response.* Evaluation is always an important step in administrative processes. It helps organizations and elected officials learn and improve.

FURTHER READING

The literature on emergency management is limited, but there are some good recent books to consult, including David E. Alexander, *Principles of Emergency Management* (New York: Oxford University Press, 2002); George Haddow, Jane Bullock, and Damon P. Coppola, *Introduction to Emergency Management*, 3rd ed. (Burlington, MA: Elsevier Science, 2008); Ronald W. Perry and Michael Kl. Lindell, *Emergency Planning* (Hoboken, NJ: John Wiley & Sons, 2007); and Richard Sylves, *Disaster Policy and Politics: Emergency Management and Homeland Security* (Washington, DC: Congressional Quarterly Press, 2008).

Overview of Exercise

Your instructor will assign roles to perform in a tabletop exercise, simulating a shooting on your campus. As in other tabletop exercises and in actual emergencies, you will have limited information about exactly what happened. In fact, your instructor may change some or all of the information provided here to simulate further the element of surprise. Emergency management is about the unexpected. The objective is to establish an ad hoc organization very quickly and to take as many of the steps outlined in this chapter that apply.

- County public health director
- Federal Bureau of Investigation
- 911 dispatch
- Local hospital director
- American Red Cross
- State National Guard Commander
- Federal Emergency Management Agency
- State patrol
- City police
- Campus police

INSTRUCTIONS

Step One
Your instructor will assign to you one of the following roles:

- Cafeteria staff
- Federal Department of Homeland Security
- County sheriff
- Governor
- City fire chief
- State Department of Emergency Government
- City mayor
- University or college chancellor
- Local radio station

Step Two
The following have instructions on Forms 49 and 50 that should be read and followed:

- Cafeteria staff
- Local radio station

Other roles do not have specific instructions. Do what you think you should and when you think you should do it.

Step Three
Your instructor will lead you in a debriefing and evaluation discussion. The questions on Form 51 can be used as a guide for this discussion.

Role Information: Cafeteria Staff

You are in the part of the cafeteria where students, faculty, and other university/college employees are getting food and paying for it. Suddenly, there are gunshots both in the kitchen and where people are seated and eating their meals. You hear screams and cries of pain. You have a cell phone. Use it.

Role Information: Local Radio Station

Play the role of investigative reporter(s). Follow rumors and leads about what is going on, and periodically interrupt the role play with a "breaking news" announcement. Allow elected officials to hold a press conference if they so desire.

Questions

1. Did you organize quickly and appropriately? If not, why? Were any agencies crucial to the emergency not included? Were some agencies not crucial included?

2. How did agencies communicate with one another? How did you find out what was happening? How did you offer your services? Did you think this was the most effective way of communicating?

3. What was the role of the various federal agencies? Do you think federal agencies could or should play a different role in emergencies of this nature?

4. What are the differences between emergency management and the kinds of administration considered in Exercises 3 and 6 through 9?

PART III
Human Resource Management

WHAT IS HUMAN RESOURCE MANAGEMENT?

The heart of any government agency, or any organization for that matter, is its personnel. How effectively an agency accomplishes its mission is heavily determined by the skill, determination, and morale of its employees. These are the central concerns of human resource management, a subfield of public administration sometimes known as "public personnel management." The main job of the personnel administrator is to make sure that an agency has working for it the most capable people possible. This means not only hiring the best candidates for each job to begin with but also ensuring that the people who already work for any agency have the requisite knowledge, skills, and abilities to perform their jobs effectively. Thus, human resource management involves all of the following administrative processes: determining organizational needs, recruiting and hiring appropriate employees, evaluating performance, training and developing personnel, and disciplining and compensating employees. The exercises in Part III are designed to give you an opportunity to learn firsthand some of the techniques used by human resource managers.

RANK-IN-JOB VERSUS RANK-IN-PERSON

Before we learn specific techniques, however, we would do well to consider some general theory. The foundation of human resource management, the wellspring from which all the techniques flow, is the idea of the *job*. Recruitment, training, compensation, evaluation, and so forth are all rooted in this very basic construct. This may seem perfectly obvious, but it really isn't. What it means is that in the minds of personnel administrators, almost all government agencies and most other organizations are conceived of as sets of jobs, not as collections of people. In fact, we might say that the first law of American human resource management is that *jobs exist independent of their occupants.*

The name given to this theory that underlies American public personnel administration is *position classification,* also known as the *rank-in-job* system. Position classification entails two related assumptions. First, the only things relevant to a personnel decision are the knowledge, skills, and abilities that a person brings to a job; all else is ignored. Second, the status and compensation an employee receives are solely a function of the job the person holds. This means that if I want a job as a carpenter, only my carpentry skills will be considered; moreover, even if I have a degree in analytical chemistry, speak seven languages fluently, and an accomplished concert pianist, I will be treated and paid as a carpenter (assuming I get the job).

Contrast this, for a moment, with the major alternative system of human resource management, known as *rank classification* or *rank-in-person.* In this system, which is used by many other countries in the world, narrowly defined jobs are not nearly so determining. Although an effort is made to match a person's skills to a job, far more attention is paid to the general qualifications and assets a person has. Given a certain level of education, skill, or experience, a person is assigned a rank, which is held regardless of the particular job that person is performing.

Not all organizations in the United States use the rank-in-job system, but most do. Noting the few exceptions may help explain the differences between the two systems. The military, the teaching profession, and the foreign service are prominent examples. Most paramilitary organizations, like police and fire departments, also use rank-in-person. Whether a person works in the motor pool or as a clerk in a company headquarters, a private is a private; whether a person teaches "Introduction to American Government" or a graduate seminar in political theory, an assistant professor is still an assistant professor; and whether a person approves visas in our embassy in Cairo or analyzes political developments from a desk in the State Department, a Foreign Service Officer-8 is still a Foreign Service Officer-8. In all these cases, pay and status go with the rank a person holds, not the job he or she performs.

WHY RANK-IN-JOB?

Again, most public personnel systems in the United States are based on the rank-in-job concept. One reason for this emphasis derives from Frederick Taylor and the impact of scientific management theories on public administration: Taylor and his disciples saw industries and governments as machines established to accomplish particular purposes. Just as an engineer designs and assembles separate components to create a complex mechanical device, so a builder of organizations stitches together jobs to create a network of activity to accomplish some broader purpose. In both cases, the parts—mechanical components or jobs—are important only insofar as they contribute to the efficient functioning of the whole machine.

A second reason for the focus on jobs rather than people is the legacy of the battle waged by the civil rights movement in the 1960s. By forcing employers to pay attention only to job-related characteristics of potential employees, reformers felt that they could exclude gender, racial, and religious considerations from human resource decisions. The 1964 Civil Rights Act in effect made what had been called the "merit system" actually focus on merit as the basis for personnel decisions. The Pendleton Act of 1883, often credited for establishing the merit principle, outlawed the spoils system and hiring or firing people based on their political party affiliation. The Pendleton Act did not, however, insist on job-related criteria for selecting people. Until after 1964, for example, there was a single exam that most applicants for government jobs took, regardless of the specific requirements of the job they were seeking.

Does all this mean that human resource managers are heartless automatons who are unconcerned with people? Of course not. It does mean, though, that personnel administrators make a deliberate effort to ignore individual characteristics that are not job related. Only by focusing on the job and its requirements, it is argued, can we ensure high quality for an agency and fair treatment for its employees.

FURTHER READING

Good, comprehensive overviews of human resource management in the United States may be found in any one of a number of textbooks. Two of the most useful ones are Dennis L. Dresang, *Personnel Management in Government Agencies and Nonprofit Organizations*, 5th ed. (New York: Pearson Longman, 2009); and Norma M. Riccucci and Katherine C. Naff, *Personnel Management in Government: Politics and Process*, 6th ed. (New York: CRC Press, 2007). Good collections of readings in the field may be found in Steven W. Hays, Richard C. Kearney, and Jerrell D. Coggburn, eds., *Public Personnel Administration: Problems and Prospects*, 5th ed. (Englewood Cliffs, NJ: Prentice Hall, 2008); and Frank J. Thompson, ed., *Classics of Public Personnel Policy*, 3rd ed. (Pacific Grove, CA: Brooks/Cole, 2003).

Exercise 11

Job Analysis and Job Description

A SHORT FABLE

Imagine for a moment that you are T. R. Hardy, head of a medium-size regulatory agency in a midwestern state. You are working quietly at your desk late one Friday afternoon, trying to get some paperwork finished before the weekend. Suddenly, there is a knock at your door, and before you can even say, "Come in," Frank Johnson, your agency personnel director, rushes into your office. "T. R.," he says, "we've got a problem. I've just heard that most of the clericals are threatening to sue us for sex discrimination. They claim that the only reason they're getting paid less than the maintenance staff is because they're women. I tried to tell them how silly . . ."

"T. R.? Listen, I need to talk to you. Oh, sorry, Frank. I didn't know you were in here." The source of this latest interruption is Sonia Fletcher, chief economist in the agency's rate division. "I hope I'm not interrupting anything important. But this really can't wait," she continues, with only a glance at a clearly perturbed Frank Johnson. "One of my senior economists is threatening to quit. He says he didn't get as big a merit increase as he thought he should. I tried to explain that I didn't feel he was working up to standard, but he . . ."

"Frank? Sonia? I didn't know we were having a staff meeting this afternoon." Alan Bateson, the agency's Equal Employment Opportunity (EEO) officer, moves quickly into the room. "Well, anyway, I guess it's just as well we're all here. Remember our last round of recruitment for junior rate analysts? I've just learned that one of the unsuccessful applicants is going to challenge the process. Maybe even go to court. He maintains that we had no business demanding advanced degrees for these positions, that this requirement wasn't related to the job and . . ."

"Excuse me, Alan, but I hadn't finished," interjects Sonia.

"*You* weren't finished!" says Frank, raising his voice. "I was here first and you interrupted me."

As the voices of your three aides merge in a cacophonous babble, you sit back, close your eyes, and try to concentrate. Sex discrimination? Unfair evaluation? Unreasonable hiring standards? What to do? The promise of a quiet, relaxing weekend seems very far away.

THE MORAL

We may justly sympathize with T. R. Hardy. None of these problems will be simple to resolve. But if T. R. is a perceptive manager and thinks carefully about these questions, a useful lesson that may forestall future difficulties can be learned. Although each problem is different, a common thread runs throughout, a thread that may well reflect a fundamental gap in the agency's personnel structure. Note that each dispute involves disagreements about the nature of the job in question. The clerical workers are arguing that their jobs are undervalued by the agency, at least in comparison with the maintenance workers'; Frank Johnson disagrees. The senior economist believes that his job performance has not been assessed properly; Sonia Fletcher disagrees. The unsuccessful applicant for the job of junior rate analyst feels that the requirement for an advanced degree is unreasonable; whoever set the requirement disagreed. In each case, there is disagreement about what a particular job requires, either in terms of qualifications needed (the junior rate analyst), behaviors expected (the senior economist), or the level and value of effort exerted (the clericals). One thing this may indicate is that the agency has not adequately analyzed its jobs. That is, it has not systematically identified all the tasks that an employee occupying each position must perform. If we can't identify job tasks systematically, we don't have much to go by, as managers, employees, or applicants. We certainly can't evaluate someone's performance fairly, because we don't have any standards that are clearly related to the job itself. We can't decide what level of compensation is equitable, because we aren't really sure what one class of jobs involves in comparison with another. Nor are we able to set appropriate qualifications to use for recruitment; without knowledge of day-to-day job requirements, how can we say whether a Ph.D. rather than a high school diploma is needed?

WHAT IS JOB ANALYSIS?

Job analysis may be formally defined as the collection and collation of information regarding the tasks performed in various positions in an organization and assessments of the knowledge, skills, and abilities necessary to perform those tasks successfully. To state it more simply, job analysis means figuring out what a particular job involves and what qualifications someone needs to do that job. Job analyses are important, as our story about T. R. Hardy makes clear, because almost all other personnel processes depend on them.

HOW ARE JOB ANALYSES DONE?

There are many different ways to conduct job analyses. Some techniques are quantitative and involve evaluating the tasks performed by a worker (the *job incumbent*) against a preset general checklist of job tasks. Other techniques rely on relatively unstructured interviews with job incumbents and their supervisors to try to get a picture of what a job involves. Whether quantitative and structured or qualitative and unstructured, all thorough job analyses require the person doing the analysis to become as familiar as possible with the job being studied.

The best source of information for a job analysis, by far, is the person who is doing the job. A job incumbent can provide details about the daily and seasonal demands of a job, what it takes to do the job well, and what affects job performance. Interviews

with job incumbents must, however, be supplemented by a discussion with supervisors. The person in charge of the unit can tell you whether the job incumbent is doing all the tasks that are assigned to the job. Also, the supervisor can let the analyst know if there are changes about to be made in the job, perhaps due to reorganization or to the introduction of new technology or new processes. In some cases, it is useful to observe how the job is being done to supplement or even reconcile the information obtained from incumbents and supervisors.

Job analysis also requires becoming acquainted with organization charts and statements of organizational mission. A review of an existing job description can be useful, but it is important to consider the possibility that what is in the file is old or only partially accurate. For many jobs, a good reference is the *Dictionary of Occupational Titles* (*www.occupationalinfo.org*), published by the U.S. Department of Labor; this volume provides general descriptions of more than 25,000 jobs.

FURTHER READING

The literature on job analysis and position classification is generally fairly technical. Good overviews may be found in the personnel administration textbooks cited in the introduction to Part III. The near-official handbook for position classifiers is Harold D. Suskin, ed., *Job Evaluation and Pay Administration in the Public Sector* (Washington, DC: International Personnel Management Association, 1977). This volume contains many useful articles on the subject but is quite technical in orientation. Another classic is Jay M. Shafritz, *Position Classification: A Behavioral Analysis for the Public Service* (New York: Praeger, 1973). The National Academy of Public Administration produced a report discussing concerns and reforms in the federal government in *Modernizing Federal Classification: An Opportunity for Excellence* (Washington, DC: National Academy, 1991). A more recent critique is Katherine C. Naff, "Why Public Managers Hate Position Classification," in Steven W. Hays and Richard C. Kearney, *Public Personnel Administration: Problems and Prospects*, 4th ed. (Upper Saddle River, NJ: Prentice Hall, 2003).

Finally, you may find it useful to put the American system of position classification in comparative perspective by considering its major alternative, rank classification. Ferrel Heady, *Public Administration: A Comparative Perspective*, 6th ed. (New York: Dekker, 2001), provides an excellent introduction to alternative personnel systems.

On the Web

www.opm.gov Job analysis and classification information is available from the Office of Personnel Management in the federal government, as well as in specific agencies. www.occupationalinfo.org As mentioned above, the federal Department of Labor's *Dictionary of Occupational Titles* plays a critical role in job analyses in most public- and private-sector organizations.

Overview of Exercise

In this exercise, you will conduct a job analysis and write a job description. Your instructor may want you to select a position in your college community or hometown and analyze an actual job. If so, this requires interviewing the job incumbent (this usually takes about 30 minutes) and then discussing the position with the incumbent's supervisor (another 15 minutes). You should also get any existing job description, organization chart, mission statement, and the like. Use Form 53 as the basis of your interviews and information search.

Alternatively, your instructor may have this exercise completed in class. If this is the case, several members of your class who actually hold or have held jobs will be designated "job incumbents." The remaining members of your class will be designated "job analysts." Working in small groups, job analysts will interview a single job incumbent and complete Form 53, "Job Analysis Questionnaire." Each job analyst will then prepare a Job Description (Form 56) for the job analyzed.

Note that the in-class exercise is an abbreviated version of job analysis because it is based mainly on a single interview with a job incumbent. You are not required to observe the job incumbent's work or to talk with his or her supervisors and coworkers, although your instructor may ask you to do some background library research on the occupation being analyzed. Remember that if you were working as a professional personnel analyst, you would need to take all these additional steps to conduct a sound job analysis and prepare a valid job description.

Whether you are doing the exercise in-class or out-of-class, it is important to remember that you are an analyst, not a recorder. The information you provide on Form 53 should represent your integration and assessment of what you have learned from the job incumbent (the most important source of information), supervisor, organizational website, and the like. If you get conflicting information that you, as the analyst, cannot reconcile, then you should include the disparate messages in the relevant section on Form 53 and note the conflict. There might be times when information that you receive may relate more to an individual than the job or may simply not make sense. A common example is when you are told that someone needs a certain number of years of experience or a certain degree to do a job. These "requirements" are frequently arbitrary and reflect what the current incumbent has, not what the job actually requires. At best, a position may require *some* experience or some *specific* coursework or training, rather than 4 years of experience or a master's degree. As analyst, you need to be skeptical and to make your own assessment.

INSTRUCTIONS FOR OUT-OF-CLASS EXERCISE

Step One

Select a position in a government or not-for-profit agency, and schedule an interview with the job incumbent and his or her supervisor.

Step Two

Gather information about the agency mission and structure and learn about the kind of job that you are analyzing.

Step Three

Read Forms 52 and 54.

Step Four

Conduct interviews with the job incumbent and supervisor, being sure to get the information needed on Form 53. Ask the job incumbent or supervisor for a copy of an existing job description for the position, if there is one.

Step Five

Complete Form 53.

Step Six

Complete Form 56.

Step Seven

Answer the questions on Form 57.

INSTRUCTIONS FOR IN-CLASS EXERCISE

Step One

Your instructor will select members of the class who actually hold jobs to play the roles of job incumbents. Remaining members of the class will play the roles of job analysts.

Step Two

Job analysts should read Form 52, "Instructions for Job Analysts," carefully and familiarize themselves with the items on Form 53.

Step Three

A team of job analysts should be assigned to each job incumbent. Analysts should interview the incumbent to whom they have been assigned and complete Form 53.

Step Four

Job analysts should read Form 54, "Instructions for Writing Job Descriptions," and review the sample job description on Form 55. (If you are a job incumbent, your instructor may ask you to step out of your role at this point, obtain a completed copy of Form 53 either for your job or for another incumbent's, and complete a job description.)

Step Five

Each job analyst should complete Form 56, "Job Description," for the job that he or she has analyzed.

Step Six

Answer the questions on Form 57.

Instructions for Job Analysts

The major tasks of a job analyst are to describe as accurately and thoroughly as possible the duties performed by a job incumbent and to assess the skills, knowledge, and abilities necessary to perform those duties satisfactorily. Form 54 will help you do this by directing your attention to the key elements of the job being analyzed. The following detailed instructions explain how to complete Form 54.

A. *General Information:* Fill in agency name, job title, and job incumbent's name.

B. *Job Duties:* List each discrete job duty separately, and estimate the amount of time the job incumbent spends on each duty. Be as specific as possible in identifying job duties, focusing on actual job behaviors. For instance, job duties of an administrative assistant might include "types correspondence and reports; answers telephone; operates photocopy machine; operates fax machine." Be sure to specify whether the time basis is daily, weekly, monthly, or annual and use the same basis for all duties.

C. *Job Relationships*
  1. *Supervision Received:* Provide the name(s) of the job incumbent's immediate supervisor(s), and describe how closely the job incumbent is supervised; that is, how much autonomy, or independence, does the job incumbent have in performing his or her work?
  2. *Supervision Given:* Provide the title(s) of employees supervised by the job incumbent and the total number supervised. Specify whether the incumbent supervises other employees, volunteers, inmates, students, etc.
  3. *Other Job Relationships:* Describe any significant nonsupervisory interactions the job incumbent has with other employees or with customers in performing his or her job duties. For instance, do the incumbent's duties require extensive cooperation with other workers? Does the incumbent have extensive contact with the public?

D. *Job Qualifications*
  1. *Knowledge, Skills, and Abilities Required:* Describe the knowledge, skills, and abilities required to perform each of the job duties identified in part B, including, where possible, acceptable levels of performance. To use the administrative assistant example, a job incumbent might need the ability to type 65 words per minute, to respond knowledgeably and pleasantly to telephone inquiries, and to operate basic office

(continued)

machinery. Note that where specific duties require the same underlying skills ("operate photocopy machine" and "operate fax machine"), the skill or skills need be mentioned only once ("operate basic office machinery").

2. *Education or Training Required:* Describe here the level of education (e.g., high school diploma, civil engineering B.S., chemistry Ph.D.) or type of training (vocational courses in laboratory technology, nursing, etc.) required to perform the job duties. Make sure that whatever education or training you specify is in fact job related. It may be necessary, for example, for someone to have courses in accounting, but not strictly necessary to complete a college degree to do an accounting job. Also specify here any training or education that may be possible after a person has been hired to fill the job (e.g., "on-the-job training provided").

3. *Experience Required:* Describe any previous work (or nonwork) experiences necessary to perform the job duties (e.g., "intermediate-level accountancy experience required"). As with education and training, be sure that any experience you specify is, in fact, job related. It is, for example, far more precise to state the kind or level of experience than some arbitrary number of years.

4. *Other Requirements:* Describe any additional requirements necessary to perform the job duties. These might include such things as holding certain licenses or permits, willingness to relocate, or owning an automobile.

Job Analysis Questionnaire

A. GENERAL INFORMATION

    1. Agency/Organization Name _____

    2. Job Title _____

    3. Job Incumbent Name _____

B. JOB DUTIES

<table>
<tr><td></td><td>Duty</td><td>Percent of Time Devoted to Duty
Time Basis (daily/weekly/monthly/annual)</td></tr>
<tr><td>**1.**</td><td></td><td></td></tr>
<tr><td>**2.**</td><td></td><td></td></tr>
<tr><td>3.</td><td></td><td></td></tr>
<tr><td>**4.**</td><td></td><td></td></tr>
<tr><td>**5.**</td><td></td><td></td></tr>
<tr><td>**6.**</td><td></td><td></td></tr>
<tr><td>**7.**</td><td></td><td></td></tr>
<tr><td>**8.**</td><td></td><td></td></tr>
</table>

C. JOB RELATIONSHIPS

    1. Supervision Received:

        a. Title of Supervisor(s):

        b. Extent of Supervision:

    2. Supervision Given:

        a. Titles of Employees (volunteers, inmates, etc.) supervised:

            i.

            ii.

(*continued*)

     iii.

     iv.

     v.

    b. Total Number of Employees Supervised:

  3. Other Job Relationships:

D. JOB QUALIFICATIONS

  1. Knowledge, Skills, and Abilities Required:

    a.

    b.

    c.

    d.

    e.

    f.

    g.

    h.

  2. Education or Training Required:

  3. Experience Required:

  4. Other Requirements:

Submitted by: _____

Name of Job Analyst

Instructions for Writing Job Descriptions

A job description is a narrative summary of a particular job's duties and responsibilities, together with a statement of qualifications necessary to perform the job satisfactorily. Job descriptions provide the foundation for myriad personnel processes, including recruitment, performance evaluation, and compensation.

Because job descriptions are based on job analyses, you might ask what the difference is between a job description and the completed version of Form 53. The difference is chiefly one of how the material is organized and written; substantively, they will be very similar. A job description summarizes a great deal of information. It is the job description, not the pile of paperwork generated during a job analysis, which constitutes the real currency of human resource management. Consequently, it is worth learning how to write one clearly, accurately, and succinctly.

You should observe the following general rules:

1. Begin with a general statement of job duties and responsibilities that encompasses job relationships. See the statement of "General Responsibilities" in the example on Form 55.

2. List the major duties of the job, in descending order of importance, together with any relevant performance standards. See "Major Duties" in the example on Form 55.

3. Identify the relevant knowledge, skills, and abilities required. See the corresponding section in the example on Form 55.

4. Specify the levels of education, training, and experience required for appointment. Note on-the-job training if relevant. Be sure that the qualifications specified are appropriate to the job.

5. Keep the description as concise as possible by avoiding unnecessary words. Use a "telegraphic" writing style: the subject of the description, the job incumbent, is assumed; thus, a simple verb–object form (e.g., "Analyzes financial data," "Supervises three-person maintenance staff") can be used.

Sample Job Description

Job Title:	**Police Dispatcher**
General Responsibilities:	Under general supervision, a dispatcher performs skilled emergency service work that includes receiving emergency 911 and non-emergency requests for police assistance, determining the nature and urgency of calls, initiating police and other emergency personnel action and maintaining contact with field units to monitor response and needed support requirements.
	This is a civil service position, and is not filled by a ranked police officer.
Major Duties	**1.** Receives and responds to emergency and non-emergency calls.
	2. Evaluates information received, prioritizes calls and dispatches required units and/or agencies.
	3. Monitors police unit activity.
	4. Creates and maintains logs of public safety communications.
Required Knowledge, Skills, and Abilities:	**1.** Knowledge of telecommunications technology and equipment.
	2. Skill in operating a variety of communications equipment.
	3. Skill in reading and interpreting maps.
	4. Ability to speak clearly and concisely.
Qualifications:	This is an entry-level position and assumes no previous experience or training in police dispatch work.

Job Description

Job Title:

Responsibilities:

Major Duties:

Required Knowledge, Skills, and Abilities:

Qualifications:

Questions

1. Why is it important to be as precise as possible in identifying specific job duties when conducting job analyses and writing job descriptions?

2. What drawbacks, if any, do you see with efforts to define jobs in this way? Is it really possible—or desirable—to ignore the individuals who occupy the jobs?

3. Would you rather work for an organization that defined your job very carefully in writing or for one that left things more open?

Exercise 12

Performance Evaluation

PERFORMANCE EVALUATION: WHAT, WHY, AND HOW?

Most members of organizations—employers and employees—embrace performance evaluation with all the enthusiasm usually shown a bad case of the flu. Few people enjoy having their work evaluated, especially when they think their pay, their promotion chances, or their very jobs depend on the outcomes. Probably not many more enjoy evaluating the work of others; even if you think you know what other employees are doing wrong, and even if you have supervisory responsibility for their work, it is seldom easy to summon the courage to tell them, no matter how constructive the criticism. A major reason for the dread most people experience in the face of performance evaluation is that these assessments, especially but not exclusively in the public sector, are rarely linked to rewards. The common linkage is to discipline and dismissal. In addition, organizations are more than the cool lines of authority and neat boxes that appear on organizational charts. In organizations, social relationships develop quickly; informal norms of interaction become established, often cemented by close working relationships and even friendships that pull at formal organizational roles.

Yet, performance evaluation is unavoidable. In many governments, law requires annual evaluations. Also, we naturally and instinctively evaluate one another's performance. We desire, as well as fear, feedback. And personnel decisions about opportunities and sanctions are, in fact, based at least in part on performance.

Although almost all organizations evaluate their employees' performances, not all do so in a systematic and conscientious manner. Valid performance evaluations require time and guidelines. Managers must be convinced that the results of the evaluations will be useful for achieving organizational goals; employees must believe that the method of evaluation is fair and unbiased. It should be clear that there are some employee performances that essentially are graded on a pass–fail basis. Obviously, embezzlement, theft, sabotage, and the like are not only criminal, but also grounds for dismissal. In a few jobs, the standard of acceptable employee performance is at the highest level and there are no allowances for errors or flaws. The police dispatcher position, for example, demands immediate and appropriate responses to some emergencies. Errors can cause deaths. But even in this example, the pass–fail standard that might be applied to urgent, emergency calls is separate from other dimensions of the job, like keeping a log. Performance evaluation is needed even when a job includes a responsibility that does not allow for error.

What exactly do we mean by "systematic performance evaluation"? What distinguishes sound from unsound methods of evaluating employee performance? While no one method will be right for every job in every organization, all systems of performance evaluation worthy of the name are distinguished by one central idea: those employee traits or behaviors—and only those employee traits and behaviors—directly related to the performance of job duties are measured. For the evaluator, this requires two kinds of information. First, he or she needs to understand the exact nature of the job; second, he or she needs to have accurate knowledge of what the job incumbent has actually been doing. The first requirement should be familiar to anyone who completed the preceding exercise. It is by reading a valid job description, based on a thorough job analysis, that evaluators know the nature of a job. More precisely, job descriptions provide detailed specifications of job duties. Each of these job duties, which in the language of performance evaluation are called *job dimensions,* can be used as a yardstick against which to measure the actual performance of job incumbents.

The nature of the yardstick varies widely, however. In fact, we may identify two broad types of performance appraisal systems, each of which focuses on very different measures of performance.

TWO APPROACHES TO PERFORMANCE EVALUATION

The first approach focuses on employee *behaviors.* Here, we evaluate not the person, but what the person does (a distinction that owes much to child psychology: "Johnny isn't a bad boy," his mother notes as she surveys the smoking ruins of her house; "he just exhibits bad behaviors"). In the most popular of the behavioral systems—Behaviorally Anchored Rating Scales, or BARS—for each of the job dimensions identified in a job analysis, a series of statements is generated that describe the behavior—from excellent to execrable—of hypothetical job incumbents. If we were to develop BARS for the police dispatcher job described in Exercise 11 (Form 55), we would have to write "anchor" statements for the four job dimensions of receives and responds to calls; prioritizes calls and dispatches units; monitors activity; and keeps log. Some examples for prioritizing calls might be "always considers urgency appropriately," "sometimes confuses a non-emergency situation as an emergency," and "fails consistently to communicate with all relevant units needed to respond to a situation."

Once arrayed on weighted scales, the statements provide relatively objective points of comparison in the evaluation process. A supervisor simply reads the statements and decides which set best describes the behavior of the employee in question. It is easy to quantify BARS evaluations, with a certain number of points awarded for each level of performance (e.g., 5 for "excellent," 4 for "good," with each dimension subject to some multiplier that reflects the relative importance of the dimension to the job); once each employee is evaluated on each dimension, a total performance score can easily be determined.

Proponents of the behavioral approach cite not only its relative objectivity but its instructional character as well. By looking at a BARS form or similar instrument, an employee can learn exactly what behaviors are expected and change his or her own conduct accordingly.

Still, behavioral approaches are not without weaknesses. They are, to begin with, time consuming to design. This investment, however, applies only initially. Revisions are relatively easy to make. A good BARS system requires the generation of scores of anchor statements for each job. And every job class requires a new set of scales: Sets of anchor statements developed for a clerical job cannot be used to evaluate a welder. Some critics also argue that behavioral systems are too rigid and directive. Not only do jobs change from year to year (even day to day), but seldom is there one "best" way to do a job, as such approaches seem to assume. The corollary assumption, that what is important is how a job gets done, not what is actually accomplished, clearly misses the point, critics argue.

The second approach to performance evaluation responds to these criticisms, at least in part, by focusing on *results.* Here, attention shifts away from the behaviors in which employees engage to the things that they accomplish. Instead of specifying how a salesperson makes contacts with potential customers ("seldom returns phone calls," "keeps accurate records of visits made"), we would simply ask, "How many widgets did Zander sell last quarter?" If Zander sells a lot of widgets, we may not care much about his sales "behavior": He is welcome to wear a gorilla suit, speak in limericks, and ride to appointments on a unicycle, as long as sales volume stays high.

The most popular and best known of these results-oriented systems is management by objectives (MBO). Although MBO may take various forms, differing in degree of formality, most MBO systems consist of four basic steps:

1. Setting goals and objectives.
2. Working toward the goals and objectives.
3. Reviewing performance.
4. Linking rewards or sanctions to performance.

Although MBO does not logically require heavy employee participation in goal setting, most systems rely on it on the assumption that employees need to "buy in" psychologically. Indeed, heightened motivation and creativity through employee participation and "empowerment" are usually cited as the chief benefits of results-oriented systems like MBO.

Like behavior approaches, result-based systems have problems. Depending on the design of the system, it may be difficult to compare the performance of employees on a common metric. Objectives, after all, will vary with the employee. Therefore, it may be hard to link evaluations to pay and promotion decisions—at least in any way that is perceived as fair. Furthermore, an overemphasis on results may lead to employee confusion and uncertainty about the hows of getting the job done. Worse, it may lead to an "anything goes" philosophy in which ethics and legality are skirted as long as the objective is achieved. How a job gets done matters. Also, results-based systems require special efforts on the part of raters to weigh and filter out extraneous factors—factors beyond the control of the employee—in writing evaluations.

Organizations and jobs differ. While you may prefer either a behavior or a results-based approach, it may be inappropriate to use the same approach for all jobs. If, for example, we are evaluating social workers or teachers, we know that we can measure some results, such as number of cases closed or student scores on a standardized examination, but those results are due to some important factors beyond the employee's control—like the economy, family influences, and the health and abilities of individuals. In these situations, we might be better off using behaviors and making the inference that good job behaviors are going to contribute to desired results. And there is no reason a performance evaluation system for a given job cannot be a mixture of some results measures and some behavior scales.

FURTHER READING

One of the classic statements on the problems of performance evaluation, with particular emphasis on the importance of employee participation, is Douglas McGregor, "An Uneasy Look at Performance Appraisal," *Harvard Business Review*, May–June 1957. Dennis Daley provides an updated analysis in "The Trials and Tribulations of Performance Appraisal: Problems and Prospects on Entering the Twenty-First Century," in Steven W. Hays and Richard C. Kearney, eds., *Public Personnel Administration: Problems and Prospects*, 4th ed. (Upper Saddle River, NJ: Prentice Hall, 2003). For overviews of performance appraisal systems, consult Gary Latham and Kenneth Wexler, *Increasing Productivity through Performance Appraisal* (Reading, MA: Addison-Wesley, 1994). Also of interest are William Swan and Phillip Margulies, *How to Do a Superior Performance Appraisal* (New York: Wiley, 1991); William J. Bruns, Jr., *Performance Measurement, Evaluation and Incentives* (New York: McGraw-Hill, 1992); and Jacky Holloway, Jenny Lewis, and Geoff Mallory, *Performance Measurement and Evaluation* (Newbury Parks, CA: Sage, 1995). More information on BARS can be found in R. S. Atkins and E. T. Conlon, "Behaviorally Anchored Rating Scales: Some Theoretical Issues," *Academy of Management Review* 3 (January 1978): 119–128; and D. P. Schwab, H.G. Heneman, and T.A. Decotiis, "Behaviorally Anchored Rating Scales: A Review of the Literature," *Personnel Psychology* 28 (Winter 1975): 549–562.

On the Web

www.opm.gov   The federal Office of Personnel Management provides assistance to agencies, as well as state and local governments, on the design of performance evaluation systems.

Overview of Exercise

In this exercise, you will construct a performance evaluation system for the job you analyzed and described in Exercise 11. Because you will not have the opportunity to observe employee performance, your task is to *design* the evaluation instrument, not apply it.

INSTRUCTIONS

Step One
Review the job description you prepared for Exercise 11. If you played the role of job incumbent and did not write a job description, obtain completed

copies of Forms 53 and 56 from one of your classmates who served as a job analyst.

Step Two

Decide which approach to performance evaluation—behavior based or results based—you wish to take in designing an appraisal instrument for this job. You will need to weigh a variety of factors—some inherent in the approach, some peculiar to the job in question—in making your choice. Think about the advantages and disadvantages of each approach discussed in the introduction to this exercise.

- If you decide to use a *behavior-based system,* review Form 58.

- If you decide to use a *results-based system,* review Form 60.

You may, if you like, use some combination of these systems, in which case you will probably want to review all of these forms before you design your own evaluation form from scratch.

Step Three

Use the appropriate worksheet (Form 59 or 61) to design your appraisal form.

Step Four

Answer the questions on Form 62.

Designing a Behavior-Based System

This form describes how to implement an abbreviated version of Behaviorally Anchored Rating Scales (BARS), which is the most common example of a behavior-based performance evaluation system.

1. Read through your job analysis and job description and identify the major job dimensions.

2. Make a judgment about the relative importance of each job dimension, and express it as a percentage. For instance, if the four job dimensions of a police dispatcher are responding to calls, prioritizing responses, monitoring activity, and keeping a log, after reading the job analysis we might decide to weight them as follows: responding to calls, 30 percent; prioritizing responses, 40 percent; monitoring activities, 20 percent; and keeping a log, 10 percent.

3. *For each job dimension,* create one copy of Form 59 (or another like it of your own design). If you are working with five job dimensions, you need to create five blank forms; if you are working with three job dimensions, you need to create three blank forms.

4. Fill in the appropriate information at the top of each copy of Form 59 that you made: indicate the job title, the job dimension, and the factor weight (from step 2).

5. Write a series of statements that describe a range—from excellent to unacceptable—of behaviors for each job dimension. Be creative and make them up. For instance, if you are generating statements for the job of waiter (for the job dimension "food service"), you might write statements like "frequently spills food on customers" and "always remembers to mention special menu items." The main idea is to compose statements that would describe real, observable behaviors of someone doing that job (not necessarily the person you used for the job analysis—*any* person who might hold that job).

6. Arrange the statements you wrote in step 5 in the corresponding blank spaces on the various versions of Form 59 that you copied. Clipped or stapled together, these scales constitute your completed performance evaluation form.

Behavior-Based Evaluation Worksheet (Model)

Incumbent: _____

Job Title: _____

Job Dimension: _____

Factor Weight: _____

5. Excellent   _____
_____

4. Good   _____
_____

3. Fair   _____
_____

2. Poor   _____
_____

1. Unacceptable   _____
_____

Designing a Results-Based System

This form explains how to design an MBO-style, results-oriented performance evaluation system.

1. Read through your job analysis and job description and identify the major job dimensions.

2. Generate one or more measurable performance goals for each of the major job dimensions, and write the goals in the appropriate spaces on Form 62 (or another form that you design). The goals should be directly related to the job dimension and must be measurable in objective, quantifiable terms. For the job of administrative assistant, for instance, with its job dimensions of word processing, photocopying, and telephone answering, we would generate such goals as "type final drafts of technical reports at an average rate of one page every 4 minutes" or "provide average turnaround of less than 1 hour on top-priority photocopy requests."

3. If possible, discuss the goals with the job incumbent (the person who provided the basis for the job analysis). The performance level expected should be *reasonable* from the perspective of both the individual and the organization.

Results-Based Evaluation Worksheet (Model)

MBO WORKSHEET

Incumbent: —————————————————————————————

Job Title: ——————————————————————————

		Performance Evaluation			
Performance Goal	Goal Weight (%)	Superlative	Successful	Marginal	Not Acceptable

Questions

1. How do you suppose the job incumbent would react to your instrument or to the evaluation method that you chose? Would the supervisor find this useful?

2. How would you feel about having your own work (perhaps even your work as a student) evaluated in this way?

3. What are the strengths and weaknesses of the various methods of performance evaluation discussed in this exercise? Are there any approaches that you can think of that might be better? If so, what makes them better?

Exercise 13

Succession Planning

RETIREMENT FALLOUT

In 2011, the largest generation in American history will be gray. According to the U.S. Census Bureau, the number of people in the United States who will be celebrating their 65th birthday will jump to 3.3 million, an increase of 21 percent from the year before. The ranks of the retired will grow from one in eight in 2006 to one in five in 2030. The recession that began in 2008 severely devalued retirement accounts and personal savings and prompted many to delay planned retirements. But that delay has pushed the big surge that had been expected in 2011 off for a few years. Retirements have been postponed, not cancelled.

Already some employers, private and public, are hosting retirement parties for almost one-third of their employees. In the federal government, the number of people over 50 years old was 34 percent in 2005. More than one-third of the civilian workers in the federal government will be eligible for retirement in 2010.[1] The pattern is similar in state governments. Some occupations, especially in the managerial, transportation, environmental, and health fields, will have retirement rates near 50 percent.[2]

One way of responding to these demographic facts is to worry about how organizations are going to fill so many positions. The challenge is especially serious because retirements naturally mean the exodus of the most experienced, senior staff. Another response is to celebrate the significant increase in opportunities for young people, especially for those who have recently earned college degrees. Both responses are equally valid.

SUCCESSION PLANNING

To varying degrees, organizations have been preparing for the retirement of baby boomers. The conscious efforts of assessing the effects of retirements and designing strategies for filling impending vacancies is known as "succession planning." This process has been available to personnel managers for more than two decades. Initially, it was touted as a way of taking steps to get more women and minorities in middle and senior positions. But succession planning has been on the shelf, collecting dust, until now. Even with the obvious challenges of replacing baby boomers, serious succession efforts are increasing, but not common.[3]

Succession planning follows the following basic steps:

1. Identify expected vacancies.
2. Determine critical positions and functions.
3. Identify current employees who might be developed to fill vacancies.
4. Provide training and mentorships to develop current employees with potential.
5. Develop strategy for recruiting employees with needed skills and abilities for jobs where current employees are not available.
6. Evaluate results and determine what further measures are needed.

[1] Office of Personnel Management, www.opm.gov/hr/employ/products/succession/succ_plan_text.

[2] www.bls.gov/opub/ted/2000/Aug/wk4/art04.htm.

[3] General Accountability Office, "Succession Planning and Management Is Critical Driver of Organizational Transformation," October 2003, pp. 5–9.

Succession planning begins with not only cataloging positions that will be open because of expected retirements, but also with assessing organizational needs. Given the number of people who will be retiring, it is almost inevitable that agencies and firms will have to consider not filling every vacancy and doing their work in a different way. Organizational assessments may suggest redesigning workflow, as was done in the total quality management exercise (Exercise 6). Agencies may want to use new technologies. Perhaps contracting with other firms for some work is the answer.

The usual response to a vacancy is to treat it individually and to try to find a replacement who is someone like the recent incumbent. The focus is typically on a position, as in the job analysis and selection exercises (Exercises 11 and 14). Clearly, individual positions and individual employees are the building blocks of organizations. The point is that succession planning invites considering the whole when dealing with the individual parts. The position analyses are critical to developing an inventory of the skills and abilities that are being lost when incumbents leave. The assessment of current employees and job candidates is essential for knowing what pool of talents and experiences an organization has and what holes it needs to fill.

INDIVIDUAL CAREER PLANNING

Part of succession planning by an organization is to groom individuals who are currently employed with the organization to step into positions that become available because of retirements and to hire individuals from outside the organization with skills and abilities that are needed. You, however, do not need to be a passive object in these processes. In fact, you would be well advised to be active. The needs of employers are your opportunities. Remember, not all agencies and organizations are doing succession planning—or doing it well.

To take full advantage of the opportunities presented by the expected surge of retirements, you could do some planning of your own. In doing this, you will follow steps similar to what analysts do for an organization. You need to think systematically about your personal goals, your strengths and interests, and what you need to do to enhance the possibility that you can have the kind of career you consider most desirable.

A personnel manager analyzes a position and assesses a person to get a good match between the two in the hiring process. Likewise, you need to analyze a job and assess yourself to match your interests with career possibilities. In doing this—even though, for planning purposes, you need to look at specific jobs—you might want to think of positioning yourself for a category of job opportunities rather than targeting a single position. There are too many factors beyond your control to pin all your hopes and efforts on just one particular job.

FURTHER READING

A summary description of the implications of the retirement of the baby boomers is provided by Shari Caudron, "The Looming Leadership Crisis," *Workforce*, September 1999, pp. 72–80. The federal General Accountability Office completed a report, "Succession Planning and Management Is Critical Driver of Organizational Transformation," linking the pending labor shortage to succession planning in October 2003.

The most widely cited and used guides to organizations for succession planning are William J. Rothwell, *Effective Succession Planning*, 4th ed. (New York: American Management Association, 2010); and Robert Slater, *The GE Way Fieldbook: Jack Welch's Battle Plan for Corporate Revolution* (New York: McGraw-Hill, 2000). A discussion of opportunities presented in succession planning can be found in Roger T. Peay and Gibb Dyer Jr. "Power Orientations of Entrepreneurs in Succession Planning," *Journal of Small Business Management* 27:1 (1989): 47–52.

For the perspective of someone seeking a job or a job change, rather than a manager filling expected job vacancies, see Shoya Zichy and Ann Bidou, *Career Match: Connecting Who You Are with What You'll Love to Do* (New York: AMACOM, 2007) and Richard N. Bolles, *What Color Is Your Parachute? 2010: A Practical Manual for Job-Hunters and Career-Changers* (Berkeley, CA: Ten Speed Press, 2009).

On the Web

www.opm.gov   Again, the federal Office of Personnel Management provides information and assistance for succession planning.

Overview of Exercise

This exercise is an opportunity for you to develop a basic plan for preparing for a career. This exercise is similar to a step in a succession career planning procedure initiated by an employer. It is also a plan that you can carry out independently of any agency's or company's efforts. To have a realistic, feasible plan, it is most important to think of what you would like to be doing and where you would like to be in the near term (5 to 10 years). You may, of course, also want to think about the long term, but that is important primarily because of what it suggests you should do now.

It is important, perhaps outside the framework of the course you are taking, to include other people in career planning. Ideally, you will complete this exercise and then share it with family and close friends and, if relevant, with trusted coworkers, supervisors, and, importantly, a mentor or mentors. These discussions are important not only for frank, realistic feedback, but also to inform those with whom you live and work about the career and personal development objectives that you have and that they can help you achieve.

INSTRUCTIONS

Step One
Answer the questions on Form 63. These questions include important information about your career objectives as well as personal concerns.

The answer to question 7 can be found in a job analysis and job description (like the one you completed in Exercise 11) and in job recruitment announcements (like in Exercise 14). List the competencies required in Form 64.

Step Two
Complete Form 64, which assesses the extent to which you have the competencies required for the kind of positions you would like to fill and invites you to specify how you will get those competencies that you need but do not have now.

Step Three
Complete Form 65, which lists skills and abilities that have been found generally to contribute to success in professional and managerial positions. Indicate which of these factors are relevant to your career objectives, and then specify how you will increase your preparedness in areas where you need further development. Examples of how to increase some skills and abilities include taking certain courses, getting training, gaining experiences, and volunteering for tasks and responsibilities. Be as specific as possible.

Step Four
Answer the questions on Form 66.

Career Objective

1. Title and brief description of desired position:

2. Agency or type of organization:

3. Desired community location (geographic area or type of community):

4. Type of career opportunities that need to be available for partner or spouse, if any:

5. Time frame(s) in which desired positions are likely to become vacant (time available to get prepared):

6. Changes—in mission, technology, and organizational structure—likely by the time the desired positions become vacant:

7. Skills, abilities, and other competencies required (or potentially required) for the desired positions:

Position Requirements and Personal Competencies

Personal Competencies				
			Need	
Position Requirements	Have	How to Acquire	When	Cost

General Success Factors

Success Factor	Required in Career Objective	Have	Personal Abilities	
			Need to Improve	Plan for Improvement
Managing projects				
Organizing				
Planning				
Supervising staff				
Budgeting				
Making decisions				
Communicating				
Evaluating programs				
Innovating				
Influencing others				
Representing organization				

Questions

1. What are the similarities and the differences between succession planning and individual career planning?

2. Think about (or learn about) the career paths of people who are 20 to 30 years older than you are. To what extent did these people plan their career and get themselves in a position to take advantage of job opportunities? What lessons might you draw from their experiences?

3. What are the challenges of a surge in retirements to organizations that you know? How might these organizations respond to these challenges?

Exercise 14

Recruitment and Selection

ANGST AND THE JOB INTERVIEW: A ONE-HALF-ACT PLAY

THE TIME: The not-too-distant future
THE SCENE: A college placement office
You have gotten dressed in your best business attire. You now sit nervously in the placement office, waiting for your name to be called, eyes scanning for the hundredth time a résumé you're convinced is too thin. I really want this job, you think. What will they ask me? Are my grades high enough? Why did they pick me for this interview, anyway? Do I have any skills I can offer this organization?

Relax. A little anxiety in the face of a job interview is to be expected. You wouldn't be sitting there if there weren't some evidence to suggest that you were qualified for the job. In any event, consider how the world must look from the perspective of the person on the other side of the interview table: How can we get the best person to fill this position? What sorts of questions should I ask to make sure I really get to know this candidate? Will I be able to avoid making judgments on superficial characteristics that have nothing to do with the job? If I focus too much on grade-point averages, will I be screening people out who might well be perfect for our organization?

Recruiting and selecting candidates for employment is not easy for the candidates or the employer. Although both parties have a common interest in making a good match, the information needed to do that is often difficult to obtain. As was noted in the introduction to Part III, human resource decisions should be guided solely by reference to a person's capabilities. This avoids illegal discrimination and, importantly, enables us to fill a position with the right person. We need to ask whether the knowledge, skills, and abilities required for a job are matched by the knowledge, skills, and abilities embodied in a candidate. If we have done a sound job analysis, we know what knowledge, skills, and abilities a job requires. Our problem now is to address the other half of the equation: How do we assess a candidate's qualifications?

TYPES OF SELECTION DEVICES

Employers use a wide variety of techniques to assess the qualifications of prospective employees and to help them make hiring decisions. Which device or set of devices any particular agency adopts will depend on the size and sophistication of the organization, any general personnel rules that govern the jurisdiction, and the nature of the job being filled.

For most organizations, the first cut through a pool of candidates is made by a review of *job applications.* Typically, job applications ask candidates for general identity information, education and employment histories, and references. Although some agencies use very general application forms to cover a wide range of positions, the most useful forms are those designed especially for particular jobs. When seeking to fill the position of accountant, for instance, an organization would be well advised to ask a series of questions specific to accounting skills and qualifications. These questions can (and should) be derived from a thorough job analysis.

Some organizations request *résumés* instead of or in addition to job applications. Résumés usually provide the same general information as an application form but in a format designed by candidates rather than employers. Because they are not standardized, it is more difficult to make systematic comparisons among candidates with résumés than it is with job applications. The use of résumés rather than applications may be particularly appropriate when attempting to fill professional (e.g., city manager, county budget director, social worker) or unique (e.g., limnologist, utilities economist) positions.

Regardless of whether applications or résumés or both are used, it is important that the applicant be sure to include and even highlight all relevant information. Your overall grade point average and the title of your major are important, but you should also make clear what courses and projects you completed make you especially qualified for the job you are seeking.

Also, it is critical that individuals reviewing them take care to apply appropriate standards when making judgments about the suitability of candidates. A concerted effort must be made to ensure that the criteria applied are (1) job related and (2) the same for all candidates. One way employers do this is by developing a written scoring system, again derived from a job analysis, which can be applied to the applications or résumés. It might be determined, for instance, that each relevant college course is worth 5 points or that demonstrated mastery of a particular skill is worth 10 points. Such a system helps guard against bias in the initial stages of the selection process.

Many organizations use some form of paper-and-pencil *test* as part of their selection process. This technique can be used as an initial screening device (all applicants take the test) or can be restricted to a later stage of the process. Depending on the nature of the job, tests may be aimed at assessing either achievement (how much do you already know about this field?) or aptitude (how likely are you to be able to learn?).

In addition to written tests, other forms of examination are available. *Work sampling* and *assessment centers* are two examples. Work sampling requires that the applicant actually perform some of the tasks used on the job—typing is a common example. Assessment centers are simulated work experiences—the term *center* is misleading because it does not refer to a location or program. Depending on the job in question, candidates are required to make decisions about complex, hypothetical problems; demonstrate an ability to budget their time; and

interact effectively with other people in a group exercise. Assessment centers are expensive and thus used only for a select number of professional and managerial jobs.

By now it should be clear that the answer to the question "How do we assess a candidate's qualifications?" involves more than simply gathering all the information about the candidate that we can. Our task is not just to gather information; it is to gather *job-related* information. This is a point that must constantly be borne in mind, regardless of the selection device used. The reasons for the focus on job-relatedness should also be clear: it ensures a certain level of fairness to the prospective employee and helps the employer choose the person who will make the best contribution to the mission of the organization.

CERTIFICATION AND VETERANS' PREFERENCE POINTS: THE SHORT LIST

Based on a review of applications and the administration of examinations, human resource specialists will develop a short list (usually 5–10 people) of the best applicants and invite them for an interview with whomever is making the hiring decision. Interviews are time consuming, and short lists are essential to keep interviews down to a manageable number. Having personnel specialists instead of hiring authorities develop the short list is especially critical in government to avoid the appearance or the substance of political patronage or of favoritism. The process of developing a short list in government is referred to as *certification*. Each jurisdiction has its own certification rules—some specify a certain number that can be certified (e.g., the individuals with the top 5 or 10 scores); some use a percentage (e.g., the top 5 or 10 percent); and some use a combination (e.g., the top 10 or the top 5 percent, whichever is smallest). In civil service jobs, only people on the certified list can be hired.

Almost all government employers have a policy of providing an advantage to veterans who are applying for jobs. This is done through adding *veterans' preference points* to examination scores. Typically, veterans get an additional 5 points. Disabled veterans get 10 points. Again, each jurisdiction has its own rules for defining who is a veteran or disabled veteran and how the points are applied. Most jurisdictions add the points before certification. Some first certify based just on examination scores and then add to the certified list any veteran who, with examination score and veterans' preference points, gets the same number of points, as those certified based only on exams. Once the final list of certified candidates is compiled, in whatever way veterans' preference points are applied, job interviews can be scheduled.

THE INTERVIEW: THE ONE-HALF-ACT PLAY RESUMED

Back to the job interview. Interviews are fundamentally unstructured discussions. Someone conducting job interviews does not have to ask the same questions of every candidate. Interviews allow employers to ask more subtle and detailed questions than are posed in applications and examinations. Interviews also provide the opportunity to assess candidates' personal characteristics and social skills. The only requirement of interviews is that they must not discriminate on the basis of race, religion, gender, and the like.

So, can you rehearse? Although job interviews vary in the details, we can predict that there will be some basic features:

1. The most important question you will be asked—although frequently it is not asked directly or even clearly—is "Why do you want this job?"
2. Interviewers tend to reach a final decision within the first four minutes of the interview, although interviews usually last 30 minutes.
3. Unfavorable responses and impressions have a greater impact on judgments than do favorable responses.
4. Visual cues or "body language" have more of an effect than verbal cues.

When rehearsing, it is a good idea to think of a question or two that you can ask the interviewer. Good questions are those that indicate you know something about the agency and that you are really interested in the job. Remember that the interviewer is trying to determine whether you will be a good fit for the job, and in large part that determination will focus on subjective characteristics like attitude and

commitment. The examination and certification stages of the selection process have already presumably answered the more objective questions about skills, knowledge, and abilities.

PROBATION: ENCORE

You have been offered the job! Congratulations! But wait . . . it's not over. The last step in the selection process is the probationary period. This last step is, in fact, the best step. The employer no longer has to infer from your qualifications and from your performance on an examination or a job interview that you will be a good employee. Now you will actually be in the job and you can show in a very direct way how good you are. Likewise, you no longer have to guess that you will like this job. You will have a chance to experience it and work with others in the agency and you can see for yourself.

When someone does not pass probation, employers do not have to provide the justification and evidence that are required when they fire someone. Passing probation is passing a test. Employers have the right to set the standards and determine what is a passing score. Once someone has passed probation, then the rules, procedures, and standards for dismissal apply.

So, plan on having two parties: one when you get the job offer and one when you pass probation.

FURTHER READING

The literature in the field of personnel selection and test validation is more technical and specialized than that in most other areas of human resource management, and much of it is concerned with fairly arcane questions of personnel psychology and statistical analysis to determine the validity and reliability of tests administered to relatively large numbers of people. Although not recommended for the casual reader, perhaps the most authoritative guide to this subject is *Principles for the Validation and Use of Personnel Selection Procedures*, 2nd ed. (Berkeley, CA: American Psychological Association, 1980). More accessible treatments can be found in Mark Cook, *Personnel Selection: Adding Value Through People*, 5th ed. (New York: Wiley, 2009) and Robert M. Guion and Scott Highhouse,

Essentials of Personnel Assessment and Selection (New York: Taylor and Francis, 2006).

For a review of recent developments in the federal government's hiring practices, see Carolyn Ban, "Hiring in the Federal Government: The Politics of Reform," in Carolyn Ban and Norma M. Riccucci, eds., *Public Personnel Management: Current Concerns, Future Challenges*, 3rd ed. (New York: Longman, 2002). Gary Roberts provides a look at the public sector more generally in "Issues, Challenges, and Changes in Recruitment and Selection," in Steven W. Hays and Richard C. Kearney, eds., *Public Personnel Administration: Problems and Prospects*, 4th ed. (Upper Saddle River, NJ: Prentice Hall, 2003).

Neal Schmitt provides a good review of research on job interviews in "Social and Situational Determinants of Interview Decisions: Implications for the Employment Interview," *Personnel Psychology* 29:3 (May/June 1976): 79–101. See also, Bradford D. Smart, *Selection Interviewing: A Management Psychologist's Recommended Approach* (New York: John Wiley & Sons, 1983).

On the Web

www.usajobs.opm.gov This website has been commissioned by the federal Office of Personnel Management to provide agencies and job seekers with an opportunity to make matches.

www.governmentjobs.com This is a job board that includes some federal agencies and agencies in state and local governments throughout the country.

Overview of Exercise

In this exercise, you will first devise and discuss a selection strategy for the job you analyzed in Exercise 11. You will then simulate a selection process by interviewing job applicants for the police dispatcher job described in Exercise 11.

INSTRUCTIONS

Step One

Review the job analysis and job description you completed for Exercise 11. Assume that this position is vacant and you have been put in charge of filling it. Use Form 67 to outline and justify the set of selection procedures you plan to use.

Step Two

Review the job description of the police dispatcher provided on Form 55 (Exercise 11). As directed by your instructor, arrange yourselves in groups of 2 to 4 people. One of you assume the role of the interviewer and others assume the role of job applicants. Spend about 15 minutes on each interview, unless given other limits by your instructor. Job applicants may be creative in answering questions about background and preparation for the job.

Step Three

Have a group discussion about the interviews, including how the interviewer performed. Whom would you have hired? Why?

Step Four

Answer the questions on Form 68.

Employee Selection Strategy

Job Title: _____

1. How and where will you let potential applicants know that this job is available?

2. What kinds of information do you want applicants to provide in their applications? Will you use this information to screen applicants and determine that some are not eligible for further consideration? If so, how?

3. What kinds of examinations are most appropriate for filling this job? Provide some sample questions or exercises. Will you score these as pass–fail or will you rank applicants based on their performance?

Questions

1. What means have the employers for whom you've worked (or sought to work), including summer or part-time jobs, used to screen job applicants? Do you think their selection procedures helped identify good employees (yourself excluded, of course!)?

2. Looking ahead to jobs you may apply for in the future, what selection procedures do you hope will be used? Are there particular devices you consider particularly fair or unfair?

3. Based on your experiences and on the interview simulation, what advice would you give to someone preparing for a job interview?

(*continued*)

4. Some seasoned managers believe that their subjective judgments about people are a better guide to their personnel decisions than any formal system of testing or quantitative scoring. Do you think this view has any merit?

Exercise 15

Collective Bargaining

BILATERALISM AND PUBLIC MANAGEMENT

Students who have completed the preceding four exercises may have come away with the impression that public personnel administration is an activity dominated by white-collar managers in business suits who, after careful and dispassionate analysis, issue edicts that determine the shape and structure of an organization's personnel system. Although there is perhaps some truth to this picture, there is considerably less now than there was before the 1960s. Public personnel management is typically no longer unilateral management. That is, no longer (or at least less often) can personnel managers simply write rules and regulations, set compensation levels, or make other significant decisions that affect public employees without considerable consultation with those employees. The extent of such consultation varies widely from jurisdiction to jurisdiction, to be sure. But as a general rule, public workers across the nation have become well organized and have forced public employers to recognize their rights and interests as employees.

This is not, by any means, to suggest that the tools and techniques of public personnel administration discussed earlier (e.g., job analysis, performance evaluation, and succession planning) have been rendered outdated or unnecessary by the advent of public employee unionization and collective bargaining. Rather, it is to say that the manner in which these tools and techniques are used in particular situations may be subject to collective negotiations with employees. Some jurisdictions, for instance, allow employees to bargain over the process of position classification; others permit bargaining about the system of performance evaluation to be used and determine whether employees can appeal a poor rating on a performance evaluation. Many state and local governments allow employees to bargain over wages, salaries, and fringe benefits. (The federal government continues to prohibit bargaining over these issues.) Other items that often fall within the scope of bargaining agreements are work schedules, disciplinary procedures, grievance processes, training and promotion opportunities, and union security provisions (dues checkoff, exclusive representation rights, use of public facilities for union activities, etc.). Thus, human resource administrators and other public managers increasingly need to recognize that they work in a complex environment of bilateral authority. The tools and techniques of personnel administration must be adapted to this environment.

THE RISE OF PUBLIC EMPLOYEE UNIONS

Although public employee unions have been in existence in the United States since the 1830s, they did not begin to have a serious and continuing impact on public personnel administration until the 1960s. One reason was that state and federal governments either ignored public employee unions or placed heavy restrictions on their activities. It was not until 1959 that Wisconsin became the first state to pass a law requiring its municipalities to bargain with unions their employees organized. Even though a series of executive orders dating to 1962 conferred limited bargaining rights on federal workers, the federal government did not enact a statute protecting bargaining rights of its employees until 1978. When the Department of Homeland

Security was established in 2002, the federal government backed away from this commitment.

Thirty-seven states have now passed laws authorizing some sort of collective bargaining with public employees. Most municipal, state, and federal employees today are covered by union contracts. Despite the late start for public-sector unions, a higher percentage of public- than private-sector workers are now organized.

THE BARGAINING PROCESS

Public-sector bargaining, like private-sector collective bargaining, is *bilateral*. This means that there are two distinct parties, employers and employees, involved in the bargaining, each of which has a separate and opposing set of interests. Hard, good-faith bargaining between the two sides should produce an agreement, or a contract, at the point of equilibrium of their interests. Note, however, that public-sector managers, especially elected officials and their appointees, may not always view union members as adversaries. After all, union members vote; this creates a complication that doesn't arise in the private sector.

The first step in the bargaining process involves identifying the parties. In effect, it is necessary to answer the question, Who's going to be doing the bargaining for whom? This is done by defining the *bargaining unit.* In some cases, all employees in an agency are lumped together in a single bargaining unit; in other cases, employees are grouped by occupation or position (clerical workers, technicians, prison guards, etc.). Once bargaining units are defined, employees are allowed to vote on whether they want to be represented by a union and if so, which one. Called a *certification election,* this process is usually overseen by a special state or federal agency charged with ensuring that workers are not intimidated into voting one way or another. Once a union is certified as the bargaining agent for the employees in a unit, it may, again depending on the laws of the jurisdiction, be allowed to collect dues or a "fair share" of representation costs from all employees in the unit.

Following certification, *contract negotiations* can begin. Typically, the union will assemble a negotiating team, drawn from specially elected (or selected) rank-and-file union members, union officers, and, occasionally, professional negotiators from the state or national union of which the local union is an affiliate. The union team will put together a list of contract proposals or demands and will meet with a corresponding team from management, which will have its own set of proposals. The management team may consist of top agency officials, labor relations administrators from specialized agencies, or combinations thereof. Through a series of face-to-face bargaining sessions, interspersed with private discussions within each team, the two parties seek to reach accord and to agree on the language of a contract. Once the parties have produced a tentative contract, each side must seek the formal approval of its constituency—the full union membership ratifies the agreement for the employees and a school board, city council, state legislature, Congress, or similar legislative body ratifies the agreement for management. A source of tension sometimes is that legislative bodies are typically distinct from the executive branch, and it is the latter that is present at the negotiating table. Thus, legislators feel like they are almost an afterthought in the bilateral bargaining process. And they usually are. Although collective bargaining is essentially a bilateral process between unions and executive branches, there really are three parties (unions, executive branch, and legislators) that need to agree before there is a contract.

IMPASSE RESOLUTION PROCEDURES

Bargaining does not always produce contracts in a straightforward manner. Occasionally, the two negotiating parties are simply unable to come to terms. Such a stalemate is called an *impasse.* When an impasse is reached, several things can happen. First, employees may decide to strike or to take some other job action (work slowdowns, "sick-outs," "working to rule," etc.). Although strikes by public employees are illegal in most jurisdictions, they are hardly uncommon.

More often, attempts are made to resolve the impasse through *third-party intervention.* This refers to the intercession of a neutral and independent person into the stalemated bilateral negotiations. There are three main types of third-party intervention. The first and least intrusive of the three is *mediation.* The job of a mediator is to try to convince both parties to be more flexible and to return to serious bargaining. Lacking the formal power to impose a settlement, a mediator must rely solely on persuasion and his or her reputation as a fair and unbiased individual.

The second type of third-party intervention, sometimes used when mediation fails, is called *fact-finding.* Like a mediator, a fact finder is a neutral, disinterested person called in to help resolve an impasse. A fact finder does not, as the term implies, find facts. He or she makes a recommendation based on a review of the proposals of each side. Usually, a fact finder holds a formal hearing and then publicly issues a recommended settlement. The proposal of a fact finder is *not* binding, but it is intended to place public pressure on the two sides to accept the recommendation and end the impasse.

The third type of third-party intervention is *arbitration.* Arbitration differs significantly from both mediation and fact-finding in that an arbitrator has legal authority to *impose* a settlement. Actually, there are several varieties of arbitration. The first, often termed *general binding arbitration,* permits an arbitrator to review the proposals of both sides and then pick and choose among the positions of labor and management to create a contract the arbitrator considers fair. The arbitrator may, if he or she deems it necessary, write new provisions or even draft a new contract.

The second and more common type of arbitration, *final offer arbitration (item selection),* limits the power of the arbitrator in an important way: Although he or she can still impose a settlement, the contract must be constructed from provisions actually proposed by one side or the other; the arbitrator may not exercise creativity and draft wholly new or compromised provisions. Many people believe that this limitation on the power of the arbitrator encourages labor and management to submit more reasonable and temperate proposals because they will fear that anything less than reasonable and temperate will drive the arbitrator to the position of the other side.

The third type of arbitration is a variation on the second. Its name—*final offer arbitration (package selection)*—effectively summarizes the difference. In this type of arbitration, the arbitrator must choose, without modification, either the entire package submitted as a last, best offer by management or the entire package submitted as a last, best offer by labor.

This type of arbitration creates a high-stakes game for the two parties. Even more than with the item selection variety, each side knows that it must submit a moderate and reasonable last, best offer to the arbitrator. Anything less than that is likely to produce an unalloyed victory for the other side.

Sentiment is strong among labor relations specialists in favor of bilateral negotiations. Third-party intervention is viewed as a last resort, something to be used only when labor and management are truly stalemated. Similarly, once it is determined that a third party must be called in to break an impasse, there is a bias in favor of the least intrusive intervention. One major reason is that labor and management, whatever their fundamental differences, share a long-term interest in coexistence. It is better for them to work things out for themselves than to rely on an outside referee; after all, there won't be a referee around on a day-to-day basis as the work of the organization proceeds through the year. Also, the third party is typically not a member of the community who will have to live with the consequences of the settlement in the same way that workers, managers, and legislators will.

It is certainly better for labor and management to bargain their way to a contract, even if they have to use a mediator or a fact finder, than it is to have one imposed by an arbitrator. Most people involved in labor relations believe that arbitration is useful only for preventing strikes. And even then, some would argue that strikes are to be preferred.

FURTHER READING

The literature on public-sector labor relations is vast and varied. A good place to begin is Richard C. Kearney, *Labor Relations in the Public Sector,* 4th ed. (New York: CRC Press, 2008), which provides a textbook overview of the major issues in the field. Also good as an introduction is Charles J. Coleman, *Managing Labor Relations in the Public Sector* (San Francisco: Jossey-Bass, 1990).

An excellent edited volume is Joyce Najita and James Stern, eds., *Collective Bargaining in the Public Sector: The Experiences of Eight* States (New York: M.E. Sharpe, 2001). For a detailed look at municipal labor relations, with an emphasis on very practical questions of determining bargaining units, selecting representatives, assessing unfair labor practices, and so forth, see Joan E. Pynes and Joan M. Lafferty, *Local Government Labor Relations: A Guide for Public Administrators* (Westport, CT: Quorum Books, 1993).

On the Web
www.nlrb.gov The National Labor Relations Board monitors and regulates labor–management relations. Most states have an equivalent agency and these are usually responsible for public-sector labor relations.

The major public employee unions are the American Federation of State, Local and Municipal Employees (www.afscme.org), the American Federation of Government Employees—for federal workers (www.afge.org), American Federation of Teachers (www.aft.org), National Education Association (www.nea.org), and the Service Employees International Union (www.seiu.org). There are many other unions that include public employees, some of them are part of other, larger unions and others are relatively small, independent organizations.

Overview of Exercise

This exercise simulates a round of collective bargaining between the City of Barnswallow and the Barnswallow chapter of the International Federation of Firefighters (IFF). Playing the role of a member of the city's bargaining team, the union's bargaining team, or a neutral third-party mediator or arbitrator, you use the current contract between the city and the union as a baseline and attempt to negotiate a new agreement.

INSTRUCTIONS

Step One
Your instructor will assign to you one of the following roles in this exercise:

    H. Rodriguez, Mayor of Barnswallow
    J. Symes, City Personnel Director
    N. Rich, City Budget Director
    D. Raucher, Fire Commissioner
    T. Sweeney, IFF Local 492 President
    P. Jeffries, Union Bargaining Team Member
    G. Rank, Union Bargaining Team Member
    F. Martin, IFF Representative
    I. M. Fair, Mediator
    B. Just, Arbitrator

Classes larger than 10 students will subdivide into two or more sets of bargaining teams. Read the information about your role provided on Forms 69a through 69j. Use the information provided as a general guide to behavior throughout the exercise. Feel free, however, to embellish your role as you see fit. Use your imagination!

Step Two
Read through the provisions of the current contract (Form 70), and familiarize yourself with the characteristics of the City of Barnswallow, IFF Local 492, and the other background information provided on Form 71.

Step Three
Meet with the other members of your bargaining team, and establish an initial bargaining position. Decide which provisions of the current contract should remain intact, which should be altered, and which should be thrown out. You may, if you like, propose entirely new provisions or even draft a wholly different contract. Each member of the bargaining team will probably have slightly different perspectives on what items to stress, what positions to take, and what overall strategy to adopt in dealing with the opposing bargaining team. Try to work out reasonable compromises. Students playing the role of mediator or arbitrator should await further directions from the course instructor.

Step Four
Arrange a face-to-face bargaining session with the opposing bargaining team. Each side should present its demands and receive reactions from the other side.

Step Five
Review the proposals submitted by the opposing team in a private session with your bargaining team. Reformulate your positions as you deem appropriate.

Step Six

Arrange further bargaining sessions and conduct private meetings with your team as needed. Work to produce a new contract satisfactory to your team.

Step Seven

Once agreement between the two sides has been reached on all provisions of a new contract, each side should complete Form 72. Obtain appropriate signatures on Form 72, and present it to the instructor.

Step Eight

In the event that agreement between the two sides on all provisions of a new contract cannot be reached by the time specified by your instructor, an impasse will be declared. At this time, the two parties to your negotiation will be subject to one of several impasse resolution procedures (mediation, general binding arbitration, final offer arbitration with package selection, or final offer arbitration with item selection); your instructor will inform you at the outset of the exercise which impasse resolution procedure governs your negotiations. Parties governed by mediation will return to bargaining with the intervention and assistance of a mediator; bargaining will continue until a contract has been negotiated or time ends, whichever comes first. If a contract is successfully negotiated, complete Form 72, obtaining the required signatures. Parties governed by arbitration should read and follow Steps Nine and Ten.

Step Nine

If an impasse has been declared and your parties are governed by any form of arbitration, each bargaining team is to complete Form 72 independently. This form now represents the last, best offer your team is willing to make with respect to each of the provisions under negotiation. Be sure to complete this form fully and carefully, especially the final section that allows you to add provisions or provide the full text of any altered provisions; you need not obtain signatures from the opposing team for this step. Upon completing the form, submit it to the arbitrator designated by your instructor.

Step Ten

After reviewing the submissions from both parties, the arbitrator will hold a hearing at a time designated by the instructor. At this hearing, the arbitrator will take testimony from both parties regarding their submissions. The arbitrator may raise any questions he or she likes about the submissions. Following the hearing, the arbitrator will review all materials; complete and sign a clean copy of Form 72, summarizing his or her judgment; and, at a time set by the instructor, announce this judgment. Representatives of both parties will then sign the arbitrated version of Form 72.

Step Eleven

Answer the questions on Form 73.

ROLE:
H. Rodriguez, Mayor of Barnswallow

Mayor Rodriguez believes that continued economic prosperity in Barnswallow depends on creating a hospitable tax environment for businesses and citizens. To that end, the mayor has instructed city administrative officers to pare spending wherever possible. While recognizing the importance of first-rate fire protection, Rodriguez believes that the current fire department is too large and that Barnswallow firefighters already receive more than generous compensation. The mayor's major goal in the present round of negotiations is to see at least a modest decrease in the fire department's operating budget. Although Rodriguez does not participate in direct, face-to-face negotiations with union representatives, the mayor's approval is required before any contract proposals can be formally offered to the other side.

ROLE:
J. Symes, City Personnel Director

J. Symes has worked for the City of Barnswallow for almost 30 years and has spent the last 15 years as city personnel director. Symes grew up with a personnel system that was heavily management oriented and has never completely adjusted to the complexities of collective bargaining. Consequently, Symes is very sensitive to the management rights and prerogatives covered by the contract and believes that the city has given up too much of its authority to set policy without union "interference." Symes is especially interested in revising the grievance procedure to make it more difficult for firefighters to challenge departmental decisions. Symes would also like to see a 2- or 3-year contract negotiated, rather than another 1-year contract, and is in favor of abolishing across-the-board salary increases in favor of a pure performance-based pay system.

ROLE:
N. Rich, City Budget Director

N. Rich, like J. Symes, is a professional public administrator, although Rich is considerably younger and does not share Symes's thinly veiled hostility toward the city's unions. Rich is interested only in the "bottom line." The budget director's goal, like the mayor's, is to hold down costs. With an eye toward the city's long-term financial health, Rich is especially interested in excising "time bombs"—items that aren't expensive now but whose costs will explode later on—from Barnswallow's labor contracts. Hence, the budget director worries about total staffing levels and pension rights, as well as short-term wage and benefit expenses. Rich would like to cut at least 25 positions from the department. Like Symes, Rich is in favor of longer-term contracts; the budget director believes that the longer the contract, the greater the savings for the city.

ROLE:
D. Raucher, Fire Commissioner

D. Raucher has been commissioner of the Barnswallow Fire Department for 4 years. Most of his/her career was spent as a firefighter and officer in a large city in a nearby state. Although Raucher feels considerable empathy for the men and women of the department and indeed was once active in another IFF local, he/she recognizes the commissioner's role as a member of the city's management team. As top administrative officer of the department, Raucher's main goal is to increase managerial autonomy and especially to enhance the authority of departmental officers to establish work rotations and effect transfers as they deem necessary. Moreover, Raucher has been promised by the mayor, off the record, that any savings in the department's operating budget will be rewarded by support for new capital expenditures in new firefighting equipment, including new pumper and ladder trucks. Raucher thus has considerable interest in holding down contract costs as well.

ROLE:
T. Sweeney, IFF Local 492 President

T. Sweeney is serving a third 2-year term as president of the Barnswallow chapter (Local 492) of the IFF. Although he/she is interested in running for a fourth term, Sweeney is being pressured by a group of younger, more militant firefighters (Sweeney is 47) to step aside at the end of the current negotiations. Sweeney's major goal is to shore up support among union members by negotiating a contract with substantial wage and benefit increases.

ROLE:
P. Jeffries, Union Bargaining Team Member

P. Jeffries is a 48-year-old engineer who entered the department the same year as T. Sweeney and who has remained a close friend and supporter of Sweeney. Jeffries was very active in the old Barnswallow Firefighters Association (the predecessor of the union) but has not taken a leading role in the activities of the local since the advent of collective bargaining. Jeffries has publicly bemoaned the "lack of cooperation" between the city and the IFF in various union meetings, although a recent dispute over sick pay with an assistant chief, which led to Jeffries's filing a grievance, has softened his/her attitude toward the union and its role. Jeffries agreed to run for a seat on the bargaining team at Sweeney's request. Jeffries's main goal is to improve the provision of the contract dealing with pensions and press for improved insurance coverage for retired employees. Jeffries is also sensitive to problems in the grievance procedure and is supportive of higher pay.

ROLE:

G. Rank, Union Bargaining Team Member

G. Rank is a 27-year-old firefighter who has worked for the Barnswallow Fire Department for 5 years. Rank is one of the leading "young turks" who has been pressuring President Sweeney to step down. Rank has been mentioned prominently as a candidate for the job of union president in the next election. Rank's major goal in the negotiations is to press for increased fringe benefits, especially in the area of job training and education. Rank also supports a substantial increase in wages and salaries and is sympathetic to the demands of F. Martin, the IFF representative. Rank is opposed to any contract that runs more than 1 year unless specific cost-of-living adjustment (COLA) provisions are negotiated.

ROLE:
F. Martin, IFF Representative

F. Martin is a professional union negotiator employed by the national office of the IFF. Martin's job is to assist local chapters, such as Barnswallow's, in contract negotiations and other proceedings affecting IFF members. Martin has a reputation as a tough, no-nonsense negotiator and has been accused by municipal officials elsewhere of being an instigator of strikes and other illegal job actions. Martin's goal is to strengthen virtually all contract provisions, especially those dealing with union rights and grievance procedures. Martin would like to restrict management prerogatives to transfer workers from one firestation to another without their consent, replace discretionary merit raises with across-the-board increases, require strict adherence to seniority in promotion decisions, and mandate a four-platoon work rotation system (24 hours on, 72 hours off). Martin insists that the union refuse to accept a contract that runs for more than 1 year, arguing that any step-up of inflation would lock workers into low wage scales.

ROLE:
I.M. Fair, Mediator

Fair's job is to act as a neutral third party and try to persuade union and management to compromise and come to terms when an impasse has been reached. Fair has no authority to impose a settlement but must instead rely on his/her skills of persuasion. Once an impasse has been declared, Fair may be as active as he/she wishes; that is, Fair may propose contract provisions to each side that he/she feels will garner agreement or may simply act as a go-between in stalemated discussions.

ROLE:
B. Just, Arbitrator

Once an impasse has been declared, Just's job is to receive the final contract proposals from each side and to reach a fair and reasonable judgment regarding a new contract. Just's precise powers as arbitrator will be determined in advance by the instructor. Just may have virtually unlimited power to write a new contract (general binding arbitration) or may be limited to either accepting, as a whole, the set of proposals of one side or the other (final offer arbitration with package selection) or choosing among the various provisions proposed by each side (final offer arbitration with item selection). In any event, Just should use the arbitration hearings to gather as much information as possible to reach an equitable settlement.

Agreement between the City of Barnswallow and the International Federation of Firefighters, Barnswallow Chapter

Effective January 1, 2010–December 31, 2010

ARTICLE I
AGREEMENT

This agreement is made and entered into this 22nd day of December, 2009, by and between the City of Barnswallow, hereinafter referred to as the "City," and the Barnswallow Chapter of the International Federation of Firefighters, hereinafter referred to as the "Union" or the "IFF."

ARTICLE II
RECOGNITION

The City recognizes the IFF (Barnswallow Chapter) as the sole and exclusive bargaining representative as certified by the State Department of Labor in respect to matters concerning wages, salaries, hours, vacations, sick leave, grievance procedures, and other terms and conditions of employment as specifically set forth in this Agreement, for all employees of the City in the collective bargaining unit designated by that certification dated April 23, 1971, as follows: all employees of the Barnswallow Fire Department in the job classes Firefighter, Hose Operator, Engineer, and Driver.

Excluded from the collective bargaining unit are all administrative and line officers of the Barnswallow Fire Department, including all Battalion Chiefs, Captains, and Lieutenants.

ARTICLE III
UNION DUES

During the term of this Agreement, the City agrees to deduct monthly membership dues, proportionately each pay period, from the wages and salaries due all members who individually and voluntarily give the City written authorization to do so. The City shall forward such dues for the previous month's salaries to the Treasurer of the Union on or before the tenth day of each month. The Union assumes full responsibility for the disposition of monies so deducted once they have been remitted to the Treasurer.

ARTICLE IV
MANAGEMENT RIGHTS

The Union recognizes that, except as hereinafter specifically provided, the operations and administration of the Barnswallow Fire Department, including, but not limited to, the right to make rules and regulations pertaining thereto, shall be fully vested in the Commissioner of the Barnswallow Fire Department and his/her designees, as the executive agent of the City of Barnswallow. Except as hereinafter specifically provided, nothing herein stated shall be construed as a delegation or waiver of any powers or duties vested in the Commissioner of the Barnswallow Fire Department, the Mayor of the City of Barnswallow, or any administrative official or their designees by virtue of any provision of the laws and ordinances of the State or the City of Barnswallow.

ARTICLE V
UNION REPRESENTATIVES AND PRIVILEGES

5.1 The Union, its officers and members, shall not engage in union activities, hold meetings on City property, or utilize City facilities in any way that interferes with or interrupts normal City operations or the obligations and duties of Union members as employees.

5.2 The Union shall have the right to make reasonable use of City space, facilities, and equipment for proper activities related to its position as the recognized representative of Department employees.

5.3 The Union shall have the right to post at appropriate locations in City firestations bulletins and notices relevant to official Union business.

ARTICLE VI
GRIEVANCE PROCEDURE

6.1 A grievance is defined as any dispute or difference concerning the interpretation, application, or claimed violation of any provision of this Agreement.

6.2 Every attempt will be made to resolve any grievance speedily and informally by meetings between affected parties.

6.3 In the event that informal resolution procedures fail to satisfy the aggrieved party, the following formal procedure is to be followed:

Step 1

An aggrieved member of the bargaining unit (hereafter called "the appellant") shall present an appeal in writing and signed by the appellant in the first instance to the Company Captain. The Captain shall discuss the grievance with the appellant. The Union will be notified by the Captain and may send representatives to all meetings where the grievance is discussed with the appellant. The Captain shall consider the appeal and reply in writing within seven (7) workdays after receipt of the appeal. For the purposes of this procedure, Saturdays and Sundays shall not be counted as workdays.

Step 2

If the matter is not resolved, the appellant shall file a written appeal to the Battalion Chief within seven (7) workdays after receipt of the Step 1 decision, with copies to the Captain and the Union. The Battalion Chief shall discuss the appeal with the Captain and the appellant. The Union will be notified by the Battalion Chief and may send representatives to all meetings where the grievance is discussed with the appellant. The Battalion Chief shall consider the appeal and reply in writing within ten (10) workdays after receipt of the appeal.

Step 3

If the matter is not resolved, the appellant may appeal in writing to the Commissioner of the Barnswallow Fire Department within fifteen (15) workdays after receipt of the Step 2 decision. The Commissioner of the Barnswallow Fire Department, sitting with a panel composed of one member from the City of Barnswallow Personnel Department and two members designated by the Union, shall conduct a hearing within fifteen (15) workdays after receipt of the appeal. Such hearing shall be conducted with concern for due process. The appellant shall have the right to testify, introduce documentary evidence, and present witnesses on his/her behalf. The Commissioner of the Barnswallow Fire Department shall render a decision on the appeal, in writing, within ten (10) workdays after the hearing, with copies to the appellant and Union. The other members of the hearing panel may state their views in separate opinions, which shall be appended to the decision of the Commissioner of the Barnswallow Fire Department. Said separate opinions are advisory only and are not to be construed as binding on the City of Barnswallow or the appellant.

Step 4

If the matter is not resolved, the Union, acting on behalf of the appellant, may file a written appeal within seven (7) workdays to the American Arbitration Association (AAA) for binding arbitration under its rules. The arbitration shall be by a neutral arbitrator selected under AAA rules, and the decision of the arbitrator shall be final and binding. The costs of arbitration shall be borne equally by the parties.

ARTICLE VII
NO STRIKES OR LOCKOUTS

The Union and the City subscribe to the principle that any and all differences under this Agreement be resolved by peaceful and legal means without interruption of City services. The Union therefore agrees that neither it nor any of its officers, agents, employees, or members will instigate, engage in, support, or condone any strike, work stoppage, or other concerted refusal to perform work by any employees in the bargaining unit during the life of this Agreement. The City agrees that there shall be no lockout during the life of this Agreement.

ARTICLE VIII
WAGES AND BENEFITS

8.1 For the period January 1, 2010, through December 31, 2010, *salaries* of members of the bargaining unit shall be adjusted in the following manner:

a. Each member of the bargaining unit shall have his/her salary increased by an amount equal to 2% of his/her base salary as of December 31, 2009.

b. In addition, an amount equal to 1% of the base salaries as of December 31, 2009, of all employees in the bargaining unit shall be allocated to a special merit pool. This pool shall be used to provide additional salary increments to members of the bargaining unit. Decisions about allocation of merit money rest solely with the Commissioner of the Barnswallow Fire Department, who will seek the advice of his/her subordinate line officers.

8.2 Employees shall be required to work no more than four (4) of the following ten (10) holidays:

New Year's Day	Independence Day	Christmas
Thanksgiving	Good Friday	New Year's
Easter	Labor Day	Eve
Memorial Day	Martin Luther King, Jr. Day	

Decisions as to which holidays an employee shall work are to be understood as a prerogative of management. When required to work on one of the holidays designated above, employees shall be compensated at one and one-half times their normal hourly rate.

8.3 Employees shall receive paid vacation according to the following schedule:

1st year through 5th year	2 weeks
6th year through 10th year	3 weeks
11th year through 15th year	4 weeks
16th and later years	5 weeks

8.4 Employees are responsible for purchasing and maintaining their own uniforms and personal equipment. The City shall, however, provide an annual *uniform allowance* of $1,200 to all uniformed personnel to defray purchase and maintenance costs.

8.5 Employees required to report for duty at times other than their regularly scheduled rotations shall receive *overtime pay* of one and one-half times their normal hourly rate.

8.6 The City agrees to pay one-half the *tuition and fee expenses*, up to a total of $2,000 per employee per year, of any employee enrolled in an approved course of study related to firefighting or fire safety. Approval of the course of study rests solely with the Commissioner of the Barnswallow Fire Department or his/her designees.

8.7 The City shall pay the entire cost of the employee's *Blue Cross Blue Shield Major Medical coverage.* Should the employee elect family coverage, the employee shall pay a monthly contribution of $200.

8.8 The City shall pay the entire cost of a group *disability insurance* policy for each employee. Said policy, to be selected by the City of Barnswallow, shall provide benefits of not less than $4,000 per month to any disabled employee.

8.9 The City shall provide *term life insurance* at no cost to the employee in the amount of two times the annual salary of the employee. Choice of a policy and insurance company rests solely with the City of Barnswallow.

8.10 *Paid sick leave* accrues to employees at the rate of five (5) days per year for the first year of employment and ten (10) days per year for each succeeding year. Sick leave may not be carried over from one year to the next.

ARTICLE IX
PENSION RIGHTS

The City shall contribute an amount equal to 5% of each employee's salary to the State Employees Pension Fund on behalf of the employee. Each employee shall contribute a minimum of 5% and a maximum of 10% to said Fund. Full pension rights are available at age 60 or following 30 years of employment, whichever comes first.

ARTICLE X
MAINTENANCE OF PRACTICES

The parties agree that there is a body of written policies and of practices and interpretations of those policies that govern administrative decisions concerning wages, salaries, hours, workload, sick leave, vacations, grievance procedures, transfers, suspension, and dismissal not explicitly covered in this Agreement. Such policies and practices shall be continued for the life of this Agreement. An administrative action not in accordance with the past application or interpretation of the above policies shall be grievable.

ARTICLE XI
NONDISCRIMINATION

The City and the Union, to the extent of their respective authority, agree not to discriminate against a Union member with respect to the application of the provisions of this Agreement because of race, creed, color, sex, religion, national origin, veteran or handicapped status, or membership or nonmembership in the Union.

ARTICLE XII
CONTRACT PERIOD AND FURTHER NEGOTIATIONS

This agreement shall be binding on both parties for the period January 1, 2010, through December 31, 2010. Both parties agree that negotiations to extend or modify this contract for any period beyond December 31, 2010, should commence no later than August 1, 2010.

Background Information

THE CITY

Barnswallow is a medium-size city (population 350,000) in a Middle Atlantic state. Although city finances are now fairly stable, like many older cities in the Northeast, Barnswallow experienced considerable economic distress from the mid-1960s through the late 1990s as large numbers of middle-class whites moved to the suburbs, causing a serious erosion of Barnswallow's tax base. Deteriorating neighborhoods, increases in the city's crime rate, including rates of arson, and rising joblessness placed great strains on city services.

By 2009, things began to turn around for Barnswallow. An energetic young lawyer, H. Rodriguez, defeated the candidate of the city's political machine for mayor. Rodriguez assembled a small team of able, professional administrators and, often with intense opposition from the city council, began to reform Barnswallow's administrative apparatus: Budgeting procedures were rationalized, a civil service system was installed for city workers, and procurement practices were modernized. Through these reforms, and by discharging almost 200 city workers, Rodriguez managed to balance the city's budget and improve its bond rating. Barnswallow's fiscal health was also assisted considerably by a general increase in economic prosperity and by an influx of young, well-to-do professionals back into the city. In a recent interview with the *Barnswallow Evening Chronicle,* Rodriguez hinted that next year's city budget would include a significant reduction in the property tax rate. Knowledgeable observers are convinced that Rodriguez will announce a reelection bid shortly.

THE UNION

Local 492 is an affiliate of the International Federation of Firefighters (IFF), one of the largest unions of firefighters in America. Although Barnswallow's firefighters have been organized for nearly 60 years, collective negotiations with the city have taken place only since the early 1970s, following a change in state law authorizing bargaining with uniformed municipal employees. Prior to this time, the Barnswallow Firefighters Association, the predecessor of Local 492, acted largely as a social organization and as an informal lobby for fire safety and other firefighter concerns in the city. The union today represents 296 people at 18 firestations. Support for the union among members is high, although there is a growing rift between older and younger firefighters: the younger members have been pressing the union leadership to take a hard line against the Rodriguez administration's budget policies and have advocated militant job actions, including strikes, in dealing with the city.

CITY–UNION RELATIONS

Relations between the city and the union were relatively harmonious during the first 25 years of collective bargaining. Support for Barnswallow's political machine by union members was rewarded with generous contracts. Agreements were negotiated promptly and smoothly, with no serious threats of disruptions in city services. With the advent of the Rodriguez administration, relations took a turn for the worse. Negotiations on the 1999–2001 (2-year) contract were marked by acrimony and distrust on both sides, with the union charging that the Rodriguez administration was trying to "balance the city budget on the backs of its employees." A strike (still illegal under state law) by firefighters was threatened in 2004 when the city refused to budge from its proposal to close three firestations and eliminate 37 jobs. The 2007 contract (1-year) was finally settled when the State Public Employee Relations Board intervened and brought the case to an arbitrator.

BARNSWALLOW FIRE DEPARTMENT: ORGANIZATION AND STAFFING

The head of the Barnswallow Fire Department is the fire commissioner, an official appointed by the mayor and confirmed by the city council; the fire commissioner is responsible for planning and coordinating the work of the department. Directly below and responsible to the commissioner are a series of professional fire administrators who are in charge, respectively, of fire prevention, fire extinguishment, finance and budgeting, training, equipment, and personnel. The most important of these administrators is the chief fire marshall, the official responsible for the Division of Fire Extinguishment. The chief fire marshall is the principal "firefighter" of the department, in direct command of Barnswallow's firefighting and rescue operations. Reporting to the fire marshall are five battalion fire chiefs, who in turn supervise the city's 34 fire captains. Each captain commands a fire company; the city's 34 fire companies are deployed at 18 separate firestations.

The 296 men and women represented by IFF Local 492 are organized into specialized companies (pumper, hose, ladder, rescue, etc.) attached to the firestations. Depending on the size of the area it serves, each firestation has from one to four companies. Four job classes form the basis of Local 492: firefighter, engineer, hose operator, and driver. Table 15.1 provides a breakdown of the numbers of people filling each job class, together with their average annual salaries.

Table 15.1 Distribution and Salaries of Local 492 Members

Job Class	Number of Employees	Average Salary (2009)
Firefighter	127	$41,000
Engineer	40	43,500
Hose operator	74	41,000
Driver	55	43,000

CURRENT CONTRACT COSTS

Basic salary costs of the Barnswallow Fire Department can be estimated from the data provided in Table 15.1. Additional information that may be used to gauge the cost of the 2010 contract as well as proposals under negotiation is as follows:

1. Under current department procedures, each fire company is organized into three platoons, designated A, B, and C. Each platoon works a 24-hour shift and is then off for 48 hours. Overtime rates apply whenever an employee is required to work more than 24 hours in any 72-hour period. Employees are typically required to work an average of 60 hours of overtime pay per year.

2. An average of 42 employees per year have taken advantage of the contract provision providing tuition assistance. Of these, 34 receive the $2,000 maximum grant, as their costs equal or exceed the limit set by the contract. The eight remaining employees have been granted an average of $675 each.

3. Individual Blue Cross Blue Shield major medical coverage costs the city $6,000 per year per employee. Blue Cross Blue Shield family coverage costs $9,000 per year (see contract provision 8.7). Currently, 210 employees opt for family coverage.

4. The city's current disability policy costs $350 per year per employee. Each $100-per-month increase in benefits adds $15 to the cost of the yearly premium.

5. The city's term life insurance policy costs $150 per year per employee given the current benefit structure (see contract provision 8.9). There is a direct relationship between the annual premium per employee and the projected average benefit, such that an increase in benefits to three times annual salary would raise the premium to $200 per employee; an increase to four times salary would cost $300 per employee.

6. For the purposes of this exercise, the inflation rate and other aggregate indicators of national economic well-being are assumed to be the same as those actually prevailing at the time the exercise is conducted. Although this information has no direct bearing on the costs of the 2010 contract, it may influence the course of negotiations on a new agreement.

Outline of the Contract between the City of Barnswallow and the International Federation of Firefighters, Barnswallow Chapter

Instructions: This form provides a skeletal outline of the current (2010) contract between the City of Barnswallow and IFF Local 492. Each number on this form corresponds to a provision in the current contract. In the space provided after each number, write "retain," "delete," or "alter," depending on how the new contract you have just negotiated (or are submitting for arbitration) differs from the 2010 contract. Wherever you write "alter" (i.e., whenever a new provision differs from a previous provision), provide a brief summary of the changes. Enter the complete text of the altered provisions as well as any completely new provisions you may negotiate (or propose) at the end of this form. Obtain signatures as required.

I. AGREEMENT _____

_____

II. RECOGNITION _____

_____

III. UNION DUES _____

_____

IV. MANAGEMENT RIGHTS _____

_____

V. UNION REPRESENTATIVES AND PRIVILEGES _____

_____

VI. GRIEVANCE PROCEDURE _____

_____

VII. NO STRIKES OR LOCKOUTS _____

_____

VIII. WAGES AND BENEFITS _____

_____

IX. PENSION RIGHTS _____

_____

X. MAINTENANCE OF PRACTICES _____

_____

XI. NONDISCRIMINATION _____

_____

XII. CONTRACT PERIOD AND FURTHER NEGOTIATIONS _____

_____

XIII. ADDITIONAL PROVISIONS AND/OR TEXT OF ALTERED PROVISIONS _____

_____

SIGNATURES

The undersigned are duly authorized representatives of the City of Barnswallow and the Barnswallow Chapter (Local 492) of the International Federation of Firefighters.

IN WITNESS WHEREOF THE PARTIES HERETO HAVE SET THEIR HANDS AND SEALS ON THIS ———— DAY OF ————, 20 ————:

For the City	*For the Union*
J. Symes	T. Sweeney
N. Rich	P. Jeffries
D. Raucher	G. Rank
	F. Martin

For Cases That Go to Arbitration Only

The undersigned, being a duly authorized representative of the State Public Employee Relations Board and a certified arbitrator empowered by Section 317.6(a) of State Statutes to resolve impasses in labor disputes, does hereby warrant that the attached is a fair and legal contract binding the two parties for the period specified.

B. Just

Questions

1. How effective was your bargaining team? Did you achieve any or all of your aims in the contract? To what do you attribute your success or failure?

2. Assuming that more than one set of bargaining teams was operating in your class, what were the major differences in the contracts that were negotiated? Did the method of impasse resolution used (if any) have any systematic effect on outcomes?

3. What types of third-party intervention, if any, do you think are most appropriate to resolve impasses? Would you support the use of any type of arbitration?

4. Do you think public employees should be allowed to strike? If you think strikes by public employees should be illegal, what would you do as a public administrator if your employees struck anyway?

PART IV

Budgeting

WHAT IS A BUDGET?

A budget is a document that sets forth how money is to be spent. Although budgets come in a bewildering variety of shapes and sizes, all budgets—personal, corporate, and governmental—have one central and simple element in common: they tell us what we plan to buy and how much it is likely to cost.

Budgets are usually written for a fixed period of time called a *fiscal year,* which is any consecutive 12-month period that an organization uses to plan its expenditures. A complicating feature of governmental budgeting is that the fiscal years of different jurisdictions usually do not coincide. The fiscal year for the federal government is October 1 to September 30. Many states and localities operate on a July 1 to June 30 fiscal year. Some states and local governments use the January 1 to December 31 calendar year.

Of course, budget administrators and elected officials are always interested in shorter and longer periods of time as well—is there enough left in the budget to buy a new computer, or what is the implication of this expenditure for the next five years? Nonetheless, the fiscal year is the basic unit of time for casting a budget.

WHY DO WE BUDGET?

If we had all the money we wanted, we probably wouldn't need to write budgets. Given a limitless checking account, for instance, you wouldn't have to worry about setting aside enough to pay the rent each month. The fact is, however, that there is never enough money to do everything we want to do. Money is scarce. As a result, we must forgo or postpone some things we want in favor of other things we must have. Even national governments, with their access to presses for printing money, have to make choices about what to buy and what not to buy. This is where budgets come in. By listing clearly and systematically all the things we plan to buy, we can make sure we make our purchases sensibly so that there is rent money.

Guarding against financial imprudence is not the only reason to budget, however. A second reason governments budget is to ensure that money is spent only in accordance with specified public purposes. That is, budgets provide the means for citizens and public officials to control or account for the expenditure of public funds. Instead of just sending truckloads of cash from the Treasury to government offices at the beginning of each fiscal year and saying, "Go administer," we draw up a budget that specifies in detail what things should be purchased and how much should be spent on them. Then we say, "Go administer." But we add, "And we want to see the receipts!"

As the exercises in Part IV make clear, budgets are useful for a third reason as well: they help us make decisions. By classifying alternative expenditures in ways that allow systematic comparison, we can make informed choices about which investments of public funds promise the best return. It is possible to devise budget systems that help officials weigh the relative merits of two different job training schemes, for instance, or decide whether building a new state park is worth the cost.

HOW DO WE BUDGET?

There are as many different ways to construct budgets as there are organizations that seek to do so. Fortunately for the student of budgeting, however, the many different specific approaches used by various units of government are really variations on a few simple themes. This set of exercises introduces the fundamental approaches that constitute the building blocks of all budget systems. Once the logic of these systems is mastered, we can understand and reproduce virtually any budgetary system; it is necessary only to take an organizing pinch from one and add a conceptual dash or two from another. There are five basic budget systems:

    Line-item budgeting

    Performance budgeting

    Program budgeting

    Zero-base budgeting

    Outcome-based budgeting

The five represent a historical progression in ideas about budgeting, with line-item budgeting the earliest and outcome-based budgeting the most recent. This is not to say that later ideas have displaced earlier ideas, at least not completely. Line-item budgeting is a fundamental building block for all budgeting systems. Many of the concepts of performance and program budgeting are widely incorporated into today's approach to budgeting. Generally speaking, the line of progression has been from less complex to more complex, as we have asked our budgeting systems to undertake more and more tasks.

FURTHER READING

Useful discussions of public budgeting in the United States are Robert D. Lee, Jr., Ronald W. Johnson, and Philip G. Joyce, *Public Budgeting Systems*, 8th ed. (Sudbury, MA: Jones and Bartlett, 2008); Charles E. Menifield, *The Basics of Public Budgeting and Financial Management: A Handbook for Academics and Practitioners* (Lanham, MD: University Press of America, 2008); and Irene Rubin, *The Politics of Public Budgeting: Getting and Spending*, 6th ed. (Washington, DC: Congressional Quarterly Press, 2009).

On the Web

www.omb.gov   The Office of Management and Budget (OMB) is the federal agency responsible for compiling the budget of the federal government and presenting it to Congress on behalf of the president. OMB also provides central direction in managing the budget once passed by Congress.

www.cbo.gov   The Congressional Budget Office (CBO) is a nonpartisan, professional agency that provides Congress with analyses independent of those presented by the executive branch.

State and local governments have agencies similar to OMB and CBO.

Two professional associations provide analyses, recommendations, and support for the public budgeting process:

www.nasbo.org   National Association of State Budget Officers

www.gfoa.org   Government Finance Officers Association

These general sources are relevant to all of the exercises presented next on different approaches to budgeting.

Exercise 16

Line-Item Budgeting

BUDGETING FOR CONTROL

Line-item budgeting is the oldest and most ubiquitous form of budgeting. So widely used is this technique, in fact, that to most people a budget *is* a line-item budget, even if they've never heard the term.

Table 16.1 is an example of a line-item budget. Note that it contains two basic elements: a *commodity to be purchased* (employee salaries, office supplies, telephone, etc.) and a *cost*. Although line-item budgets can be organized in many different ways, similar commodities are usually classified together. This makes it easier for the budget to be read and interpreted.

Some line-item budgets are more detailed and include more information than others. For instance, the "Office Supplies" category in this Department of Parks and Recreation budget might, in another organization's budget, be broken down into "pencils," "paper clips," "staples," and so forth. The amount of detail in a line-item budget is a function of the amount of control that central budget administrators wish to extend over their operating units. The more autonomy and discretion granted, the less detailed the line-item budget. The idea of control is central to line-item budgeting. Line-item budgets were developed initially and have retained their popularity precisely because

Table 16.1 Budget Request Form: Department of Parks and Recreation

Item	FY 2011–2012	FY 2012–2013 (Request)
Salaries		
Classified positions		
Administrative	$84,000	$92,000
Secretarial	32,000	34,000
Maintenance	53,000	56,500
Unclassified positions		
Seasonal recreation	23,600	25,300
Seasonal maintenance	17,000	19,400
Total Salaries	**$209,600**	**$227,200**
Other Operating Expenses		
Computer supplies and service	$11,600	13,000
Telephone and postage	2,750	3,200
Printing and advertising	12,300	14,000
Office supplies	2,600	3,250
Equipment maintenance	9,350	10,300
Grass seed, fertilizer	4,500	5,750
Contingencies	3,700	4,800
Total Other Operating Expenses	**$46,800**	**$ 54,300**
Total Departmetal Expenses	**$256,400**	**$ 281,500**

they provide such an effective means of controlling public expenditures. The information that a line-item budget offers can also be expanded by providing extra data on costs or expenditures. The budget in Table 16.1 shows actual expenditures for FY (fiscal year) 2011–2012, as well as the FY 2012–2013 request. Some line-item budgets require the organization to show expenditures in earlier years (e.g., FY 2010–2011) or to provide a column of figures that show the percentage change from one year's expenditure to the next. Information of this kind is often used by public officials, especially legislators, to help them decide whether to grant a budget request.

FURTHER READING

Line-item budgeting is included in the readings suggested for Part IV as a whole.

Especially, enterprising students may wish to read through the report of the Taft Commission of 1912 and the Budget and Accounting Act of 1921. These two documents, which had formative effects on budgeting in the federal government, are presented in Albert C. Hyde and Jay M. Shafritz, eds., *Government Budgeting: Theory, Process, Politics* (Oak Park, IL: Moore, 1978).

Overview of Exercise

The Adams County Board of Supervisors recently approved a plan to consolidate library services in the county. In an effort to cut costs and improve services next year, the public libraries from the county's six incorporated towns, four villages, and one city are to be merged and operated as one system. Complicated negotiations by county officials, municipal officials, and representatives of two public employee unions have produced an agreement for a single new organizational structure known as the Adams County Library.

As deputy county budget director, it is your responsibility to prepare an initial line-item budget for the new consolidated library system. Your task is complicated because there is no single budget base on which to build. Because the system is new, you basically have to start from scratch. You do have two sources of information to guide your efforts, however. The first is a memorandum from the budget director outlining her expectations and those of the county supervisors with respect to the new

library system. Second, you have a line-item budget of the operating expenses for each of the 11 units to be consolidated.

INSTRUCTIONS

Step One
Read the memo from the budget director (Form 74) and review your budget survey data (Forms 75A–75K).

Step Two
Use Budget Request Form 76 to construct a line-item budget for the new Adams County Library. Make sure you take Budget Director Johnson's directives into account. Note: if your instructor agrees, you may want to use the spreadsheet available for this step.

Step Three
Answer the questions on Form 77.

October 14, 20___

TO: A. C. Andrews
         Deputy Budget Director

FROM: Sarah T. Johnson
         Budget Director

RE: Library Budget

As you know, the supervisors voted last night to approve the consolidation plan for the county library system. I'd like you to take charge of putting together a preliminary first-year budget for the board's review.

Your budget should take the following points into consideration:

1. All existing public libraries in the county, including the branches in the city of Waynesfield, are to remain open.

2. The county's cost-sharing agreement with the municipalities assumes that there will be an overall savings of three percent (3%) from the aggregate of the existing library budgets.

3. Cuts—defined either as elimination or reduction in hours—to full-time library employee positions are limited to five at the professional level and eight among support staff. There are no restrictions on cuts in other expenditure categories.

4. As per the county's agreement with the public employee unions, salary scales within job classifications are to be standardized at the highest levels currently paid by any of the newly consolidated units. This policy is to be applied to all positions.

5. All township and village librarians previously designated "head librarians" (full- or part-time) are to be redesignated "branch librarians" and are to be compensated accordingly.

6. A new position, director of county libraries, is to be created, budgeted at $90,000.

As the start-up date for the new system is July 1, we'll include this in our regular budget cycle. Please have all documentation completed by December 15.

Adams County Library Budget, Fiscal Year 1

City of Waynesfield	Job Title	Salary	Number or Hours	Cost
Professional Staff				
Full-time	Head librarian	$70,000.00	1	$70,000.00
	Branch librarian	$55,000.00	6	$330,000.00
	Reference librarian	$51,000.00	5	$255,000.00
	Assistant librarian	$46,000.00	9	$414,000.00
Part-time	Reference librarians	$24.50/hour	2,100 hours	$51,450.00
	Assistant librarians	$22.00/hour	3,000 hours	$66,000.00
Support Staff				
Full-time	Administrative assistant	$34,000.00	1	$34,000.00
	Circulation clerk	$24,960.00	8	$199,680.00
	Computer technician	$30.000.00	3	$90,000.00
	Secretary	$22,880.00	2	$45,760.00
	Maintenance worker	$22,880.00	4	$91,520.00
	Page	$16,640.00	3	$49,920.00
Part-time	Circulation clerk	$10.00/hour	7,000 hours	$70,000.00
	Maintenance worker	$11.00/hour	2,000 hours	$22,000.00
	Page	$8.00/hour	13,250 hours	$106,000.00

Other costs

Acquisitions—books, DVDs, etc.	$400,000.00
Computer supplies & service	$180,000.00
Utilities	$120,000.00
Maintenance	$40,000.00
Bookmobile	$21,000.00
School programs	$11,000.00
Summer children's prog.	$6,500.00
Travel	$4,500.00

Adams County Library Budget, Fiscal Year 1

Village of Clear Creek	Job Title	Salary	Number or Hours	Cost
Professional Staff				
Full-time	Head librarian	$55,000	1	$55,000.00
Support Staff				
Part-time	Maintenance worker	$9.00/hour	780 hours	$7,020.00
Other costs				
Acquisitions—books, DVDs, etc.				$4,500.00
Computer supplies & service				$1,000.00
Utilities				$4,200.00
Maintenance				$1,500.00

Adams County Library Budget, Fiscal Year 1

Village of Woolfords	Job Title	Salary	Number or Hours	Cost
Professional Staff				
Full-time	Head librarian	$57,000.00	1	$57,000.00
	Assistant librarian	$41,000.00	2	$82,000.00
Support Staff				
Full-time	Circulation clerk	$21,000.00	1	$21,000.00
	Maintenance worker	$20,000.00	1	$20,000.00
Part-time	Page	$7.00/hour	1,040 hours	$7,280.00
	Computer technician	$12/hour	1,040 hours	$12,480.00

Other costsT				
Acquisitions—books, DVDs, etc.			$16,000.00	
Computer supplies & service			$2,500.00	
Utilities				$4,400.00
Maintenance				$3,750.00

Adams County Library Budget, Fiscal Year 1

Village of East Woolford	Job Title	Salary	Number or Hours	Cost
Professional Staff				
Full-time	Head librarian	$55,000.00	1	$55,000.00
	Assistant librarian	$39,500.00	1	$39,500.00
Support Staff				
Full-time	Circulation clerk	$19,760.00	1	$19,760.00
	Maintenance worker	$19,500.00	1	$19,500.0
Part-time	Circulation clerk	$9.50/hour	850 hours	$8,075.00
	Computer technician	$10/hour	1.044 hours	$10,400.0

Other Costs				
Acquisitions—books, DVDs, etc.				$20,000.0
Computer supplies & service				$3,500.00
Utilities				$4,700.00
Maintenance				$2,000.00

Adams County Library Budget, Fiscal Year 1

Village of Glenridge	Job Title	Salary	Number or Hours	Cost
Professional Staff				
Full-time	Head librarian	$54,000.00	1	$54,000.00
Support Staff				
Part-time	Maintenance worker	$9.75/hour	600 hours	$5,850.00
Other Costs				
Acquisitions—books, DVDs, etc.			$1,600.00	
Computer supplies & service				$600.00
Utilities				2,500.00
Maintenance				$300.00

Adams County Library Budget, Fiscal Year 1

Town of Littleton	Job Title	Salary	Number or Hours	Cost
Professional Staff				
Full-time	Head librarian	$62,000.00	1	$62,000.00
	Reference librarian	$50,000.00	1	$50,000.00
	Assistant librarian	$43,680.00	2	$87,360.00
Part-time	Assistant librarian	$21.00/hour	1200 hours	$25,200.00
Support Staff				
Full-time	Circulation clerk	$19,760.00	4	$79,040.00
	Computer technician	$19,850.00	1	$19,850.00
	Maintenance worker	$19,500.00	1	$19,500.00
	Page	$15,080.00	1	$15,080.00
Part-time	Circulation clerk	$9.50/hour	550 hours	$5,225.00
	Page	$7.25/hour	1,500 hours	$10,875.00

Other Costs		
Acquisitions—books, DVDs, etc.	$30,000.00	
Computer supplies & service	$6,500.00	
Utilities		$2,700.00
Maintenance		$1,500.00
Great Book programs		$10,500.00

Adams County Library Budget, Fiscal Year 1

Town of Keeler	Job Title	Salary	Number or Hours	Cost
Professional Staff				
Full-time	Head librarian	$54,500.00	1	$54,500.00
Support Staff				
Part-time	Circulation clerk	$9.50/hour	1,200 hours	$11,400.00

Other Costs				
Acquisitions—books, DVDs, etc.			$1,500.00	
Computer supplies & service			$200.00	
Utilities				$2,300.00

Adams County Library Budget, Fiscal Year 1

Town of Mt. Tom	Job Title	Salary	Number or Hours	Cost
Professional Staff				
Part-time	Head librarian	$27.00/hour	1,600 hours	$43,200.00
Support Staff				
Part-time	Page	$7.25/hour	600 hours	$4,350.00

Other Costs				
Other Costs				
Computer supplies & service				$350.00
Utilities				$1,800.00
Book donation drive				$500.00

Adams County Library Budget, Fiscal Year 1

Town of Warren	Job Title	Salary	Number or Hours	Cost
Professional Staff				
Full-time	Head librarian	56,500.00	1	$56,500.00
Part-time	Assistant librarian	$22.00/hour	1,040 hours	$22,880.00
Support Staff				
Full-time	Circulation clerk	$19,760.00	1	$19,760.00
Part-time	Computer technician	$10.50/hour	1,000 hours	$10,500.00
	Maintenance worker	$9.60/hour	1,000 hours	$9,600.00

Other Costs		
Acquisitions—books, DVDs, etc.	$16,000.00	
Computer supplies & service	$2,200.00	
Utilities		$3,500.00
Maintenance		$2,750.00

Adams County Library Budget, Fiscal Year 1

Town of Lansdale	Job Title	Salary	Number or Hours	Cost
Professional Staff				
Full-time	Head librarian	$60,000.00	1	$60,000.00
	Reference librarian	$49,920.00	1	$49,920.00
	Assistant librarian	$45,760.00	1	$45,760.00
Part-time	Reference librarian	$24.00/hour	900 hours	$21,600.00
	Assistant librarian	$22.00/hour	750 hours	$16,500.00
Support Staff				
Full-time	Circulation clerk	$20,500.00	1	$20,500.00
	Computer technician	$27,600.00	1	$27,600.00
	Maintenance worker	$20,100.00	1	$20,100.00
Part-time	Page	$7.25/hour	3,300 hours	$23,925.00

Other Costs		
Acquisitions—books, DVDs, etc.	$165,000.00	
Computer supplies & service	$35,000.00	
Utilities		$7,000.00
Maintenance		$3,600.00
Foreign film series		$12,500.00

Adams County Library Budget, Fiscal Year 1

Town of New Bremen	Job Title	Salary	Number or Hours	Cost
Professional Staff				
Full-time	Head librarian	$57,500.00	1	$57,500.00
	Assistant librarian	$46,650.00	1	$46,650.00
Support Staff				
Full-time	Circulation clerk	$19,760.00	1	$19,760.00
	Computer technician	$28,000.00	1	$28,000.00
	Maintenance worker	$19,800.00	1	$19,800.00
Part-time	Circulation clerk	$9.50/hour	1,600 hours	$15,200.00
	Page	$7.25/hour	2,500 hours	$18,125.00

Other Costs		
Acquisitions—books, DVDs, etc.		$41,000.00
Computer supplies & service		$4,250.00
Utilities		$3,800.00
Maintenance		$5,650.00
	Total County Budget	$4,147,275.00

Budget Request Form

Administrative Unit: Adams County Library

Item	FY 1 Request

Questions

1. What was the aggregate budget for all preconsolidated Adams County libraries?

2. Did you achieve the mandated 3 percent savings? If not, why?

3. Assume that you are a member of the board of supervisors. What questions would come to your mind as you reviewed this line-item budget? Is there any information you would like to have that this budget does not contain?

4. In general, what are the strengths and weaknesses of the line-item format?

Exercise 17

Performance and Program Budgeting

BUDGETING FOR EFFICIENCY

Although line-item budgets are very useful, especially in maintaining control and accountability in expenditures, they do not always provide as much information about what government is actually doing with its money as some decision makers would like to have. Budgets may tell us, for instance, that the Department of Parks and Recreation is proposing to spend $1,750 on grass seed and fertilizer but offer no clue as to whether it is an efficient use of public money. What exactly are we getting for this $1,750? Have expenses for playing field maintenance been proportionate to the number of people who use the fields? Questions like these, which line-item budgets fail to address, are made to order for a *performance budget*. Because performance budgets are built around the *activities* in which a government engages rather than the commodities it buys, a person who reviews a budget in this format is able to ascertain the relative efficiency of public undertakings. Indeed, it is for this reason that a performance budget is often called an *activity budget*.

Although the groundwork for performance budgeting was laid as early as the report of President William Howard Taft's Commission on Economy and Efficiency (1912), it was not until the New Deal that performance budgeting became prominent. As the scale of government grew and its programs became more complex and far-flung, a need was felt for a budget system that offered more than control over expenditures. Budgeting processes should help *manage* as well as control, it was argued; budgets should tell us what services we are getting for our money and point out where there are inefficiencies. This format received widespread attention from all levels of government from the 1930s through the 1950s. Many of the concepts it introduced remain part of contemporary budget practices and, as we shall see in Exercise 18, the calculation of cost per unit of activity or performance is an important building block for budgeting that establishes priorities when cutting overall spending.

CLASSIFYING ACTIVITIES

How exactly do performance budgets work? The key is the way expenditures are classified. Instead of listing, line by line, every item that an organization buys, expenditures are grouped according to the organizational function or task they help fulfill. Thus, the first step in the preparation of a performance budget is to pose and answer the following simple question: What exactly are the activities or functions of this organization? If you ask this question of the city sanitation department, for example, you will probably get answers such as "collects trash," "cleans streets," and "removes snow." If you are dealing with a state department of agriculture, answers might include "inspects farms," "certifies organic produce," "encourages soil conservation," "promotes exports," and "preserves farmland." Note that the answers always begin with active verbs: *collects, cleans, removes, issues, certifies, encourages, promotes, preserves,* and so on. These are the activities or—to use the professional jargon—the *outputs* of government.

Having determined the activities of the unit to be budgeted, the next step in constructing a performance budget is to identify the expenditures that are necessary to produce the various activities. These are the "items" in a line-item budget or the "inputs" that correspond to the "outputs." All of the commodities that an organization buys should be allocated, in whole or in part, to one of the activities in the performance budget. Obviously, this is not done randomly. In compiling a performance budget, one seeks to assign all the costs—and only those costs—that actually go into performing an activity. The key calculation in performance budgeting is to determine *unit costs*—the average cost of serving each citizen or paving each mile of road or issuing each license. By comparing the unit cost for a particular activity from one year to another, one can then get some idea of whether an agency is generally making better, worse, or the same use of its funds. In other words, are they being more efficient, less, or about the same.

To illustrate this process, let us reexamine the budget for the Department of Parks and Recreation used in Exercise 16. Suppose that our research has found that the department engages in the following activities: it maintains playgrounds, runs an adult softball program, coordinates summer arts and crafts programs for children, manages one public golf course and four tennis courts, and operates an outdoor swimming pool; of course, it also engages in certain general housekeeping or administrative functions. Our identification of these programs or activities represents the first step in the process. For the second step, we have investigated and learned that the costs of the programs are as presented in Table 17.1.

Table 17.1 represents the bare bones of a performance budget for the Department of Parks and Recreation. Note that all of the cost data from the original line-item budget (Table 16.1) have been reassigned to the various activity classifications. How exactly was this done? Although for the purposes of this illustration the calculations are not shown here, we simply determined which expenditures were necessary to complete each of the activities. For instance, the $36,200 required by the playground maintenance

category had appeared in the line-item budget (Table 16.1) as parts of four different lines: $16,000 for maintenance, $14,300 for seasonal maintenance, $4,600 for equipment maintenance, and $1,300 for grass seed and fertilizer. This gives us a budget that tells us not just what things we plan to buy but what specific activities will be accomplished by our expenditures.

One more step is necessary to produce a true performance budget, however. The third step requires the budget maker to devise specific measures of performance for each activity in which an organization engages and to calculate the unit cost of each. In the Department of Parks and Recreation, we might want to measure the performance of the tennis program by estimating the number of hours the courts are actually used; when this number is divided into the overall cost of the program ($15,800 in FY 2011–2012), we get a unit cost for each court-hour. Alternatively, we could determine a unit cost for each person served in a tennis instruction program.

This process is repeated for each activity. The idea, of course, is to identify meaningful measures that managers can use to judge the efficiency of the organization's operations. It accomplishes little to generate statistics unrelated to the central purposes of the agency's programs. Table 17.2 provides a more complete version of a performance budget for the Department of Parks and Recreation, including unit cost information.

It should be emphasized that the techniques of performance budgeting are used not simply to display data in budget requests but to allow legislators and elected executives to evaluate the performance of agencies. If we find, as Table 17.2 seems to indicate, that the arts and crafts program is costing markedly more over time for each child taught, we

Table 17.1 Program Costs: Department of Parks and Recreation

	Activity	FY 2011–2012	FY 2012–2013 (Request)
01.	Administration	$54,000	$62,000
02.	Playground Maintenance	33,500	36,200
03.	Adult Softball	11,000	11,500
04.	Arts and Crafts	21,300	23,000
05.	Golf Course Maintenance	37,675	38,700
06.	Tennis Court Management	15,800	21,400
07.	Swimming Pool Operations	66,125	69,700
	Total	**$239,400**	**$262,500**

Table 17.2   Program and Unit Costs: Department of Parks and Recreation

Activity		FY 2011–2012	FY 2012–2013 (Request)
01.	Administration	$ 54,000	$ 62,000
	Cost per citizen	1.08	1.23
02.	Playground Maintenance	33,500	36,200
	Cost per acre	42.66	46.12
03.	Adult Softball	11,000	11,500
	Cost per player	25.04	25.00
04.	Arts and Crafts	21,300	23,000
	Cost per child	87.22	106.18
05.	Golf Course Maintenance	37,675	38,700
	Cost per round played	7.35	7.82
06.	Tennis Court Management	15,800	21,400
	Cost per court-hour	5.67	6.73
07.	Swimming Pool Operations	66,125	69,700
	Cost per user-hour	4.21	5.09
	Total	**$239,400**	**$262,500**

may want to investigate why unit costs are rising so precipitously. Conversely, once we are able to identify a stable pattern of unit costs, we can use estimates of demand for compiling our budget requests. If we know that it costs approximately $25 for each adult who participates in the softball program and can estimate that 460 people will sign up for the leagues next year, we know our budget request must be $11,500 for the program.[1]

BUDGETING FOR PURPOSE

Performance budgeting assesses the efficiency of government operations by examining and comparing the unit costs of public services. But, we can walk through the woods very efficiently but get lost nonetheless. With government programs as with walking in the woods, we need to know if we are

headed in the right direction, not just how fast we are getting there.

Program budgeting is designed in large part to tell us just that. A program budget forces policymakers to identify and evaluate the goals of public programs and to develop means that are optimally suited to reaching those goals. Where performance budgeting focuses on inputs and outputs, program budgeting encompasses inputs, outputs, *and impacts or results*. Program budgeting encourages public officials to weigh alternatives systematically and to choose policy strategies that most effectively meet public purposes.

Program budgets are distinguished by the fact that budget requests are arranged, as the name suggests, by programs. That is, rather than grouping together all personnel costs and all supply costs as line-item budgeting requires or classifying activities after the fashion of performance budgeting, program budgeting requires that budget managers think in terms of agency missions or goals. The broad set of goals for an organization provides a set of categories for organizing and evaluating public expenditures. This arrangement is designed to serve as a reminder that day-to-day operating costs or even organizational activities are not ends in themselves. The purpose of government is to provide certain services to accomplish things. Program budgets focus attention

[1]These calculations have been simplified for the purpose of this illustration. Most performance budgets distinguish between fixed and variable costs. Fixed costs are those that remain constant regardless of the level of the activity performed; variable costs fluctuate as activity levels change. Certain costs are fixed in operating a public swimming pool, for example, even if very few people use it: insurance and utilities must be paid, certain basic pool maintenance must be undertaken, basic lifeguard costs must be absorbed. Other costs vary with the number of users: additional lifeguards must be hired or more chlorine must be purchased, and so on.

on what those things are and make it easier for officials to determine if government is delivering what it is supposed to deliver.

The structure and logic of program budgeting can be illustrated by reference to our hypothetical Department of Parks and Recreation. You will recall that the final performance budget for the department (Table 17.2) classified expenditures according to seven key activities, such as playground maintenance, adult softball, and arts and crafts; moreover, for each of these activities, unit costs were calculated. To create a program budget for this department, we have to refocus our thinking and ask ourselves, "What are the goals or purposes of this unit of government with respect to parks and recreation?" Each goal or purpose is considered a "subgoal." Subgoals might include providing recreational opportunities for adults and supervised recreational opportunities for children,

maintaining public spaces for general public enjoyment, and offering various instructional sports programs. The various subgoals provide a framework for our program budget.

Each subgoal would then be further broken down into more detailed goals, for which specific programs would be planned and developed. The terms used to describe this nested hierarchy of goals and subgoals are *program, subprogram, element,* and *subelement,* with program the most general and subelement the most specific. A summary budget for the recreation program might appear as illustrated in Figure 17.1.

Note that the various subprograms identified in Figure 17.1 may be understood as more carefully specified goals to be pursued in furtherance of the general goal of "providing a wide range of recreational opportunities and services to area residents." Note also that the overall budget is framed without

---

PROGRAM:	5.0 Recreation
DESCRIPTION:	This program provides a wide range of public recreational opportunities and services for county residents. The goal of the program is to make possible structured and unstructured leisure-time activities that promote health, physical fitness, and social interaction.
ADMINISTRATIVE UNIT(S):	Department of Parks and Recreation
SUBPROGRAM:	5.1 Athletic Instruction This subprogram provides basic and intermediate instruction for residents of the county in several different sports, including tennis, golf, and swimming. The goal of this subprogram is to encourage residents to pursue vigorous and healthful physical activity by teaching skills basic to such sports.
SUBPROGRAM:	5.2 League Sports This subprogram provides coordination of and support for athletic leagues in the county. The goal of this subprogram is to create opportunities for residents to participate in team sports.
SUBPROGRAM:	5.3 Open Recreation This subprogram provides for the maintenance and operation of public recreational space in the county. The goal of this subprogram is to ensure the availability of public space, including playgrounds, parks, and athletic facilities, for the pursuit of recreational activities by county residents.

Figure 17.1
Sample Program Budget Summary

regard to a specific organizational unit or department: the focus is on recreation, not on a particular agency. Although some governments may be organized in a way that permits program budgets to be constructed with a one-to-one correspondence with departments and agencies, pure program budgets often cut across organizational lines, with various units contributing to each of the program categories. This means that budget officials must create additional documentation (called *crosswalks*) that translate program data into departmental operating budgets.

To appreciate the distinctiveness of program budgeting, however, it is necessary to look beyond such a broad summary of planned expenditures. Figure 17.2 provides a sample page from the program budget of our fictional municipality that focuses on a specific subelement of the recreation program.

Figure 17.2 presents budget information of subelement 5.111, tennis instruction. If we had the full budget in front of us, we would find a separate page for subelements 5.112 (golf instruction), 5.113 (swimming instruction), and so on. Indeed, there

---

PROGRAM:	5.0	Recreation
SUBPROGRAM:	5.1	Athletic Instruction
ELEMENT:	5.11	Lifelong Sports (Adult)
SUBELEMENT	5.111	Tennis Instruction

Description: This subelement is concerned with the provision of tennis instruction to adult residents of the county for the purpose of encouraging participation in a vigorous, lifelong activity that enhances fitness and social interaction.

Objective: To provide introductory and intermediate group tennis lessons to all interested adult residents.

Administrative Unit: Department of Parks and Recreation, Division of Recreation.

	Five-Year Plan				
	2007–2008	*2008–2009*	*2009–2010*	*2010–2011*	*2011–2012*
Residents served	700	750	790	825	850
Hours of instruction	1,400	1,500	1,580	1,650	1,700
Cost	$9,800	$11,200	$11,950	$12,560	$13,230

Summary Analysis: To meet the anticipated increase in demand for tennis instruction over the next 5 years, the department initially considered four alternative strategies: (1) maintain the current level of service at no charge to students, (2) maintain the current level of service with a small user charge, (3) increase the size of the instructional groups so as to instruct more students in the same number of hours, and (4) eliminate all intermediate lessons.

The department recommends that alternative 1—maintain the current level of service at no charge to students—be fully funded as indicated in the 5-year plan. This will require two additional seasonal staff positions.

Alternative 2 was rejected because the calculated costs of administering a user fee system would require that the fee be set at a level that would exclude a significant percentage of interested residents.

Alternative 3 was rejected because analysis of comparable public and private instructional programs indicates that adequate instruction cannot be provided to groups larger than five students.

Alternative 4 was rejected both because it was deemed inconsistent with subelement objectives and because a survey of area residents indicates increasing interest in instruction beyond the introductory level.

Figure 17.2
Sample Program Budget Page

would be detailed information provided for every subelement of every element of every subprogram of every program in the county. Note that the entry defines the subelement, specifies its objective, and identifies the administrative unit responsible for meeting the objective. Note that it also displays cost and service data for a 5-year period. Such multiyear cost projections are a central part of program budgets; their purpose is to force decision makers to weight long-term costs when considering program alternatives.

Perhaps the most important part of Figure 17.2 is the section titled "Summary Analysis." It is here that we find the heart of program budgeting. Given the goal of providing introductory and intermediate group tennis lessons to all interested area residents, budget officials have systematically analyzed various alternative strategies. The first alternative—maintaining the current level of service at no charge to the student—is recommended for funding because it most effectively meets the specified objective. The other three alternatives—instituting a small user charge, increasing the size of the instructional groups, and eliminating intermediate lessons—were found wanting for the reasons specified.

Of course, what we see here is only a brief summary of the analysis that was done; depending on the relative importance of the issue and the rules of the jurisdiction, a fuller and more detailed analysis might well accompany the budget request. This summary makes our point effectively, nevertheless: Program budgets are designed to draw the attention of decision makers to the relationship between the goals or purposes of government and the means available to reach them. Public officials are thereby encouraged to evaluate goals, weigh alternative programs systematically, and choose policy strategies that best meet public purposes. It should be stressed in this context that there is no single methodology or analytical tool that can be used to sort out alternatives in a program budget. Some budget problems lend themselves readily to highly quantitative decision-making devices, such as cost–benefit or cost-effectiveness analysis (see Exercise 1). Other questions require budget officials to rely on "softer," qualitative analyses. Which tool is used will depend mainly on how easy it is to quantify the impact or benefit of a particular set

of programs (costs can almost always be calculated or estimated in "hard," dollar terms, of course). Although some advocates of program budgeting have been criticized for their excessive attachment to quantification, program budgeting itself does not require any such excess.

As with other budget formats, variations on program budgeting are multitudinous. In general, though, governments that use program budgeting follow the basic pattern described here. That is, all budget requests must be justified in terms of their effectiveness in reaching agency goals. The initial use of program budgeting places heavy demands on agency officials and requires them to spend considerable time and energy gathering and analyzing information. Subsequent years, using program budgeting requires considerably less effort. The time and energy expended can pay great dividends. After all, a Department of Parks and Recreation that relied only on performance or efficiency measures might never even think about the adequacy of its tennis instruction program. From an efficiency standpoint, the more people on a court, the better!

Program budgeting became popular in the public sector in the 1960s, following Robert McNamara's use of the system to aid his management of the Department of Defense in the Kennedy administration. McNamara's system, officially termed PPBS (for planning programming budgeting system), was extended to all federal agencies by President Lyndon Johnson in 1965. Although PPBS met great resistance from many agency officials, who found it overly complex and cumbersome, and although the formal use of PPBS in the federal government was suspended in 1971 by Nixon Budget Director George Shultz, the logic and at least some of the techniques of program budgeting have thoroughly penetrated the routines of government and not-for-profit budgeting systems throughout the country.

FURTHER READING

Accounts of the operation of program budgeting in the Pentagon are offered in Alain C. Enthoven and K. Wayne Smith, *How Much Is Enough?* (New York: Harper & Row, 1971); Charles J. Hitch and Roland

N. McKean, *The Economics of Defense in the Nuclear Age* (Cambridge, MA: Harvard University Press, 1967); and Allen Schick, "A Death in the Bureaucracy: The Demise of Federal PPB," *Public Administration Review* 33 (March–April 1973), 25–41.

Good general treatments of PPBS are found in the readings suggested for Part IV as a whole and the relevant chapters in Aaron B. Wildavsky and Naomi Caiden, *The New Politics of the Budgetary Process*, 5th ed. (New York: Longman, 2004).

Overview of Exercise

In this exercise, you will first identify performance budget indicators for the newly consolidated Adams County Library. The key challenge is to define the basic output *units* for the various library activities. Then you will design an overall program structure for the Adams County Library system. To do so, you must outline a set of program goals that the library is trying to achieve to serve as a framework for the budget. You will then review a request from a member of the library staff to buy a new bookmobile and to fund associated operating expenses. In response, you will write a memo explaining how the request should be stated in terms of a program budget.

INSTRUCTIONS

Step One

Review the preliminary activity classification developed by the library administrative staff as presented on Form 79. Note any modifications you think necessary. (Hint: is "personal services" an activity?)

Step Two

Using the data provided on Form 80, together with the budget data you compiled in Exercise 16, recast your FY 1 budget into a performance format on Form 81. This is mainly a process of deciding how to allocate line-item costs to performance categories. Be sure to include appropriate performance measures and unit costs. (Because the line-item budgets prepared in Exercise 16 can differ, each student will be working with slightly different numbers in this exercise, unless your instructor chooses to reproduce and distribute a standardized budget.)

Step Three

Complete Form 81 by preparing budget projections for FY 2. Again, use the data provided on Form 80 to make your estimates. Assume a 3 percent increase in all staff salaries as well as a 3 percent increase in supply, utility, and maintenance expenses. Assume no increases in average book prices.

Step Four

Assume that you are A. C. Andrews, deputy budget director for Adams County. Read the memo addressed to you from Budget Director Johnson (Form 82), and use Form 83 to outline a set of subprograms for the Adams County Library that could be used as a program budgeting framework. Because the purpose of this exercise is simply to get you to think in program budgeting terms, there is no expectation that you have any detailed knowledge of library administration. Just draw on your general experience with public (or college) libraries, and ask yourself: What do libraries do? What services do they try to provide? (Note: although this information isn't necessary to complete this exercise, to provide continuity with Exercise 17, assume that you are now in FY 2; if you like, fill in appropriate dates on memos.)

Step Five

Review Form 84 and formulate a response to Budget Officer Tome on Form 85. Remind Tome that such requests must be submitted in a program format, and make some suggestions as to how this might be done. (Hint: are there any alternative ways to meet these service goals?)

Step Six

Answer the questions on Form 86.

Budget Request Form

Administrative Unit: Adams County Library

Activity	FY 1	FY 2 (Request)
01. General Administration		
02. Acquisitions		
03. Cataloging		
04. Circulation		
05. Reference		
06. Special Programs		
07. Personal Services		

Adams County Library Data Sheet

- At the time of the merger, the Adams County Library system had total holdings of 1,652,000 volumes. In FY 1, 18,000 additional volumes were acquired. It is anticipated that 21,500 volumes will be acquired in FY 2.
- In addition to cataloging all new volumes, the library system has met and expects to continue to meet its goal of recataloging 10 percent of its holdings each year to convert to the Library of Congress system.
- The combined circulation figures (in volumes) for all branches of the system are as follows: FY 1, 752,000; FY 2, 776,000 (anticipated).
- In FY 1, 421,000 patrons used the library system (including repeat visits). It is expected that 423,400 visits will be recorded in FY 2.
- In FY 1, the reference departments of all library branches answered 67,800 patron questions. It is expected that the reference departments will handle 71,500 questions in FY 2.
- Twenty-four special after-school programs were conducted by the system in FY 1 attended by 1,200 elementary and secondary school pupils. The same figures are expected for FY 2. In addition, the Great Books discussions for adults over a 10-week period in FY 1, with a total participation of 127; this program will be discontinued for FY 2. A foreign film series attracted 4,500 viewers in FY 1; approximately 6,000 are expected in FY 2.
- Total staff levels in the library system have remained constant since the merger, with no changes in the distribution of job classification (that is, you can assume that the figures from Form 80 are still accurate).
- A recent time study of library employees indicated that branch librarians spend 35 percent of their time on general administration, 25 percent on reference, 20 percent on special programs, 15 percent on acquisitions, and 5 percent on circulation. Assistant librarians devote 30 percent of their time to cataloging, 25 percent to reference, 25 percent to circulation, and 20 percent to special programs. The director of county libraries devotes all his or her time to general administration, as do his or her secretaries and administrative assistant. Pages and circulation clerks spend 100 percent of their time on circulation, reference librarians 100 percent of their time on reference.
- It may be assumed that maintenance, supply, and utility costs are borne equally by all library activities in proportion to their share of staff costs (as measured by salaries).

Budget Request Form

Administrative Unit: Adams County Library

Activity	FY 1	FY 2 (Request)

February 25,:___

TO: A. C. Andrews
         Deputy Budget Director

FROM: Sarah T. Johnson
         Budget Director

RE: Revisions in Library Budget Format

Now that we finally seem to have gotten everyone to agree on program categories for the new format, we need to move ahead and devise appropriate subprograms, elements, and subelements. Although the staff in each operating unit will carry out most of this work, it is important that we provide some technical assistance at this stage of the process. Despite our training sessions, most of the department heads still do not understand program budgeting.

I'd like you to act as technical liaison with the library people. Your help with their performance budget categories gave you good insight into what's going on over there.

Here's what I would like you to do: Try to get the library staff to categorize library services by program, by what they are trying to accomplish. Disabuse them of the notion that "cataloging" is a public service! But don't develop the entire budget structure for them. Confine your efforts to the subprogram level. Identify a set of subprograms and provide a brief set of definitions and objectives.

As you know, the library has been designated the sole administrative unit responsible for the program category "Library and Information Services." The library's entire operating budget is to be presented in this category.

Draft Program Budget Summary

PROGRAM: Information and Library Services

ADMINISTRATIVE UNIT: Adams County Library

    SUBPROGRAM:

    SUBPROGRAM:

    SUBPROGRAM:

    SUBPROGRAM:

    SUBPROGRAM:

FORM 84

April 23, 20___

TO: L. C. Tome, Budget Officer
          Adams County Library

FROM: J. Stacks, Head Librarian
          Main Branch

RE: Funds for a New Bookmobile

We have received increasingly insistent requests from residents of North Waynesfield to open a new branch library. They point out, quite accurately, that the closest library facilities are more than 6 miles away and that the steadily growing population in North Waynesfield warrants better and more convenient library services.

I think we need to do something for these people this year. Consequently, I am submitting a supplemental budget request for a new bookmobile unit. The estimated costs are as follows:

Bookmobile truck	$63,000
Driver-librarian salary	37,000
Books and periodicals	11,000
Maintenance expenses	8,000

Although the total costs for the first year will be fairly high ($120,000), once we have the additional truck it won't be so expensive in future years. Also, I figure we'll have to use this truck in North Waynesfield only about half time; we can use it to fill service gaps in other areas of the county when the truck isn't in North Waynesfield.

FORM 85

May 2, 20___

TO: L. C. Tome, Budget Officer
Adams County Library

FROM: A. C. Andrews, Deputy Budget Director
Adams County

RE: Bookmobile Request

Questions

1. Do your unit cost calculations indicate that the Adams County Library is becoming more or less efficient? Is this true of all programs? What might account for this pattern?

2. What additional measures or statistics would be useful to have to assess the performance of the Adams County Library?

3. What was the problem with the budget request that Stacks submitted to Tome? Do you think a program format would help Tome make a more intelligent decision?

4. Given the analytical difficulties presented by program budgeting, do you think it is worthwhile to justify all budget requests every year in program terms? Would it be better to limit detailed program analyses to "big ticket" or expensive items and have other things presented in a simpler, incremental fashion?

Exercise 18

Zero-Base and Outcome-Based Budgeting

BUDGETING FOR PRIORITIES

Zero-base budgeting (ZBB) is a misnomer. Although the term *zero-base budgeting* implies a very comprehensive, from-the-ground-up system, ZBB does not in fact require administrators to start from zero and justify every dollar. Indeed, some of ZBB's popularity derives from its relative simplicity, especially in contrast to the intricate calculations, projections, and narratives that can comprise program budgeting. As this exercise makes clear, the heart of ZBB lies in comparing and ranking alternative packages of expenditure against one another. ZBB directs the attention of managers to the relative value of different programs by forcing them to set priorities when they make their budget requests.

Developed in 1969 for the Texas Instrument Corporation, ZBB gained widespread attention when President Jimmy Carter mandated its use by federal agencies in the late 1970s. Although subsequent administrations have not required its use, many federal agencies continue to use ZBB when preparing budget requests. ZBB is also widely used (although typically with some other label or no label at all) at state and local levels of government. This is an approach toward budgeting that is especially popular when spending has to be cut back.

Outcome-based budgeting is in many ways an extension of zero-base budgeting. It, too, emphasizes the setting of priorities through the budget process, both by conveying the message that all programs are up for serious review and that there might be serious cutbacks and restructuring. In addition, outcome-based budgeting emphasizes the use of quantitative measures to identify success or failure.

DECISION UNITS AND DECISION PACKAGES

As with all budget formats, there are many different ways to implement a ZBB system; the specific approach will vary with the needs of the particular jurisdiction. In essence, though, this approach involves four basic steps:

1. Identify decision units.
2. Analyze programs and alternatives.
3. Prepare decision packages.
4. Rank decision packages.

In the language of ZBB, a *decision unit* is the organizational entity that prepares a budget. An agency as a whole may be designated a decision unit for ZBB purposes, or an agency may be subdivided into several different units. But what constitutes a proper decision unit? Unfortunately, there is no obvious answer. According to the federal Office of Management and Budget, decision units should be designated at the lowest levels of organization where officials "make significant decisions on the amount of spending and the scope and quality of work to be performed."[1] The main idea is to involve in the budget process line officials who have major program responsibilities. In our Department of Parks and Recreation, we might decide that the Grounds and Maintenance Division constitutes one logical decision unit, the Recreation Division another, and the central administrative offices a third; alternatively, we might decide to break the divisions down into smaller decision units by designating an adult recreation decision unit and a children's recreation decision unit within the Recreation Division. What

[1]Fremont J. Lyden and Marc Lindenberg, *Public Budgeting in Theory and Practice* (New York: Longman, 1983), p. 99.

we decide will depend on the structure of the organization and on how responsibilities are arrayed. On balance, ZBB tends to decentralize budget-making design; program budgeting, by contrast, has centralizing tendencies.

The second step in ZBB, once the decision units have been designated, requires that the programs of each decision unit be identified and analyzed and that alternatives to these programs be investigated. In effect, managers ask themselves, "Why are we operating this program? What purposes does it serve? Are there better ways to accomplish our goals?" In a budget-cutting context, the central questions are "How would we operate? What would our priorities be if we had less money?"

Having identified the programs and purposes of their decision units, managers next prepare sets of *decision packages.* A decision package specifies a level of service to be achieved given a particular level of funding. Decision packages also summarize the objectives of a program and indicate alternative

methods considered by the decision unit for reaching program goals. A sample decision package prepared by the Recreation Division of the Department of Parks and Recreation for the tennis instruction program is provided in Figure 18.1.

This decision package sets an outcome for 30 residents to acquire beginning level skills for playing tennis. It also indicates the consequences of disapproving the funding request and displays alternatives to the tennis instruction program that were considered.

Generally, decision unit managers prepare several decision packages for each program within their unit. Although practices vary from jurisdiction to jurisdiction, three types of packages are common:

1. *Minimum- or reduced-level decision packages* prescribe the level of service below which program operations cease to be feasible.
2. *Current-level decision packages* specify the level of service to be delivered, assuming no change in funding from the current fiscal year.

---

(1) Decision Unit: Recreation   *(2) Package Name:* Tennis Instruction   *(3) No.* 1 *of* 3   *(4) Rank:* 1

(5) Statement of Purpose: This program is intended to provide basic tennis instruction to adult residents of the county.

(6) Outcome: This level of funding will bring 30 residents to the beginning level in tennis.

(7) Personnel Required: 1 seasonal instructor

(8) Costs (FY 2010–2011):

$4,500

(9) Consequences of Disapproval: Discontinuation of tennis program, with resultant inadequate recreational opportunities for residents.

(10) Alternatives Considered: Volunteer instructors—rejected because experience indicates problems with program reliability.

Figure 18.1
Sample Decision Package

DECISION UNIT: Recreation
DECISION PACKAGE: Tennis Instruction
UNIT COSTS: $150 to beginning level; $100 beginning to intermediate level; $150
intermediate to advanced level

Package 1 of 3 $4,500 (base cost)
Outcome: 30 residents at beginning level

Package 2 of 3 $3,200 (incremental cost)
Outcome: Additional 10 residents at beginning level and 17 at intermediate level

Package 3 of 3 $2,100 (incremental cost)
Outcome: Additional 6 residents at intermediate level and 10 at advanced level

Figure 18.2
Summary of Decision Packages

3. *Enhanced-level decision packages* project levels of service to be achieved given specified incremental increases in funding.

During budget-cutting exercises, decision unit managers may have to prepare packages that begin with a current level of funding and then assume two different levels of reductions.

In a sense, this means that managers have to prepare three spending plans for each program they supervise. Each spending plan, or decision package, says, in effect, "If you give me x number of dollars, I can provide y level of service." This is what item 3 ("No. 1 of 3") refers to in Figure 18.1: that this is the first (lowest level) of three decision packages for the program. In other words, there are two other decision packages that have been prepared for the tennis instruction program, each somewhat more costly, each providing a somewhat higher level of service. Figure 18.2 provides a summary of these three packages.

RANKING DECISION PACKAGES

To understand why budget requests are broken down into separate decision packages, we must move to the final step of the process, which is ranking. At this stage, all decision packages are ranked against one another in order of their priority. Suppose that the recreation decision unit is responsible for four programs: tennis instruction, swimming instruction, softball, and arts and crafts; we will label these, respectively, TI, SI, SB, and AC. For each program, three decision packages have been prepared, as in Figure 18.2, for a total of 12 decision packages. The decision packages may be represented as TI-1, TI-2, TI-3, and so on. The manager of the recreation decision unit must rank all 12 decision packages according to his or her priorities. Table 18.1 shows what such a ranked list might look like.

This ranking is, of course, only illustrative. A decision unit manager may submit any ranking that reflects his or her sense of what constitutes the most appropriate pattern of expenditure. The only rule that must be followed in ranking decision packages is that more basic packages must be ranked above additional increments. That is, a TI-1 must always be ranked above a TI-2, which must always be ranked above a TI-3. This rule is only common sense: there must be a minimum package (represented by the "1") before there can be increments (represented by the "2" and "3"). It is perfectly proper, though, to rank an increment of one package higher than the minimum level of another package. In other words, we might rank

Table 18.1 Sample Ranking of Decision Packages

Decision Unit(s): Recreation Division   *Manager: J. T. Smith*

Priority Ranking

Rank	Package	Incremental Cost	Cumulative Cost
1	TI-1	$ 4,500	$ 4,500
2	SI-1	16,000	20,500
3	TI-2	3,200	23,700
4	AC-1	7,500	31,200
5	TI-3	2,100	33,300
6	SB-1	6,000	39,300
7	SI-2	4,000	43,300
8	SI-3	3,250	46,550
9	AC-2	5,100	51,650
10	SB-2	2,800	54,450
11	SB-3	2,700	57,150
12	AC-3	1,750	58,900

TI-1 and TI-2 and even TI-3 above SI-1 and SB-1. This is simply a way of communicating the fact that you would rather have a lot of one program (tennis instruction) than a little of two (swimming instruction and softball).

This process of ranking decision packages is repeated all the way up the organizational hierarchy. Upper-level managers take the ranked decision packages submitted by lower-level decision units, combine them into "consolidated decision packages," and produce another ranked list. Upper-level managers are free to change the priorities set by their subordinates, although in general the lower-level judgments are respected.

It should now be apparent that the essence of ZBB lies in the process of ranking the separate decision packages. Although ZBB does not remove politics or bureaucratic game-playing from the budget process, it does tend to undercut the common budget strategy of claiming that all programs are equally crucial. Managers are forced to lay their cards on the table and set clearly stated priorities among their programs. Moreover, once managers learn how much money has been appropriated for their agency, they should be able to turn to their ranked list of packages, draw a line under the cumulative dollar figure corresponding to the

appropriation, and be prepared to discontinue any programs that fall below the line. For instance, if the Recreation Division were granted $47,000, packages AC-2, SB-2, SB-3, and AC-3 (in Table 18.1) would be excised.

Although most public managers do not actually have that much discretion because legislative appropriations often require certain programs to be fully funded, the ZBB process can be a very useful way of redirecting or refocusing an agency's attention. Several years ago, for instance, the U.S. Environmental Protection Agency decided, after a thorough ZBB review, that its noise pollution program was not worth its cost; it was deemed better to have that money go to enhanced air, water, and solid waste pollution abatement projects and to run a few programs at a high level rather than a lot of programs at a low level. Similarly, our Department of Parks and Recreation might decide that a fully funded swimming program is more important than half a swimming program plus half a tennis program. Although ZBB provides no "correct" solution to such problems of resource allocation, it does encourage decision makers to think about the issues in a responsible fashion.

OUTCOME-BASED BUDGETING

The most recent addition to public budgeting processes and analyses links the allocation of funds to measurable results. This approach goes beyond the focus of unit cost that was central to performance budgeting and specifies the long-term impacts of government programs and activities. This is done through identifying quantitative results of agency actions. This is often, but not always, done with ZBB so that legislators and chief executives know the implications of choosing one decision package over another. Several states and a large number of cities, counties, and federal agencies rely, at least in part, on outcome-based budgeting.

Again, let us use our Department of Parks and Recreation to illustrate how to apply this approach to budgeting. One application of the outcome-based model would be to establish priorities through the ZBB process, which relies on the Department manager and staff. Another approach is to administer a survey of residents, have a public hearing, or use some other form of citizen participation to set priorities. Or you could have the representatives of the people, that is, the Mayor and City Council, set priorities.

If we assume that tennis and swimming instruction were identified as top priorities, the manager of the Department of Parks and Recreation would propose some measurable outcomes that the Department would meet if funded adequately. An outcome for tennis and swimming instruction would be a specific number of individuals who have learned how to play tennis and how to swim. Outcomes could also include a number of people who have reached an intermediate and advanced level of proficiency or learned certain swimming skills, like the breaststroke, the butterfly, or the backstroke. Presumably it would cost more to hire the number and quality of instructors to reach the higher-level outcomes than to be satisfied with having city residents at the beginner's level of tennis and swimming. The Department must calculate a unit cost for reaching its outcomes, using a process similar to the one in performance budgeting in Exercise 17. The unit cost for beginning tennis might be, for example, $150 per person, for intermediate level; an additional $100 per person; and for advanced level another $150 per person.

The Mayor and City Council would then respond by funding the Department of Parks and Recreation at a level associated with specific outcomes. The Department is then obliged to meet the outcomes, with the understanding that a failure to do so will mean a reduction in funding based on the unit cost or perhaps some change in personnel. In other words, given the preceding example, if the Department fell three people short at the beginning level of tennis instruction it would lose $450 and if it were five people short at the advanced level another $750. And, of course, the Department manager might lose his or her position for not meeting targeted outcomes. (This is a community that takes tennis seriously!)

Use of outcomes for budgeting and accountability of managers begs the question of whether it is possible to measure the important things that public agencies do. We visited issues of measurement in Exercise 2 on policy evaluation, but this is an important issue to address here, too. It is relatively easy to imagine counting the number of people who learn how to play tennis or how to swim. However, if we think that an important goal of a recreation program is to keep children from engaging in delinquent behavior or to

enhance the quality of life in a community, it is going to be difficult if not impossible to measure these outcomes in a precise way. In general, it is more difficult to measure preventing something than accomplishing a task. A reduction in the crime rate is at best an indirect way of measuring the prevention of crime. This is especially true when trying to link reduction in crime to one program or factor. How can we really know that someone would have vandalized property or shoplifted merchandize but for attending tennis lessons? And while a goal like "quality of life" has a general meaning, we would have to agree on how to define and measure that.

It is important to recognize problems of measurement. Nonetheless, some important outcomes can be measured relatively easily, and the intuitive and political appeal of outcome-based budgeting challenges analysts and administrators to try to develop meaningful measures for the others.

FURTHER READING

One of the most useful references on ZBB is a short article by Peter Pyhrr, the man largely responsible for developing the system: "The Zero-Base Approach to Government Budgeting," *Public Administration Review* 37 (January–February 1977), 19–27. For a discussion of outcomes-based management, see Carolyn J. Heinrich, "Outcomes-Based Performance Management in the Public Sector: Implications for Government Accountability," *Public Administration Review* 66 (November–December 2002). The collection of essays edited by Albert C. Hyde and Jay M. Shafritz, *Government Budgeting: Theory, Process, Politics* (Oak Park, IL: Moore, 1978), contains nine pieces on ZBB, including case studies of its implementation in New Mexico, New Jersey, and Wilmington, Delaware. For a detailed how-to-do-it look at ZBB, see L. Allan Austin and Logan M. Cheek, *Zero-Base Budgeting: A Decision Package Manual* (New York: AMACOM, 1979). The most widely used and cited book on outcome-based budgeting is by David Osborne and Peter Hutchinson, *The Price of Government* (New York: Basic Books, 2006). For a general review and critique of the use of indicators like outcomes, see William T. Gormley, Jr. and David L. Weimer, *Organizational Report Cards* (Cambridge, MA: Harvard University Press, 1999).

Overview of Exercise

In this exercise, you will translate part of the performance budget you developed for the Adams County Library into a ZBB format. In doing so, you will first develop three summary decision packages for each of five specified decision units. You will then rank the 15 decision packages against one another in any order you consider reasonable given the information provided.

It should be noted that the exercise involves two major departures from the real world of zero-base budgeting. First, it is assumed that each decision unit prepares only one set of decision packages. Normally, of course, decision units prepare several sets of packages because they are often responsible for more than one program. Second, because you have only limited information about each decision unit and its activities, you are not required to prepare comprehensive and detailed decision packages (as illustrated in Figure 18.1). Instead, you will generate summary decision packages, following the stated instructions, which will provide a minimum of information about service levels and costs. Were you to prepare an actual zero-base budget for this organization, you would have to undertake far more analysis and provide considerably more detail about program objectives and alternatives.

INSTRUCTIONS

Step One

Assume again that you are A. C. Andrews, deputy budget director for Adams County. Read the memo addressed to you from Budget Director Johnson (Form 86).

Step Two

Assume that your FY 2 budget request figures from Exercise 17 (Form 81) were approved. Transfer the figures to the appropriate column on Form 87. Note that to simplify the exercise, the "General Administration" category has been excluded as a decision unit; simply ignore the costs in constructing your decision packages. If for any reason you did not complete Exercise 17, your instructor will provide you with a set of figures that you can use.

Step Three

Assume a 3 percent across-the-board increase for FY 3. Do the appropriate arithmetic and complete the second column of Form 87. The figures for FY 3 thus calculated will provide the basis for constructing your ZBB decision packages in this exercise.

Step Four

Use Forms 88a through 88e to construct summary decision packages for each of the five decision units. All the information necessary to prepare these decision packages is contained either in Director Johnson's memo or in the data you generated for Form 87. Again, you are to use your FY 3 figures from Form 87 as the basis for your decision package cost calculations. In addition, you should use the performance and unit cost measures you calculated in Exercise 17 for the unit costs in this exercise and to figure out the level of service provided by different decision packages; assume, for the purposes of this exercise, that the basic unit cost ratios have not changed since FY 2. (Note the additional implicit assumption in Director Johnson's memo that a 90 percent level of funding will yield a 90 percent level of service, a 110 percent level of funding, a 110 percent level of service, and so on. This assumption is made for the purposes of this exercise to simplify calculations, although it is unrealistic in that it fails to differentiate between fixed and variable costs. Were you to prepare an actual zero-base budget, you would have to take the distinction between these costs into account in order to calculate projected service levels. See footnote 1 in Exercise 17 for a more detailed explanation of fixed and variable costs.)

Step Five

Use Form 89 to rank your decision packages. Provide the incremental and cumulative cost data as required. Although there is no one "correct" order of priority, try to rank the packages in a way that reflects your sense of their importance.

Step Six

Your instructor may tell you how much funding you will get. If not, assume that the library winds up receiving only 95 percent of its total FY 4 requests, as represented in Form 89, for the activities encompassed by these five decision units (exclude monies for "General Administration" when you make your calculations). Draw a line on Form 89 below the last

decision package that would be funded under these circumstances.

Step Seven
Answer the questions on Form 90.

March 23, 20__

TO: A. C. Andrews
           Deputy Budget Director

FROM: Sarah T. Johnson
           Budget Director

RE: ZBB Format for Library

As you know, the board of supervisors voted last week to discontinue our program budget format. Although I remain convinced that the benefits of this approach outweigh its costs, the supervisors were sensitive to complaints that filtered back to them from department heads about the alleged administrative difficulties of program budgeting. Fortunately, I have been able to convince them that we should not return to a routine, line-item budget system. They are willing to allow us to use a zero-base and outcome-based budget format this fiscal year, at least on a trial basis.

Because you are more familiar with this approach than virtually anyone else in County government and because you have worked closely with the library staff on budget questions in the past, I'd like you to supervise a trial run for the library budget for the coming fiscal year. Use the Acquisitions, Cataloging, Circulation, Reference, and Special Programs budget categories (the principal ones we used for performance budgeting) as the bases for your decision units; ignore the General Administration category, though—this is a special case that we'll deal with later. Prepare one set of three decision packages for each of these decision units (for a total of 15 decision packages): a minimum-level package, a current-level package, and an enhanced package. Be sure to specify outcomes for each decision package.

For ease of implementation, I suggest you use a fixed 90 percent of current expenditures to calculate the minimum-level packages and a fixed 110 percent of current expenditures to calculate the enhanced-level packages—in other words, the "base" decision package in each case should be 90 percent of current expenditures, the first incremental package (the one labeled "2 of 3") should represent the difference in dollars between the base and current expenditures, and the final incremental package ("3 of 3") should represent the difference in dollars between current expenditures and 110 percent of current expenditures. You should be able to derive the level of service figures from previous library budget submissions. I will, of course, want to see your final ranking of these 15 decision packages.

Budget Worksheet

	FY 2 (from Form 80)	FY 3
Budget Categories		
Acquisitions		
Cataloging		
Circulation		
Reference		
Special Programs		

DECISION UNIT: Acquisitions Department
DECISION PACKAGE: Book Acquisitions (BA)
UNIT COST:

Package 1 of 3 <u>Outcome:</u>   <u>(Base Cost)</u>

Package 2 of 3 <u>Outcome:</u>   <u>(Incremental Cost)</u>

Package 3 of 3 <u>Outcome:</u>   <u>(Incremental Cost)</u>

DECISION UNIT: Cataloging Department
DECISION PACKAGE: Book Cataloging (CA)
UNIT COST:

Package 1 of 3 <u>Outcome:</u>   <u>(Base Cost)</u>

Package 2 of 3 <u>Outcome:</u>   <u>(Incremental Cost)</u>

Package 3 of 3 <u>Outcome:</u>   <u>(Incremental Cost)</u>

DECISION UNIT: Circulation Department
DECISION PACKAGE: Book Circulation (CR)
UNIT COST:

Package 1 of 3 <u>Outcome:</u>   (Base Cost)

Package 2 of 3 <u>Outcome:</u>   (Incremental Cost)

Package 3 of 3 <u>Outcome:</u>   (Incremental Cost)

DECISION UNIT: Reference Department
DECISION PACKAGE: General Reference (RE)
UNIT COST:

Package 1 of 3 <u>Outcome:</u>   (Base Cost)

Package 2 of 3 <u>Outcome:</u>   (Incremental Cost)

Package 3 of 3 <u>Outcome:</u>   (Incremental Cost)

DECISION UNIT: Office of Special Programs
DECISION PACKAGE: Special Programs (SP)
UNIT COST

Package 1 of 3 <u>Outcome:</u>   (Base Cost)

Package 2 of 3 <u>Outcome:</u>   (Incremental Cost)

Package 3 of 3 <u>Outcome:</u>   (Incremental Cost)

Adams County Library
Decision Package Ranking Sheet

PRIORITY RANKING			
Rank	Package	Incremental Cost	Cumulative Cost
1			
2			
3			
4			
5			
6			
7			
8			
9			
10			
11			
12			
13			
14			
15			

Questions

1. Which programs would likely be eliminated if your budget recommendations were adopted?

2. What are the advantages and disadvantages of ZBB for line managers vis-à-vis central budget officials?

3. What are the relative advantages of ZBB versus program budgeting?

4. Assume that you are a member of the Board of Supervisors. Which budget format—line-item, performance, program, or ZBB/outcomes—would you prefer that the county's administrative agencies use?